D1015128

GOVERNMENT AND
PRESSURE GROUPS
IN BRITAIN

GOVERNMENT AND PRESSURE GROUPS IN BRITAIN

A. G. JORDAN and J. J. RICHARDSON

CLARENDON PRESS · OXFORD

1987

Oxford University Press, Walton Street, Oxford OX2 6DP
Oxford New York Toronto
Delhi Bombay Calcutta Madras Karachi
Petaling Jaya Singapore Hong Kong Tokyo
Nairobi Dar es Salaam Cape Town
Melbourne Auckland
and associated companies in
Beirut Berlin Ibadan Nicosia

Oxford is a trade mark of Oxford University Press

Published in the United States
by Oxford University Press, New York

© A. G. Jordan and J. J. Richardson 1987

All rights reserved. No part of this publication may be reproduced,
stored in a retrieval system, or transmitted, in any form or by any means,
electronic, mechanical, photocopying, recording, or otherwise, without
the prior permission of Oxford University Press

British Library Cataloguing in Publication Data
Jordan, A. G.
Government and pressure groups in Britain.
1. Pressure groups—Great Britain
I. Title II. Richardson, J. J.
322.4'3'0941 JN329.P7
ISBN 0–19–876167–8

Library of Congress Cataloging in Publication Data
Jordan, A. G.
Government and pressure groups in Britain.
Bibliogrpahy: p.
Includes index.
1. Pressure groups—Great Britain. I. Richardson,
J. J. (Jeremy John) II. Title.
NJ329.P7J67 1987 322.4'3'0941 87–11209
ISBN 0–19–876167–8

Typeset by Cambrian Typesetters, Frimley, Surrey
Printed and bound in
Great Britain by Biddles Ltd.,
Guildford and King's Lynn

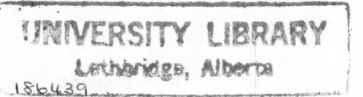
UNIVERSITY LIBRARY
Lethbridge, Alberta
186439

Preface

This book is broadly about pressure groups. As usual, qualifications and further explanations are in order. It will quickly become obvious that we use a generous definition of pressure group. This is because it is the *process* of politics that is our main interest. Such a focus quickly discovers that, in functional terms, government departments, nationalized industries, professional associations, companies, cause groups, and business associations are behaving similarly. Even local authorities will be found acting in a pressure group capacity, as when Lancashire County Council spent over £120,000 in the 1980s in opposing the Transport Act (1985).

The fundamental criticism of this approach was set out by Bernard Crick in the *American Science of Politics* (1959, p. 127), and it is periodically reinvented or borrowed. Crick argued that 'the whole theory of pressure groups may look like a tautology: that all political activity involves the clash and adjustment of interests and groups—that is what we mean by politics'.

We would not, of course, claim that group theory—even widely interpreted—encompasses 'all political activity'. However, in case study after case study the number of participants attempting to exert influence on policy (or on outputs) is routinely large. Far from being a tautology, this is a necessary restatement of the nature of politics.

We are particularly disinclined to restrict our focus to membership-based pressure groups. The conventionally used term 'pressure group'—including as it does under its rubric such varied organizations as the CBI, CND, and Greenpeace and the National Association of Local Government Officers—is itself a rather arbitrary definition. The behavioural similarities between economic actors such as the CBI, the Manpower Services Commission, British Gas, or the Ford Motor Company seem closer than those between the CBI and, say, Greenpeace.

Our starting point is, therefore, the 'normal' pressure group, but we avoid too restrictive a definition. The matter of membership-based groups does, however, itself raise several particular questions, which we address. There is the matter of the rationality of collective action; there are definitional issues; there is above all the matter of how groups fit into modern democracy.

Our concerns are principally with British politics, but much of the theoretical discussion in the literature we need to review is American. However, we have also drawn extensively on the United States because the concerns expressed in recent American empirical work—such as Berry's *The Interest Group Society* (1984)—seem to mirror our concerns, despite the differences in our constitutional systems. For example, Berry asks 'Is the sheer number of interest groups and their collective power undermining American democracy?'

Our broad assumption is that interest groups are, on balance, a strength in democracy. Des Wilson, an active campaigner of the past two decades, made the point very well: 'The country should be difficult to govern because a country that is easy to govern, is easy to dictate, it's easy to oppress'. (In Davies 1985, p. 21.) A complex society, with dispersed political power, may be difficult to govern (and describe), but who would want simplicity? We are perhaps unfashionably well disposed to this pressure group democracy. It is not that we are totally blind to its many deficiencies, but that we judge it against authoritarian regimes which have existed in the past fifty years—and currently—rather than against some unrealized ideal.

As usual, we have gathered debts: to those whose work we have quarried, to those from whose practical experience we have benefited, to those many colleagues who have steered us gently, and to those whose conclusions we do not confirm but whose work has stimulated us and provided valuable empirical material. We particularly want to thank Dr Wyn Grant, Professor Frank Bealey, and Professor Paul Pross for sharing material with us in pre-published form, and for sharing an interest in interests. We wish to acknowledge the generous support of the Nuffield Foundation, and also the help of those who have typed (and retyped) this on our behalf: Grace Hunter, Alison Robinson, Lorna Cardno, and Fiona Docherty. We are grateful to the Scottish Office for co-operation in our study of consultation practices. From the interest group side, we are particularly grateful to David Lea and Barney Holbeche. None of the forementioned has seen our account, and our appreciation of their assistance does not in the least mean that they endorse our views. We thank Gail Stedward for contributing her chapter on Women's Aid. This usefully complements our own special interest in 'producer' groups. Grant Jordan was primarily responsible for chapters 1–6 and 11, and Jeremy Richardson for chapters 7, 8, 10, and 12.

The first half of this book is mainly concerned with the literature about groups, while in the second half the emphasis is upon empirical data. Between us in the past five years we have interviewed in the order of 50 civil servants, and corresponded with many more. We are again grateful for their co-operation. At several times we deliberately sought civil servants with particular departmental experiences, but the interviews represent a range rather than a technical sample. That we tackle both theoretical and empirical approaches to the subject is deliberate: theory needs to be tested repeatedly against practice. For that reason too neither part is self-contained and each draws upon the themes of the other.

For Anne and Susan

Contents

Part One

APPROACHES

An Introduction to Pressure Politics

The Prevalence of Groups

This book may be seen as a prolonged commentary on several brief texts. In his 1983 Reith Lectures, the former joint head of the Civil Service, Sir Douglas Wass, observed how the inadequate opportunity for public participation afforded by voting had prompted the bypassing of representative government. He added:

They have associated themselves with people of similar interests into trade unions, pressure groups and lobbies. They have sought to influence government decisions not primarily by the process of influencing their representatives, but by applying pressure at the very point where policy is made, in executive government. Departments 'mark' pressure groups and special interests . . . Political decisions . . . are reached with a view, in part at least, to satisfying these pressure groups and interests . . . It is much easier politically for government to come to terms with some special interest than to oppose it. (1984, p. 105.)

In 1938, making reference to the United States, Pendleton Herring wrote that 'Government has matters other than finances to manage. Our present form of government is not to be judged simply in terms of its ineptness for fiscal control.' (Quoted in Truman 1951, p. 517.) Equally accurate a signpost of our interests might be the comments of the former director general of NEDO, Sir Geoffrey Chandler (1984, p. 16): 'Consultation and decision making are not incompatible. For decisions to endure, acceptance, to which consultation is the route, is essential.'

Governments must reconcile conflicting demands, usually expressed as group demands. Some of these demands will be economic, but there are many other sorts of demands which are held as intensely: indeed, it is arguable that economic problems can be tackled over time by incremental adjustments and growing resources, but issues such as animal welfare, abortion, and nuclear defence are less bargainable. This book, then, is about the handling of conflict. Its thrust is that the pressure group is the most significant medium of articulation of the demands, and consultation the technique for their amelioration.

In the United States as early as 1929, E. P. Herring (1929, p. 2) noted: 'Today when the voter becomes fired with an overpowering conviction as to the truth or falsity of a particular matter . . . he does not immediately look at the party as the vehicle to give support and expression to his doctrine. He finds about him numerous organized groups built around certain definite interests.' The core theme of this chapter is that pressure group activity is normal. It is commonplace. In Professor Finer's phrase, so commonplace are groups that 'they stare us in the face so obviously that we never notice they are there' (1966 edn., p. 18).

British groups will naturally enough have as their prime targets departments in government, but other bodies such as local authorities, water authorities, or even individual companies can be their focus. The Scottish National party, acting as a pressure group, in 1985 went to York to try to get Rowntree–Mackintosh to refrain from closing a Scottish factory. Occasionally the EEC will be the target, although it is common to try to use British departments to influence the EEC. On some events (such as corporal punishment) the group might wish to use European institutions to influence domestic British policy. Sometimes the British group will need to influence foreign governments, such as when in the spring of 1985 a CBI mission spent a week in the US lobbying against unitary taxation which sought to tax subsidiaries in the US for the company's world-wide operations. In Britain a Unitary Tax Campaign organization was set up, representing fifty British companies with international operations. They appointed a public affairs consultancy to provide a secretariat and organize action. The main strategy—often necessary in overseas matters as with the EEC—was to persuade the British Government to adopt their arguments, and to pursue them in International Monetary Fund meetings and other official intergovernmental meetings (see Greer 1985, pp. 28–30). The *CBI News* reported, 'The decision to mount a major lobbying exercise in California followed consultation with the Treasury.' (8 March 1985.) It will be a theme of this book that there are often, indeed usually, *shared interests* between groups and government departments.

It is routine for government departments to consult groups in the preparation of proposals. For example, the Scottish Development

Department maintains a list of 309 names interested in building control alone. A brief extract from the names listed shows how specialized, even esoteric, are the private worlds in which detailed policies are formulated:

Advocates Library
Aggregate Concrete Block Association
Architectural Metalwork Association
Association of British Manufacturers of Mineral Insulating Fibres
Association of British Roofing Felt Manufacturers
Association of British Theatre Technicians
Association of Building Component Manufacturers Ltd.
Association of Chief Architects of Scottish Local Authorities
Association of Consulting Engineers
Association of Lightweight Aggregate Manufacturers
Association of Scottish Chambers of Commerce
Association of Structural Fire Protection Contractors and Manufacturers
Association of Thermoplastic Domelight Manufacturers

The process of governing in this perspective is a process of government relations with groups. One civil servant pointed out to us the remarkable and frequent spectacle of government advertising that it faces a problem: initiatives are no longer sprung on an unsuspecting public. He added that departments make policy by consultation as a means of rallying potential supporters to the colours. And while the academic emphasis is on the problems of groups in influencing government, governments themselves, in so far as they have their own goals and agendas, will often be attempting to influence the CBI, the TUC, and individual unions and companies. Pross (1986) puts the point neatly in noting that for many groups who have established their credentials with government, 'Instead of clamouring to be consulted they are hounded for advice.'

Pressure group theory thus stems from empirical studies of how decisions are taken. Indeed, one of the important American commentators, David Truman, implied that detailed research is hardly necessary to uncover the group phenomenon: 'the fairly observant citizen sees various groups slugging it out with one another in pursuit of advantages from the Government' (1951,

p. 11). Press examples are easy to find, such as 'Following strong pressure from the heritage lobby, Barney Hayhoe, Minister of State, told the House of Commons that the Government would consider zero rating [VAT on building work for historic and listed buildings].' (*Antiques Trade Gazette*, 12 May 1984.) Or

An ambitious plan to raise hundreds of millions in tax from pensions has been abandoned . . . This outcome is a victory for one of the most intense, sophisticated lobbies that Westminster practice has seen for years . . . The campaign, masterminded by the CBI and the National Association of Pension Funds, has led to Conservative MPs being deluged with protest mail. . . . The Chancellor has also had to face representations from many companies, including the Imperial Group, BAT Industries, Unilever, Booker McConnell, ICI and Reed International. . . . (*Observer*, 24 February 1985.)

The same issue of the *Observer* ran a full-page advertisement from the Association of the British Pharmaceutical Industry protesting against the DHSS proposal to reduce costs by limiting the range of brands of drugs available on NHS prescription. The drugs industry utilized the topical argument that the Government's proposal would cost jobs.

To accept Truman's point about the prevalence of groups is not to say that all pressure group behaviour is evident at a casual glance, but that the superficial picture is sufficient stimulus to further enquiry. Indeed, much of the most important pressure group influence is wielded by groups which do not need to conduct high-profile, public campaigns. Policies are developed in private arrangements between civil servants and their pressure group peers. Douglas Yates (1982, p. 89), writing about the United States, uses the term 'silent politics' to capture the fact that there is only sporadic press interest in the technicalities of policy. He observes how there is a guild professionalism to the extent that a policy arena is dominated by a particular profession. The professionals, he says, 'will attempt to seek to confine participation in the policy making process to fellow professionals'. There is a deliberate exclusion of outsiders. We did indeed find senior civil servants using the term 'trusties' to refer to the acceptable, supportive, well-established groups.

That the major established interests are often pursuing marginal adjustments to policy in non-public, routinized relations with civil servants who share a commitment to that policy area is an observation that has implicit repercussions. If the processes are closed, there is little opportunity for participation by Parliament or parties. Eckstein (1960, p. 155) put it that group influence is enlarged by anything which restricts the influence on policy-making of anything else: 'For example', he said, 'the influence of groups . . . is enhanced by the lack of any wide public interest in an area of policy, simply because such lack of interest, apart from minimizing group competition, tends to neutralize some of the more important centres of influence which compete with private groups as such.' Later he observed, 'Negotiations nowadays tend to be confidential not so much because of any anti-democratic collusion among the negotiators but, much more important, because very few people really care about them.'

If one interprets the term 'pressure group' as representing organizations such as the Campaign for Nuclear Disarmament, Greenpeace, or the like, then Eckstein's remarks (1960, p. 888) about the BMA–ministry relationship as being 'on the whole, strikingly close and friendly' must seem a strange characterization of group–department relations. CND has not (and cannot have) such links with the Government. Our broad central argument then is *about a particular type of group*: not all groups fit into this pattern of integrated participation which is here claimed to be normal.

A version of what we present as the norm was given by a prominent member of the civil engineering fraternity, Lord Howie. In advocating improved lobbying by the construction industry, he pointed to the precedent of the National Farmers' Union (NFU) as 'the most consistently successful pressure group in British public life'. He suggested that construction needed a full-time secretariat and that the required tactic was 'to get in quick, establish a strong relationship with the civil servants, supply relevant and reliable information, never let up'. He noted that the construction industry's own federal, part-time, Group of Eight could do this only patchily (*New Civil Engineer*, 19 November 1981).

The agenda of the group–government world is not that of Parliament and the media. In concentrating on the issues of Parliament (which are easy to report), the media court the danger noted by Suleiman (1974, p. 230) in his work on France. He claimed that a focus on the sensational cases—on explosive issues when normal relationships have broken down—does not provide an understanding of the continuing process by which groups attempt to wield influence. An instance of the need to look beyond the media headline was the claim by the DHSS minister, Kenneth Clarke, to the Association of Metropolitan Authorities in the midst of the furore over the abolition of the metropolitan tier of government: 'Our political disputes must not be allowed to overwhelm our professionalism.' (*Municipal Review*, April 1985.) In other words the group–government interaction continued on other fronts.

The image of the political system adopted here is both *segmented* and *complex*. The ideas of policy community (Richardson and Jordan 1979, p. 74) or group subgovernment (McConnell 1966, p. 7) see policy being made in specialist sectors of substantial autonomy. Olsen captures the point with his characterization of the Norwegian Cabinet as 'sprawling fence posts', a metaphor that stresses the separateness of the ministers in what is usually regarded as a team situation. This interpretation of the political process is thus one which dwells on the *sectorized* negotiations between government departments and their (often) clientelistic groups rather than one which sees a collective government facing the full breadth of competing group demands. The following remarks by Olsen (1983) about Norway seem closely related to the picture which we identify in Britain: 'ministers face not only an administrative apparatus with a well developed division of labour but also agencies with routine support from strong interest groups' (p. 91); 'What has been described as governance by ministers conceals stable, functional coalitions of organized public and private interests.' (p. 101.) There results 'a segmented structure, with stable, non-hierarchical functional coalitions' (p. 116).

Group–department relationships are encouraged by the fragmentation of government itself into departments 'fighting their own corners'. One civil servant (Coates 1984, p. 157) notes that in extreme form government departments can be seen as entrenched interests. He observed that the Ministry of Agriculture, Fisheries, and Food has been accused of defending 'farmers and manufacturers in the production of more profitable food'. He added that 'any policy-maker, be he an official or a minister, is influenced by the pressures effectively brought to bear on him'. Indeed, he counters, 'were the policy-maker not affected he would be accused of insensitivity and unresponsiveness'. Heads the civil servant loses, tails his critics win.

Whiteley and Winyard (1983, p. 15) quote a civil servant remarking that it is always useful when arguing with colleagues and other ministers to be able to refer to outside pressure for a policy. Another civil servant they interviewed commented, 'There is enormous common ground between ministers, civil servants and pressure groups: there is a common interest.'

This is particularly so where there are recognized sponsor departments which are expected to put the case of producers' interests. Sir Douglas Wass, in defending the Treasury against 'ivory tower' criticisms, argued: 'we do maintain very tight lines of communication with sponsor departments of the various industries in the Department of Transport, Department of Energy, Department of Trade and the Department of Industry itself . . . And from experts in those departments, who are dealing directly with the industries they sponsor.' (Young and Sloman 1984, p. 105.) In the usual pattern of segmented politics, the minister is the patron, not the opponent, of the sectional group. When in 1970 Richard Crossman, as Secretary of State for Health and Social Security, had a row with 'his' doctors, he upbraided them in significant terms: 'How can I be your sponsor and look after you if, without a word of warning to me you slap down this ultimatum . . . How can I possibly *represent you* [our emphasis] in Cabinet if without any warning you do this to me?' (1977, p. 926.)

John Wardroper's (1981, p. 8) book on traffic problems claims that the Department of Transport has consistently seen its role as pro-lorry: for example, 'Although the 44-ton dream was postponed the departmental allies of the lorry men did a good deal to shield them from troublesome regulations.' In discussing the setting up of the Armitrage Inquiry (reported 1980) into *Lorries, People and the Environment*, Wardroper (1981, pp. 8–12) notes, 'At this point it is important to record that the freight directorate is officially not a protector and advocate of hauliers' and lorry makers' interests', but he goes on to use the following quotation: 'When they are given a particular responsibility—as for road haulage, or for Concorde or the nuclear industry . . . [civil servants] . . . almost inevitably perceive the public interest as requiring them to promote the vigorous development of their charge.'

Wardroper (1981, p. 12) quotes former transport minister

William Rodgers, who warned of the problems of civil servants 'going native': 'In my experience there are occasions when an official gets too close to the interest group with which he deals and becomes instinctively resistant to ministerial proposals hostile to it.'

Ministers and client groups can share goals. Wapshott and Brock's (1983, p. 98) biography of Mrs Thatcher describes how she defended the education budget successfully when she was Secretary of State for Education:

For an ambitious departmental minister, an expanding budget was not a disadvantage. She won an early battle in Cabinet for an increase in funds for the rebuilding of Victorian primary schools. She tenaciously pursued the commitment to raise the school leaving age—which had been delayed by the Labour Government on the grounds of cost . . . She fended off proposals to abolish the Open University . . . *Framework for Expansion*, a White Paper outlining the strategy for education resources for the coming decade, appeared in December 1972 to a good reception from most of the lobbies whose interests were at stake . . .

The image of a sectorized world is reinforced by case study after case study where issues of minor importance in general politics are of pre-eminent importance to the particular interests. As Ian Greer (1985, p. 65) has pointed out, 'A Standing Committee debate on, say, a farming issue may warrant only a few lines in the national press, but it can be front page news for *Farmers Weekly*.'

As well as being segmented we see government as being complex: the complexity is arguably increasing. For example, Moran's study *The Politics of Banking* (1984, p. 21) showed how the Bank of England attempted to restrain lending by issuing 'requests' (rather than using statutory compulsion available under the 1946 Act) to the relevant institutions. During the Second World War the requests had only to cover the 'Big Five' banks: by the 1960s they had to cover 260 institutions. Moran notes how as a consequence of this proliferation of banking bodies the bank preferred to use representative bodies and trade associations in an attempt to simplify the complex environment. He records how the bank tried to strengthen the Finance Houses Association as an instrument to control the growing number of non-clearing banks. Moran also notes how the Committee of London Clearing Bankers has in recent years been transformed from a trade association operating restrictive practices into a high level lobbyist in Whitehall. He notes how the

British Bankers' Association was roused from a dormant state in 1972 to lobby for the wider interests of all bankers. The message is of an increased number of groups, and more overtly political roles for older groups. This is the identical message to that in Wilson's (1981, p. 14) work on the USA, which documents increased lobbying both by business and public interest organizations: 'Interest groups have come closer, in short, to playing the role they always were supposed to—but did not—in American politics.' Also writing on the US, Jeffrey Berry (1984, p. 18) uses the phrase 'interest group spiral' to describe 'the sharp upturn in the number of groups'. The new technology of group mobilization in the US—through mail solicitations of support from pre-targeted clienteles—has allowed a proliferation of groups based on approving supporters rather than policy-making members. (See Berry's section 'Maintaining Interest Groups: Direct Mail'.) It is in fact difficult to *prove* this growing complexity of the group world, but if any claim stands as a self-evident truth, this may well do.

The Decline of Numerical Democracy?

This book is about interests in society and particularly the relationship between organized interests and government. Although there is no claim that everything can be explained by group interaction, it must be acknowledged that the prominence given to groups is based on the belief that groups have a substantial impact on policy outputs, and that group activity permits democratic responsiveness by government. This is not a peculiarly British concern. Recent books on exactly those themes include Pross's book on Canada, *Group Politics and Public Policy* (1986), Berry's book (cited above) on the United States, *The Interest Group Society* (1984), and Olsen's book on Norway, *Organized Democracy* (1983).

The importance of the group channel was captured by Rokkan (also writing on Norway) in 1966. He argued, 'There is certainly an electoral system, but a growth of a vast network of interest organizations and other corporate bodies means that "ruling" is not a matter of obtaining "50 per cent plus" votes, but also has to do with a bargaining process between giant alliances of associations and corporations.' In a sentence that has rolled around political science ever since, he proposed: 'votes count in the choice of governing personnel, but other resources decide the actual policies pursued by authorities'. He claimed that the negotiations between groups and government meant more in the lives of rank-and-file citizens than formal elections (1966, p. 107). He said, 'The Cabinet has increasingly had to take on the role of mediator between the conflicting interests in the national community . . . it can rarely if ever force through decisions solely on the basis of its electoral power but has to temper its policies in complex consultations and bargains with the major interest organizations.'

Examination, attempted later, of the origins and activity of groups is conducted not for its own sake but because of this conception of the group channel as being of growing importance in policy-making, and that the group channel is itself a legitimate democratic process. In Britain, at least, pressure group lobbying is still even yet a somewhat dubious activity. The director general of the CBI, in a foreword to a CBI guide advising businessmen how to exert political pressure (and defending the practice), had to concede 'The very word "lobbying" still sticks in some people's throat. They seem to think there is something improper about it; that it is a sinister (perhaps even dishonest) practice, something that starts with an expensive lunch and ends with a lucrative slice of "payola".' (CBI 1983.)

While elections determine 'governing personnel', in works such as Richard Rose's *Do Parties Make a Difference?* (1984 edn.) many commentators find the matter of *who* is elected as of less and less importance. These output studies are consonant with the pursuit of interests by groups through their particular group–government channel rather than through aggregative political parties. Therefore, instead of seeing the study of pressure groups as the study of a particular type of political actor there is perhaps more reward in seeing it as a particular, non-electoral, process of political representation and decision-making.

Professor McKenzie has made the point that the group process is an *alternative* to that of party democracy. In the *Political Quarterly* in 1958 he said that 'pressure groups, taken together, are a far more important channel of communication than parties for the transmission of political ideas from the mass of the citizenry to their rulers'. Both in Britain and the USA the thirty years since McKenzie's article have been noteworthy both for the increase in group activity and a disengagement of the public from strong party identification. This has reinforced the validity of the idea of a *two-channel* democracy.

This kind of approach denies that only the electoral channel is 'democratic'. Heisler (1980, p. 17) cites Schattschneider, who made the point that

> The classical definition of democracy as government by the people is predemocratic in its origins, based on notions about democracy developed by philosophers who never had an opportunity to see an operating democratic system . . . One consequence of our reliance on old definitions is that the modern [citizen] does not look at democracy before he defines it; he defines it first and then is confused by what he sees. (1960, p. 130.)

Schattschneider's point that a society which can be *judged* as democratic looks rather different from putative democratic societies leads to Heisler's own viewpoint that the government–electoral channel is the alternative for those whose interests are not effectively represented, or whose participation opportunities are not perceived as adequate, in the domain of organized interests. This view is perhaps akin to Samuel Beer's classic proposition in *Modern British Politics* in 1965. He claimed that the 'realities of governing' led governments and parties to bargain with organized producers and that the 'realities of winning power' led them to bid for the support of (largely) consumer groups among the voters (1969 edn., pp. 318–19). What is perhaps unreal and misleading is the impression that all this is done consciously and rationally; while Beer may be correct, he is setting out clearly the bones of confused practices. Beer himself described (1969 edn., p. 337) producer–government relations as 'a vast untidy system of functional representation that has grown up alongside the older system of parliamentary representation. It is mainly through this system that the powers of advice, acquiescence and approval are brought to bear on public policy.'

Following Heisler, one can see democracy as resting not simply in the electorcal control of government, but in any setting where (in Dahl's terms) the citizen retains a sense of competence and where opportunities to challenge policy exist and political processes are competitive. Heisler makes the point that by the time the franchise was widely extended, organized interests had already assumed prominence in what are now the Western democracies. 'Thus', he concludes, '*in practice, if not in theory*, modern democracy has entailed the admixture of electoral and organizational politics from its beginnings.' (1980, p. 12.) Dahl (1984, p. 238) has argued that although the power of groups in these group-dominated sub-governments may be 'a shocking outrage' to the vision of classical democracy, the most likely alternative is an authoritarian regime, and thus 'from a democratic perspective the untidy systems of polyarchy and pluralism begin to look more charming'.

Quite apart from the argument that representation via a group is likely to be more sensitive (less of a heterogenous category), an argument against the electoral channel as the sole version of democratic policy-making is the inappropriateness of party choice for many issues. By the nature of things the limited party choice is a crude device, and arguably, the solution to many complex problems is better contrived among those with an interest than imposed after success in an electoral contest settled on lines quite irrelevant to the particular issues.

Dahl's work can be used to establish the generally tolerant attitude of the group theorists to the prevalance of groups. This acceptance of group activity as a *means* to democratic society contradicts the view most famously expressed by Rousseau (1712–78), that associational life (i.e. groups) prevented a valid general will of the public from emerging. Dahl (1984) argued that any merit in the idea of general will was linked to small-scale contexts: it might have some chance of feasibility in the scale of the city-state. However, Dahl thought that for political units the size of modern nation states it was better to follow de Tocqueville, who, writing on the United States, was in direct contradiction to Rousseau: 'At the present time, the liberty of association has become a necessary guarantee against the tyranny of the majority . . . There are no countries in which associations are more needed, to prevent the despotism of faction or the arbitrary power of a prince, than those which are democratically constituted.' (quoted in Dahl 1984, p. 233.)

The Menu of Definitions

There are well-known and legitimate definitions of 'pressure group' available: Paul Pross (1986, p. 9), for example, defines them as 'organizations whose members act together to influence public policy in order to promote their common interest'. David Truman (disliking the term pressure group) preferred 'an interest group is a shared-attitude group that makes certain claims upon other groups in the society. If and when it makes certain claims through or upon any of the institutions of government, it becomes a political interest group.' (1951, p. 37.) Professor Finer's definition (1966 edn., p. 3) of his preferred term 'the lobby' was 'the sum of organizations in so far as they are occupied at any point of time in trying to influence the policy of public bodies in their own chosen direction; though (unlike political parties) never themselves prepared to undertake the direct government of the country'.

A rather broader type of definition from Charles Lindblom (1980, p. 85) is 'we mean by interest-group activities all inter-actions through which individuals and private groups not holding government authority seek to influence policy, together with those policy-influencing interactions of government officials that go well beyond the direct use of their authority'. It will be noted that his less restrictive version

(a) particularly dwells on groups when they are concerned with the attempted determination of public policy;
(b) accepts parts of the government machine as groups;
(c) implicitly accepts companies and corporations as groups, and explicitly extends the term to include indi-vidual behaviour.

In avoiding the membership-based sort of interpretation of 'group', we are able to consider the activities of many non-membership organizations which have an influence in public policy, for example companies, quangos, and the like. Is there a *group* of mortgage payers? In part the building societies might 'represent' their clients, but government seems able to discern an interest (with voting potential) without mediating institutions. The mortgage payer is not part of an effective existing group or potential group, but appears to count in the calculus of decision without an organizational expression. The National Consumer Council is government-funded, with no members, but employs a parliamentary lobbyist and is functionally, in our terms, a pressure group.

A reason for this sweeping interpretation of 'group' is that the emphasis of our variant of group theory is more about *pressure between* bodies than about formal groups. Group theorists are writing about how decisions are made; group theory is about the role of groups in decision-making, not merely theories about groups. Early writers such as Odegard (1928) used the term *pressure politics* rather than 'pressure group politics': the change in terminology appears to imply something more restrictive than many group writers consciously intended. There is also the matter of pressure *within* groups. Often important aspects of the process are the conflicts within groups. It is easy to credit the group with views and values which actually are only the positions of the forces temporarily in control of the organization. Thus the RSPCA has been an arena for conflict in recent years (see Thomas 1983), and in our own study of the creation of the Engineering Council one of the key episodes was a rapid alteration in the formal position of the Institution of Electrical Engineers.

The authors who are generally accepted as pioneering the study of pressure groups tended to write in reaction to what they deemed excessively institutional, constitutional, and legalistic versions of politics. Crick (1959, p. xv) dates this new emphasis on 'observation, survey and measurement' back to the 1900s. He quotes Waldo claiming that 'amorality became almost a requisite for professional respect'; the question was 'how politics *really* works'. He cited Beard, 'It was not the function of the student of politics to praise or condemn institutions or theories, but to understand and expound them.' This mood was captured by Munro in his presidential address to the American Political Science Association; 'our immediate goal, therefore, should be to release political science from the old metaphysical and juristic concepts upon which it has traditionally been based . . .' In the same year R. Spencer (1928) warned political scientists against being reformers and advised them that 'It is the function of the political scientist to observe political phenomena and to tell us what he sees.' (Both cited in Garson 1978, p. 36.)

Such a view of political investigation is open to the methodological criticism that theory determines what one sees. Hegel made the point succinctly: 'Even the average and mediocre historian, who perhaps believes . . . he is merely receptive, merely surrendering himself to his data, is not passive in his thinking. He brings his categories with him and sees his data through them.' (Quoted in Crick 1959, p. 114.) Nevertheless, the emphasis on politics as a process was valuable; politics became the analysis of that process rather than discussion of normative preferences. In later work, for example Professor Walkland's discussion of policy-making in Britain (1968, p. 7), we see the same impatience that fired the empirical reaction of the early group theorists; 'Studies of British government are peculiarly prone to be written in terms of formal constitutional notions associated with eighteenth and nineteenth-century political developments. Concepts such as the legislative supremacy of Parliament and the "rule of law", useful in limited ways, still confuse students . . .' The early pressure group work therefore did not, it is argued, start with the issue of what is a pressure group, but with the issue of how policy is made. This is still our emphasis. We are interested in all influences (membership-based and other) in the process of government.

As we concede in our preface, there is some point to Crick's claim (1959, p. 127), often echoed in hackneyed form, that pressure group theory risks tautology, that it is only saying that all political activity involves the clash and adjustment of interests and groups. It is true that this is only a restatement of the nature of politics. But even restatement is valuable, if the point is being neglected. Empirically based research tends to find government agencies, nationalized industries, and even departments engaged in making demands for themselves or their client groups.

Bentley's *The Process of Government* (1908) is the major platform in this empirically based study of decision-making. Bentley's own empirical work was thin, but there was a strong emphasis on a non-legal, non-institutional approach: for example, in discussing the regulation of steamboats—then controversial— Bentley attempts to show how a particular policy stimulates new groups into life, how government was internally divided on the issue, how the steamboat interest itself was divided, and how the Presidential policy was in reality the adoption of the strongest group position (1967 edn., pp. 344–5).

Whatever else might be posted at Bentley's door, meekness was not a failing, and many are suspicious of statements such as 'The great task in the study of any form of social life is the analysis of . . . groups . . . When the groups are adequately stated, everything is stated. When I say everything I mean everything. The complete description will mean the complete science.' (1967, pp. 208–9.)

What this means is not entirely self-evident, because Bentley used the term 'group' in an idiosyncratic and broad fashion. Certainly most pressure group theorists *do not* believe that *all* political investigation can be reduced to the study of pressure groups. Truman, for example, in an article in the *American Political Science Review* in 1960, disclaimed the description 'group theorist' and stated that his purpose was simply 'to examine interests groups and their role'. Truman was thus claiming to be in the business of a theory of interest grups rather than an interest group theory of politics. The distinction, often fudged by the term 'pressure group theory', is important, but most students of interest groups *do* see them as important, if not all-important, in policy-making.

Our position on the menu of definitions is thus that we would prefer not to begin with a strict definition of pressure group: if pressed we would go for a broad approach, as does Lindblom (above). Our reasons are manifold. Firstly, like Bentley, we do not wish to prejudice our field of interest. Secondly, hunting this snark saps the enthusiasm of the reader, and the authors. Thirdly, what we are interested in is a *process*, the interactions over time which result in public policy.

For example, in the miner's strike in 1984–5 it is not problematic to see the National Union of Mineworkers as a group. Few would object to going on to consider the National Coal Board as a group actor, though some would object to its lack of a membership base. More reservations might be made to considering the church as a group in this case, though Dr Montefiore, who was chairman of the Church of England social responsibility committee, did seem to be speaking with a group base when he intervened. More difficulties can be seen, though, when one considers the interventions of the Bishop of Durham, which might be seen as personal. We see no merit in trying to make firm rules to alleviate these problems. Following custom and practice, and for convenience, we refer to the likely participants as groups, but in practice many of the relevant actors are not very group-like. Either we construct a definition broad enough to encompass all relevant bodies, or we define a *pressure group by function*, that is, we so define all participants we find interacting in the process. It may defy popular usage to say that (say) an industrial company or a government department is a pressure group, but in so far as such bodies are active in influencing (or attempting to influence) policy, they are clearly of relevance to the analysis of pressure politics. British Rail may not be a normal 'group': it is after all within the public sector; but it still engages in press advertising, the anti-governmental nature of which is poorly disguised. For example, see advertisements such as 'in theory, a monopoly has no competition ... so much for theory'. The advertising contains lines such as 'British Rail's investment per train/km is lower than that of any other major railway in Western Europe. If Britain wants a worthwhile railway system in future, people will have to appreciate the importance of railways as they have done in other countries.' Another advertisement in the series (November 1981) said: 'Since the 60's a number of people have considered the railways to be an industry of the past. They are boring.' Such press campaigns were part of BR's pressure to persuade the Government that mainline electrification was a good idea, and it is not clear that by *function* they were not a pressure group in such instances.

Wherever the boundary between group and non-group is drawn, there is something peculiar about even considering as components of a single 'pressure group' category organizations as diverse as the National Union of Mineworkers, the Automobile Association, the Birds' Welfare and Protection Association, and the Cricket Council.

Types of Group

The literature of classification is strangely non-cumulative. Authors have repeatedly arrived at the same kind of point, though often independently, with little connection to the other discussions. There is little sense of an evolution or growing sophistication of discussion.

The British literature rediscovers two main types of group. Potter (1961, pp. 15–32) uses a sectional or spokesman versus promotional or attitude group distinction; Stewart (1958, p. 25) uses a sectional/cause group categorization. Finer distinguishes between economic or social interests and promotional or attitudinal groups (in Ehrman 1967, p. 117). The ideas underlying these (broadly) similar categorizations were expressed by Stewart. His sectional type exists to look after the common interests of a section of society, and membership is normally restricted. The cause type of group is open to anyone accepting the belief or principle that is being advanced. His sectional group is, in turn, also broadly similar to Beer's 'producer group' (1969 edn., p. 320), a term which Beer used to cover trade unions, trade associations, and professional organizations. Any simple classification will have border problems, but the 'normal' divide does usefully separate out bodies such as the National Farmers' Union and the British Medical Association from the Society for the Protection of Unborn Children or the Royal Society for the Prevention of Cruelty to Animals. Again, in broad terms, the distinction is between groups *of*, versus groups *for*. However, there is a further dimension which is usually implicit in the sectional versus cause kind of distinction. A representational body such as the Royal Society for Disability and Rehabilitation or the Royal National Institute for the Deaf is not of the kind of producer or professional group for which 'representational' is common shorthand. Such groupings might have more in common with promotional groups. This is particularly so when the representational group fails to convince the government department of its representational credentials; it tends to be the major economic interests that recruit the most convincing levels of support. The National Viewers' and Listeners' Association, so thoroughly identified with Mrs Mary Whitehouse, is another example of a body *for* promoting particular types of media, failing by low recruitment to be a representative body *of* viewers and listeners.

Moran (1985, p. 123), adapting the language of Cawson (1982, pp. 37–43), uses the terms *functional* groups and *preference* groups. Functional groups in this sense stem from the economic order and are principally business, labour, and professional groups. Preference groups are groups 'united by common tastes, attitudes or pastimes'. Such a distinction clearly has kinship with the traditional sectional/promotional ideas.

A prominent distinction in the US literature is that made by Clark and Wilson (1961, p. 135) between material, solidary (*sic*), and purposive incentives. *Material* incentives are related to tangible (usually economic) dimensions, such as discounts, tax benefits, or pay increases. *Solidary* incentives are a social or psychological benefit: friendship, group-belonging, and so on. *Purposive* goals are ideological or issue-orientated and seem very similar to the goals of cause or promotional groups: they 'do not benefit the members in any direct or tangible way'. Using this approach groups can be lotted by the sort of incentives they offer members. On the one hand the group can offer the material incentives associated with (in the main) producer groups, or on the other hand the incentives can be social (solidary) or purposive, as is mainly the case with cause groups.

Some broad generalizations can be made about the political resources available to these sectional/cause kinds of groups. Firstly, the nature of the demands made by the sectional/interest groups are likely to be particular, and often can be conceded without public controversy. The broad class of the group goal would seem to relate to the appropriate strategy. For example, one kind of clue is possibly the 'lumpiness' of the issue. If the topic is bargainable, divisible, and, in Lowi's (1964) terms, 'distributive' (that is, a concession to one interest does not directly and automatically have consequences for another, for example, subsidies on agriculture), it is easy to imagine it being pursued in the private worlds of group–department relations. The CBI guide *Working with Politicians* (1983) significantly quotes one MP arguing at a CBI seminar as follows 'Lobbying is essentially a matter of deflecting government rather than expecting the government to—a sin that dare not speak its name—make a U turn.' Clearly, the group that wishes to make 'deflections' to policy has more prospect of success than one seeking to make significant changes. The goals of producer groups are often limited. On the contrary, a high-profile policy area such as nuclear policy or abortion or constitutional reform is unlikely to be resolved without wide participation and parliamentary legitimation. Furthermore, the demands of producer groups are likely to be consistent with the general values in society. The business group does not have to change values, and it can couch its private concerns in the language of public benefits: jobs will be created, prosperity will follow. Thus the successful producer groups will be looking for long-term relationships: in the words of the CBI, 'Continuous involvement . . . Throughout the year, both in Britain and abroad, many members of the CBI's specialist committees and supporting staff are in almost daily contact with Westminster and Whitehall at all levels.' (*Working with Politicians*, p. 41.)

The promotional group is *likely* to be less well funded, less well staffed, relatively unfamiliar with internal governmental activity. It is likely to be media-orientated rather than access-orientated. The sectional group is likely to have the obverse features and to seek to build a public and media image through public relations rather than protest activity. It is likely to pursue regular contact with government departments rather than confrontation with politicians (from Pross 1981, p. 231).

The matter of group formation is clearly simpler for the producer group. Schattschneider (1960, p. 35) has pointed out that 'Special-interest organizations are most easily formed when they deal with small numbers of individuals who are acutely aware of their exclusive interests. To describe the conditions of pressure-group organization in this way is, however, to say that it is primarily a business phenomenon.'

Producer and professional groups can often be seen as being in *partnership* with departments: in the 1985 furore over the proposed restricted range of NHS drugs the Royal College of General Practitioners asked for 'a constructive partnership between government and profession rather than recrimination and conflict'. Self and Storing's 1962 book on the National Farmers' Union has the significant preface, 'to Partnership, properly understood'. The idea of partnership, though, slides easily into granting veto power to the groups.

When the Government introduced a White Paper on youth training in 1981, the Secretary of State for Employment, Norman Tebbit, announced that it was the Government's intention that unemployed sixteen-year-olds who did not take part would forfeit their right to supplementary benefit. He also proposed an allowance for trainees of about £15 per week. After controversy, particularly over the 'compulsory' aspect, a Youth Task Group was set up under the chairmanship of the Manpower Services Commission, with 'observers' from the Department of Education and Science and the Department of Employment, and representing CBI, TUC, local authorities, voluntary organizations, and educational interests. The task group opposed the 'withold' and the level of benefits, and the report was endorsed by the MSC. The Government backed down, with Mr Tebbit observing in the Commons, 'the Government has noted the firmly-held and clearly expressed views *of those on which the operation of the scheme depends* [our emphasis], that its launch could be seriously impaired by the withdrawal of supplementary benefits'. (see Moon 1986.) Moon has also described how the funding of information technology research through the Alvey steering committee and directorate meant that the Government was more or less reliant on the policy community, 'because the Government needed the compliance of the policy community in administering the programme'.

Another example where private interests are intimately involved with government is the case of the British Overseas Trade Board.

There is representation on the board by major companies, small firms, and the TUC, the CBI, and the Association of British Chambers of Commerce. What is remarkable about this field is that as well as the normal advisory role *vis à vis* the Department of Trade and Industry the board had an executive role of directing the operating decisions of a government department. The secretary to the board has written, 'The money and staff are from government but the priorities are set by businessmen for businessmen . . .' (Rumbelow 1983.)

As we examine in chapter 7, the National Economic Development Council also integrates—to a disputed degree—the TUC and CBI into decisions on economic and manpower policy. But the documented examples of the group doing something impossible (as opposed to less convenient) by direct governmental authority are limited.

It is often proposed (for example, in Ashford 1981, p. 59) that this power of the producer/sectional group is based on the resources which the group controls (usually information) and the strategic importance of the group in determining the success of policy implementation. It is true that groups often hold relevant knowledge, or can gather it less controversially from their members than can government. Sometimes it is also politically convenient (for the government) for the group to carry out governmental tasks: for example, the Association of Chief Police Officers, in running the National Reporting Centre, co-ordinated the reinforcement of local police forces during the NUM strike in 1984–5. Some 1,225 of The Law Society's 1,550 full-time staff are employed to administer the Legal Aid scheme. The deputy secretary-general of The Law Society is also the secretary of Legal Aid. (Davies 1985, p. 76.)

Ashford writes of the British Medical Association (1981, p. 59) that it has 'indispensable advice and skills', and that 'after thirty years of nationalized health and medicine, almost nothing can be done affecting the organization of care, hospitals, medical education, and medical fees without their consent'. He goes on, 'National parties have little time for the vast area of policy making involving local government, but Whitehall needs the active support of groups such as the Town and County Planning Association or the Association of Metropolitan Authorities . . .' Whiteley and Winyard (1983, p. 6), making a point about the resources of producer interests, describe how in the numerous attempts to organize an incomes policy all governments have sought the co-operation of the trade union movement in the implementation of such a policy. When the trade union movement has co-operated, incomes policies have had limited success, but the policies have invariably collapsed when that co-operation was withdrawn. The experience of the 1974–9 Labour Government is a good illustration of this.

However, the basis of group power is perhaps not so much the *threat of non-cooperation*—it is difficult to see the TCPA as one of the commanding institutions of society—but an assumption that policy will be improved through the advice of affected groups. To quote Finer again, 'The form and functioning of British Government are predicated upon the assumption that it will be advised, helped and criticised by the specialist knowledge of interested parties.' (Quoted by Beer 1969 edn., p. 322.) Beer also cited Finer to make the point about the CBI's predecessor, the Federation of British Industries, that 'overwhelmingly its persuasion is concerned with technical and administrative minutiae'. This more restricted argument is that groups are granted influence to improve policy rather than that implementation is impossible without group co-operation. Goodin (1982, p. 42) has also argued that groups are co-opted 'into issue-specific subgovernments not out of necessity but for sheer administrative convenience. While functional necessity, group possession of detailed information, and the strategic role of groups in implementation is one level explanation for the phenomenon of consultation, other explanations also count.' Goodin (1982, p. 47) says administrators in the public sector opt 'for the quiet life. They "accommodate" many groups— giving them virtual vetoes and policies—to avoid "unpleasantness" later, even though the groups in question could cause no real trouble.'

An unusual example of government having recourse to outside expertise cropped up in September 1985 when *The Times* reported that various auctioneers, dealers, and museum staff had received confidential letters asking for information about, and suggesting remedies for dealing with auction 'rings'. Unusually, the consultation was itself confidential. The phenomenon of the 'ring'—where competing buyers purchase an item collectively, and then reauction it among themselves, with a cash share of the 'excess' for those who do not end up with the item—is itself a remarkable example of how competition can coexist with co-operation, as in much public policy-making.

Sir Peter Middleton, current Permanent Secretary at the Treasury, has admitted that there is some tradeoff between granting influence (at least access) in return for the information held by groups: 'there are people who are . . . trying to bend your ear . . . If you want information, you've got to allow people to give you opinions, too.' (Young and Sloman 1984, p. 76.) However, when the medical Royal Colleges boycotted discussions with the Government because the Secretary of State at the DHSS, Norman Fowler, 'broke the rules' and failed to consult them in advance of announcing his proposals for a limited range of drugs for NHS prescription, it was politically embarrassing but not fatal to the proposals. A body of seven specialists had to be appointed as advisers on the detail of the list when the British Medical Association declined its usual role (*The Times*, 2 February 1985). But even if Fowler originally broke the pre-consultation 'rule', by the time the final list emerged it was three and a half times longer than his initial version. While policy is usually born from intimate relations between groups and departments, we, ourselves, would not wish to push too far the idea of departmental dependence on group implementation.

Sometimes, though, a *de facto* veto by the group does appear: in 1968 recruitment of doctors to the Armed Forces was 'virtually brought to a standstill' when the BMA warned off applicants in a battle over conditions of employment (see Jones in Marsh 1983, p. 98). There is, however, a possible confusion between a veto based on what is possible in a legal sense and what makes political sense. When the Government expressed the view that any extension of the power of the Health Services Commissioner/Ombudsman would require the support of the medical profession 'before any proposals could be implemented' (*The Times*, 14 February 1980), was this a statement about the administrative necessity of doctor support or the political sense of avoiding controversy? Where groups have places in the implementation machinery, their potential power is certainly enhanced. In 1985 both the Company Chemists' Association (representing multiples) and the small-shop-based Pharmacists' Action Committee were threatening mass refusal to observe terms of a new contract with the DHSS which, it was claimed, was being foisted on them in 'a process which can only be seen as thoroughly unnecessary, wholly undemocratic and much against the public interest' (*The Times*, 22 June 1985). One argument against capital punishment apparently advanced by ministers at a Conservative back-bench Home Affairs Committee meeting in 1982 was that doctors wouldn't attend the executions.

Promotional groups usually lack the blunt power claimed by one BMA chairman: 'We have the doctors: you want the doctors.' (Jones in Marsh 1983, p. 98.) Promotional goals such as redistribution of income or abolition of hunting cannot normally be attained in the private politics of consultation. In contrast, in discussing the objections of a group—the City Capital Markets Committee—to the 1985 White Paper on Financial Services, *The Times* commented, 'Without the active support of those men and others like them, the new system will be well nigh unworkable.' (1 March 1985.) Whether the impetus to consultation is the push of the veto group or the pull of being seen to act 'democratically' is perhaps unimportant given the routinization of the practice. Civil servants, arguably, do it because it is the job norm they have absorbed.

But there are other bases of the recognition granted to groups. There is the fact that these groups can mobilize protest in the country or in Parliament, which politicians, in particular, would wish to avoid. An extension of this point is the departments' wish to co-opt and hence silence protest. There is also the 'where the shoe pinches, the wearer knows best' assumption, that badly drafted or misdirected legislation will be improved by the advice of the affected interests. Furthermore, the outside group is often encouraged as the ally of the department, pursuing depratmental goals in other ways. It can help to have 'pressure'. But quite distinct from immediate functional benefits, there is the emphasis on consultation and agreement as a democratic quality. Running in tandem with the mainstream democratic belief about numerical majorities, manifestos, and mandates is a belief that policy is defensible only when applied with the consent of interested parties. This belief—as much as control of data, specialized knowledge, or strategic importance in the implementation process—seems to underpin consultation. But this second democratic norm does seem to be relevant mainly for the established, sectional group with its own political resources; promotional groups can still be heard, but they lack the resources that ensure influence.

Norwegian data reported by Christensen and Ronning (1977, p. 10) very convincingly make the point that interaction with government is related to size of full-time group secretariat (See Table 1.1).

TABLE 1.1. *Frequency of Governmental Contact by Different Groups*

Frequency of government contact:	Size of secretariat			
	11 and over (%)	6–10 (%)	1–5 (%)	0 (%)
Daily	35	21	16	4
Weekly	35	27	22	14
Monthly	12	19	35	27
More seldom	18	33	26	55

Groups with larger secretariats are likely to be the better-funded groups and hence professional or producer groups. But quite apart from noting this bias in government contacts with producer groups Table 1.1. usefully demonstrates the *range of different group–department relations*. All groups cannot be sensibly lumped together.

We would not pretend that the various forces leading to a pattern of endemic consultation can be neatly listed and packaged. The AA (*Members Handbook*, 1982–3, p. 22) claims that 'In a wide field of public affairs Governments are well aware that laws are much more likely to be observed if they have the tacit acquiescence of the governed.' This conflates the points of efficient outcomes and democratic procedures.

Some of the numbers involved in consultation are astonishing: the Green Paper on the State Earnings Related Pension (*Reform of Social Security*, Cmnd. 9517) claimed that over 40,000 consultation documents had been issued, and that 4,500 pieces of evidence had been received. But while the Government did retreat on the issue, it was probably not due to the volume of protest but to the fact that a comparatively few, powerful voices were against it. For example, Sir James Cleminson of the CBI claimed that the Green Paper's solutions were so wrong, 'it should be [put] on a bonfire'. Not a single vote in favour was recorded at the CBI's council (*CBI News*, 11 October 1985).

Some access might well not be influential. There is the anecdote of Willie Adamson, who was the first Labour Secretary of State for Scotland. When he had a troublesome deputation he advised them that their plea would get due consideration and he went on, 'd'ye see that door: it's aye open for you'. Apparently the deputation was out on the street before they realized that that was what the open door was for . . .

There can thus be a political significance in access. One example where a group lost its slight foothold of access in consequence of a breach of the 'rules of the game' involved the Standing Committee on National Parks. Although the SCNP had never acquired full consultative rights with the Department of the Environment, in 1971 it did take part in a meeting chaired by the Secretary of State. The chairman of the SCNP read a strong paper which concluded that 'we shall take all political action open to avert the proposed changes'. The Secretary of State interpreted this as a threat, and the SCNP was not circulated with the consultation paper which was the next step in the process (Kimber, Richardson, and Brookes 1974). Another neat example cropped up in the politicking over the implementation of the Finniston Report (Cmnd. 7794) on the organization and regulation of the engineering profession. The chairman of the umbrella body of engineering institutions (the CEI), which had hitherto dominated the policy field, complained, 'Now we find that the Department of Industry is consulting the CBI, the TUC, the Engineering Employers' Federation, Uncle Tom Cobley in fact.' In other words consultation with bodies other than engineering institutions was seen as destabilizing and dangerous for the dominance of groups established in the field. The issue of access does therefore require attention.

There are various kinds of boundary problems in using simple typologies. The sectional TUC can behave promotionally in supporting abortion law reform. A group like Transport 2000 was superficially a promotional group favouring the environmental merits of rail traffic, but it was, in part, a defensive measure by the (sectional) National Union of Railwaymen. Cases of ambiguity are rather different from those of deliberate masking. Truman (1951, p. 65) gives an example of a Farmers' State Rights League which was actually an organization created by cotton mill operators to 'broaden' their opposition to child labour laws. Finer gives some good instances of one *type* of group masquerading as another, for example the Road and Rail Association, which was created by a public relations organization to campaign on behalf of rail. He also cites the London Foundation for Marriage Education, which promoted 'mechanical methods of contraception'. This again was a public relations ploy on behalf of London Rubber Industries, whose product was being challenged by the birth-control pill. When this relationship became too well known London Rubber Industries gave birth to the Genetic Research Unit to argue against oral contraceptives.

A more recent example is the Campaign for Real Ice-Cream (CAMRIC), set up to look like a consumer lobby along the lines of the Campaign for Real Ale but in fact sponsored by the Milk Marketing Board to press for ice-cream containing cream and not vegetable oils. However, CAMRIC was dropped when the ice-cream manufacturers—the Ice Cream Alliance and the Ice Cream Foundation—threatened to boycott British dairy products (*Observer*, 1 July 1984).

FOREST (the Freedom Organisation for the Right to Enjoy Smoking) operates to counter ASH (Action on Smoking and Health). Peter Taylor's book on the politics of tobacco (1984, pp. 133–4) shows that while FOREST's goal and rhetoric is freedom for consumers, its financial support is the self-interested tobacco industry: 'FOREST simply sent the industry most of its bills'.

A Canadian example of the sponsored group is the environmental probird group, Ducks Unlimited. We were told that one of the major financial contributors was the American Rifle Association, which favours migrating ducks for its own unenvironmental reasons. Similarly, a study of a campaign against an oil refinery in northern Scotland reported suspicions that an environmentalist group was being aided by oil companies seeking to pose problems for competitors (Rosie 1978, p. 76).

Another variation on the front-group phenomenon is where the permanent organization, as a tactic, stimulates the one-off, *ad hoc*, campaign organization, often presenting different arguments from the 'parent'. In 1984 the Hot Takeaway Action Group (HOTAG) was set up by the Take-Away Fast Food Federation (TAFFF) to run a public campaign against the imposition of VAT on hot take-away meals.

A discussion in the literature that is distinct from the promotional/ sectional kind of categorization, but which most certainly overlaps with it, is about *legitimacy*. Legitimacy in this sense is acceptance by government departments that the group is making 'reasonable' demands which deserve attention. This point often emerges as a criticism of the system, emphasizing that not all groups have equal 'say'. The criticism has been discovered repeatedly. For example, La Palombara (1964), discussing the development of close clientele relations, argues that the principal requirements of the group are representativeness and respectability. (This is near circularity—what is respectable is what is acceptable as legitimate—but certain behaviours and beliefs are 'out'.) This aspect is also picked up by Pym (1974), Woolf (1965), Kogan (1975), Marcuse (1965), Benewick (1973), and Dearlove (1973). This is perhaps all captured by the jargon term 'trusties' mentioned on page 6.

Another of the critics (Ryan 1978, p. 23) did acknowledge that (conventional) 'pressure group theorists like Potter have been quick to identify "an inner circle" of powerful pressure groups and Finer knew well enough that those groups with a hefty "clout" would be accorded more access than others'. Of course, David Truman (1951, p. 467) had set out the problems of access in discussing 'the inflexibility of the established web'. Herring (1936) had seen that, while in theory the Government should strike a balance among conflicting forces, 'some groups are placed more advantageously than others'. (Finer (1966 edn., p. 38) puts it succinctly; 'a close relationship tends to become a closed one'.

So far then we have seen two main cleavages in the literature:

(a) sectional/functional/producer/interest vs. cause/promotional/attitude/preference
(b) respectable/legitimate/helpful/established vs. not respectable/illegitimate/unhelpful/not established.

A third possible (but still related) dimension is the *strategy* adopted by the groups. Again a coincidence of language is found. Guy Peters (1977) hit upon an insider versus outsider terminology, again seeing legitimacy (from the perspective of the bureaucracy) as the deciding factor. But it was Wyn Grant (1977) who most systematically developed the insider versus outsider strategy categories. His insider groups accept that 'it is important to develop a close relationship with civil servants and local government officials', while other, outsider groups 'either do not wish to become enmeshed in a consultative relationship with officials or are unable to gain recognition'. While the classification is intended to be based on the strategy selected by the group, Grant concedes that the choice is often made by the department in deciding whether or not to grant access. He cites the contrasting experiences of the Committee of Directors of Polytechnics, which was quickly granted recognition by the DES when it was established in 1970, and the National Union of Ratepayers' Associations (founded in 1920), which had been 'sending telegrams to the Treasury' for twenty years but whose channel of access remained the Post Office delivery boy.

One of the National Union of Ratepayers' problems in gaining access is that its recruitment is too limited. It is regarded by the department as a promotional group *for* a particular view and not a representative body on behalf *of* ratepayers. Moreover, Grant (1984, p. 137) shows that such groups may be simply too politically unsophisticated to appreciate the 'impossibilistic' nature of their demands. Thus in 1974, in its evidence to the Layfield Committee on Local Government Finance, the National Association of Ratepayer Action Groups requested that 'in any future Parliamentary debates, on this subject, a free and open vote be taken, and that an amendment be added, that, no alteration of the agreed method be permitted at any time in the future without a similar free and open vote'. Far more powerful groups than NARAG would not make demands that entailed change to the essential nature of the party-controlled parliamentary system. Whiteley and Winyard (1983, p. 19) also reported on the importance of 'recruitment', and they cite a civil servant discounting the lobbying of one-parent groups in the field of social policy because 'we are not happy that the one-parent groups are speaking for their clients. The membership is more likely to contain middle class vocal lone parents not the working class.' They also record another, arguing that 'there is no really representative group in the social security field. CPAG (Child Poverty Action Group) doesn't really talk for anyone—the Claimants' Union are probably the least representative of all.' The importance of the efficiency of the group in mobilizing its potential membership is illustrated by the case of the Farmers' Union of Wales, which was eventually conceded official status after twenty-one years in existence. Before this recognition there were extensive enquiries by MAFF/Welsh Office Agriculture Department about its representativeness, including a special audit of the union membership books.

Grant (1984, p. 137) cites Bechhofer and Elliott's work (1981) to show a group can change from an essentially outsider to an insider organization: 'An early emphasis in protest and direct action was replaced by more emphasis on contacts with government.' He quotes Bechhofer and Elliott's conclusion that 'NFSE as an organization has shifted away from the kinds of direct action which gained it much publicity in its earliest phase to more conventional, and, form the point of view of ministers and civil servants, more acceptable forms of representation. The game has changed from protest to persuasion.' However, most outsider groups lack the political resources necessary for insider status and need to use the alternative outsider strategy.

As an example of a campaigning outsider group, the Campaign for Lead-Free Air (CLEAR) shows the importance for such groups of publicity, such as media events and news conferences. A public opinion poll was organized, both to give the press a 'hook' on which to hang a story, and to convince the Government of electoral attitudes. One opinion poll in 1981 produced an *Observer* front-page headline, a second leader, a *Guardian* leader, and a *Daily Telegraph* story reporting that the Government 'was losing the lead argument' (Wilson, 1983, p. 97.) When campaigning on issues like these, such groups clearly need a different strategy in attempting to convince government of their case from a producer interest attempting to defend its place in the political system.

While not all interest groups gain regularized access, it is also true that some promotional groups do obtain 'legitimacy'. In Ryan's 1978 study of the penal lobby, one group, the Howard League for Penal Reform, is seen as having 'insider status'. Ryan contrasts the treatment given by governments to the Howard League with that given to the 'outsider' Radical Alternatives to Prison. He reports that the Home Office in 1976 refused RAP's request to visit Holloway, while conceding that the Howard League would have been admitted (p. 111). But considering that RAP not only saw prisons as 'symbols of social control and oppression in our class-divided society', but also saw criminal law as a class tool, to suppress the interests of the majority in favour of the economically or socially powerful few, and that it also condemned alternatives such as community service as 'insidious', the Home Office scope for recognition seemed limited. RAP argued that, as society is repressive, 'it is best to have the control that is exercised out in front in the nastiness of the prison system rather than performing similar functions more effectively and wrapped up in the cotton wool of community service' (*RAP Newsletter*, March 1975). Changes such as are demanded by RAP are clearly not the regular diet of consultation. The goals of the group really determined its 'outsider' position.

Grant claims that the distinction between insider and outsider strategy is not based on effectiveness—outsider groups can be effective and insider ineffective—but the strong implication is that insider groups are the legitimate groups, are the effective groups. Legitimacy is generally a characteristic to be gained over time, and hence the importance of the piggy-back campaign, where a campaigning group 'borrows' the legitimacy of others. Thus the Abortion Law Reform Association, ASH, and Action on Alcohol Abuse have been seen as trading on the legitimacy of established support groups such as the Royal College of Physicians and the Royal College of Psychiatrists (Davies 1985, p. 11). As argued above, there are several reasons for suspecting that the economic interest groups are more readily seen as legitimate and 'consultable'. For one thing, the demands they make are *not* likely to be fundamental and *are* likely to be satisfied without attracting the comment of counter-groups. Specialist, particularist, demands can be made (and settled) in 'private'.

The customarily incremental demand of the sectional (often economic) interest is a reason to expect insider tactics, and the acceptance of those tactics by the relevant department. The alternative type of demand, as used by the Abortion Law Reform Association (ALRA), has features which push it to outsider status. It is hard to negotiate if the subject matter is defined by some as child murder: incremental adjustments to numbers are beside the point. There are also active and vocal counter-groups, such as the SPUC, and civil servants will be chary of too-close involvement with ALRA-type groups when they know that protests by counter-groups will be made. When one notes Sir Douglas Wass observing, 'You have to remember that we are in continuous contact with the large pressure groups . . .', it is clear from this context that he means contacts with *representative* producer or *professional bodies*. Promotional groups are usually too politically contentious for the civil service to allow them into bed. The potentially ephemeral nature of the cause group also, in theory, inhibits regularized relations, but in practice many promotional groups, such as ALRA, often must maintain themselves to protect their policy success.

Another qualification needed to the broad sectional = insider, promotional = outsider rule is the possibility of groups changing character over time. The Farmers' Union of Wales is an example of a group being promoted to insider status: few groups would willingly move the other way. May and Nugent (1982) have identified the thresholder option as a third possibility between inside and outside strategies. They argue that the trade unions in the 1960s and 1970s fitted this thresholder category, ceasing to rely wholly on the insider strategy of the George Woodcock era. They do seem correct in suggesting that 'some pressure groups may adopt dual strategies . . . (and) swing between a "responsible" search for élite acceptance, with the close consultation with officials this implies, and more vociferous and more openly militant tactics'.

The local authority associations are another example where 'warfare' on the rate front coexists with more business-like relations elsewhere. Thus Jack Graham of the Association of Metropolitan Authorities, describing how the AMA successfully forced the Department of Transport to enforce the 38-tonne lorry weight (instead of allowing a 2-tonne overload tolerance which effectively allowed a 40-tonne weight), claimed,

It took the Association three weeks to crack this particular nut on its own . . . But there are many instances where lobbying, sometimes in conjunction with other Associations or with other non-Governmental agencies, is successful . . . The draft circular on Land for Housing in the Green Belt is . . . [an example] . . . The national press gave credit to the Council for the Protection of Rural England but in fact the campaign succeeded because of the combined efforts of a range of organisations including the AMA . . .

It is all too easy to think that the real work of the local authority Associations is related to the major policy issue of the day—be it rate-capping, *Streamlining* or Green Belt policy. The reality is very different. There is a vast range of issues affecting one or more functions . . . (*Municipal Review*, April 1984, p. 7.)

This 'business as usual' comment can be contrasted with the comment in the same issue of *Municipal Review* by the retiring chairman of the AMA, Sir Jack Smart. He complained that the Government had undermined the Consultative Council on Local Government Finance:

Since the Tories came to power it is no longer a consultative body. The Government uses it to make it look as though it is consulting but it is a charade. The Government's view of consultation is that it listens to what we say and then does what it was going to do anyway.

The two comments thus confirm the difficulty in talking about *the* relationship between a broad interest group and broad government: it is likely to differ by particular issue.

Finer's (1966 edn., p. 43) proposed 'law of inverse proportion', by which 'The clearer and snugger the lobby's consultative statutes, the more exclusive its relationship with its ministry, the less use it will make of parliamentary methods', is both neat and substantially true. He usefully points out that while for promotional groups their main target might realistically be public opinion, it would be 'impolite and imprudent' for the influential, domesticated, interest groups not to try insider methods first. Therefore their preferred targets are (1) executive, (2) Parliament, (3) party, (4) public (in Ehrman 1958, p. 130). There are many instances of a group deliberately refraining in Finer's words, from 'using Westminster for fear it offends Whitehall'.

Whiteley and Winyard (1983) suggest that successful producer groups would positively avoid ostentatious publicity: 'indeed a group forced into undertaking public campaigns would only be advertising its impotence'. They follow Eckstein (1960, p. 21), who observed, 'A group which simply does not have ready access to an executive department—which has no close clientele relationship with such a department—may be driven willy-nilly to seek its aims through other channels.' But as Kimber and Richardson (1974, p. 13) have noted, 'pressure group activity is generally more complicated than the promotional = public target, sectional = executive target suggests'. It has to be recognized that various strategies can be used simultaneously.

In Whiteley and Winyard's (1983) study, they extend the ideas of government dependence on producer groups with specialist information to their field of promotional groups in social policy. Following the dependence model (which they term the Beer–Eckstein model), they assume that government will be impressed by groups with specialized advice and by groups with votes to deliver. They thus assume that effective groups will concentrate almost exclusively on Whitehall while playing down the importance of Parliament, the media, and the public.

In fact, when they look at cases, the assumptions of the model are not confirmed. They divide their 'universe' of social policy groups into four main categories:

Whitehall oriented	14 e.g.	MIND, MENCAP
Whitehall and Parliament	17 e.g.	Disablement Income Group
Parliament	1	CHAR (Campaign for Homeless and Rootless)
Unclassified	10	

(From Whiteley and Winyard 1983, p. 16.)

but immediately have to record that practically all groups, in practice, have some sort of contact with *both* Whitehall and Parliament. They show that there is not a simple pattern of groups orientated to single targets. They cite as an example the Disablement Income Group (DIG), whose parliamentary spokesman observed, 'You can't do it just through officials; a public approach is necessary to get a groundswell.' Despite this recourse to public channels, civil servants still found DIG 'balanced and sound'. Although the 'partnership' of the NFU and MAFF is everyone's best example of an insider relationship, this does not stop the NFU maintaining regular contact with about 100 MPs: about 100 where the NFU know their briefs will not automatically be filed in the wastepaper basket. The NFU will use Parliament, and in 1985 was considering taking MAFF to court over faulty administration of the fund for disease eradication in pigs. Though basically an insider group, other strategies can none the less be used.

Whiteley and Winyard did find some groups ruled out of civil service consideration because of their strategy: for example, the National Federation of Claimants Union received the 'put down' that they came 'not to negotiate, but to get on TV'. But on the whole Whiteley and Winyard's work confirmed Kimber and Richardson's point that the pattern of type of group, target, and type of campaign is more complicated than Finer's broad rule allowed. As Kimber and Richardson (1974, p. 13) claim, in many cases groups try to use several channels simultaneously: 'It is quite common for promotional groups to submit memoranda to the relevant Department, to lobby MPs and to utilize the mass media concurrently . . . The British Road Federation, to take a sectional example, urges a continuing public campaign on the need for more roads even though it and its members have good administrative contacts.' On the issue of a restricted list of NHS drugs during 1985, the 'insider' Association of the British Pharmaceutical Industry engaged in heavy press advertising: the BMA threatened to test the Government's policies in the courts as being contrary to the Treaty of Rome. Several hundred farmers lobbied the Commons in July 1984 over EEC milk production quotas. In other words, these stalwart, insider pillars were quite prepared for campaigning politics. The key word is *credibility* and, carefully done, credibility can be maintained without total docility.

Finer noted (1966, p. 34) that 'The rule might be expressed, very simply, thus: both parties are assumed to trust one another and one another's intentions and if either party wants to be treated responsibly, it must act responsibly.' Part of the professional relationship now appears to respect that the other side—if only for reasons of the internal politics of the organization—must operate, on occasion, outside the insider style. The totally tame group lacks this useful punch of unpredictability. Whiteley and Winyard (1983, p. 17) claim that the Royal Association for Disability and Rehabilitation, which was largely instigated and funded by the Government, was ineffective because of its 'sweetheart relationship with government', whereas the Disablement Income Group (DIG), with 'distinct insider status', was highly regarded by the Civil Service, despite sometimes using public campaigns and even arranging for the defeat of the Government in the House of Lords, in spite of pleading from a senior civil servant.

When one examines the list of voluntary associations in receipt of grants from the voluntary services unit of the Home Office, one finds that around fifty groups received over £2 million p.a. between them (£2.87m.) in 1980–81 (see *Hansard*, 8 April 1981, col. 272). The groups included Child Poverty Action Group, Gingerbread, Brixton Neighbourhood Community Association, Release, and Community Service Volunteers. Even recognition to the extent of financial support does not necessarily mean that a group is in any meaningful sense 'insider'. Chapter 9 demonstrates that a group can be seen as 'useful' in service delivery but still 'suspect' in terms of policy determination.

Similarly, all business groups are not automatically and necessarily 'insider'. Thus Open Shop, which pushes for the abolition of restrictions on Sunday trading, is essentially a promotional group—with promotional tactics—despite a weighty membership list including W. H. Smith, Asda, and Woolworths (*The Times* 8 October 1984). While individually the member companies might be legitimate, the end pursued is controversial, with countervailing religious and trade union opinion, so that the Open Shop cannot pursue an insider strategy.

Paul Press's work in Canada has also attempted to break the link between goal of group and strategy of group. He has used the key terms *institutionalized groups* and *issue groups*. He defines them as:

(*a*) Institutional groups possess organizational continuity and cohesion, commensurate human and financial resources, extensive knowledge of those sectors of government that affect them and their clients, a stable membership, concrete and immediate operational objectives associated with philosophies that are broad enough to permit [them] to bargain with government over the application of specific legislation or the achievement of particular concessions, and a willingness to put organizational imperatives ahead of any particular policy concern.

(*b*) Issue groups are governed by their orientation toward specific issues . . . and have limited organizational continuity and cohesion, minimal and often naïve knowledge of government, fluid membership, a tendency to encounter difficulty in formulating and adhering to short range objectives, a generally low regard for the organizational mechanisms they have developed for carrying out their goals, and, most important, a narrowly defined purpose, usually the resolution of one or two issues or problems, that inhibits the development of 'selective inducements' . . . designed to broaden the group's membership base. (From Press 1981, pp. 288–9.)

Press's example of an institutionalized group is Greenpeace, which by our terms is a promotional group. Thus the process of institutionalization (or integration) is independent of the nature of the demand on government. None the less, in our view, rich and suggestive though the definitions are, arguably the *tendency* would be for producer groups to become institutionalized and the issue groups to be non-economic and non-professional.

Further classificatory points can be gleaned from Whiteley and Winyard's work (1984, p. 34) on 'The Origins of the "New Poverty

Lobby" '. Like May and Nugent, they argue that the various dimensions of group classification need to be disaggregated: they argue, for example, that the outsider/insider system of definitions 'confuses the two separate dimensions of strategy and status'. They claim that there are groups which are insider in terms of status, but whose use of publicity and the media mean that they are outsiders in terms of strategy. Their solution is thus to categorize groups according to four dimensions. The least familiar dimension is probably the first strategy. Their open-focused continuum of strategy is demonstrated by their contrast between DIG and CPAG. They quote a parliamentary spokesman for DIG claiming, 'when it comes to getting things done I would go for private contact with civil servants'. This they contrast with the director of CPAG: 'our main job is to shift government not to chat with civil servants . . . coverage in the media is our main strategy'.

Strategy:	(O) Open	(F) Focused
Membership:	(P) Promotional	(R) Representational
Status:	(A) Accepted	(N) Not Accepted
Activity:	(L) Lobbying	(S) Service

One merit of this approach used in a narrow field of related poverty groups is to emphasize the variety within the field, but it does run into a problem of over-sophistication. They find that many of the new lobby groups are OPALS (open, promotional, accepted, and lobbying): but it is just plain unwieldy and inconvenient to discuss DIG as FPAL (focused, promotional, accepted, lobbying). They do effectively make their point that groups of the 1960s and 1970s in the new poverty lobby tended to be of a particular type—OPALS. But different contexts might produce different dimensions of relevance, such as size, financial resources, and so on.

Two main streams thus exist in the literature; the approaches which find two major categories, and the approaches written in reaction which accept a more complex typology. One way to choose between the approaches is to consider the purpose for which the classification is made: horses for courses. Though simple twofold categories have weaknesses, the picture can become so complex when one allows for all the dimensions available that simple divisions still have a useful place.

The main focus of this book is insider (and therefore *usually*) sectional groups. The generalizations that fit these groups—which work by bargaining and the development over time of co-operative relations with politicians and administrators—are simply inappropriate when one is considering the activities of outsider groups. The following description of the sort of language and mental set of the professionalized lobbyist relates primarily to the former type of group.

Getting in the In-tray

This kind of lobbying of politicians and administrators has become professionalized in that rules of acceptable behaviour have developed. In the world of the professional lobbyist, the self-justification is that 'the most democratic thing to do is to argue your case as hard as you can so that those people who take the decisions . . . have all the information before they finally make up their minds'.

The repeated refrain is *credibility*. To pass the 'gate-keepers' certain conditions pertain: in one phrase from a lobbyist, 'No hippies'. That merely means that conventional dress and non-radical demands have easier access. 'Past track record' is another cliché, which is a different way of saying that the views expressed must be reliable. An American summary of the qualities needed was 'be pleasant and inoffensive, be well prepared and informed, be personally convinced of your arguments, pursue the soft sell, convince the official of the issue's importance to him in his constituency or in terms of the public interest, and leave a written summary behind' (Greenwald 1977, p. 63). Greenwald also quoted another survey: 'do not carry a brief-case to a meeting since the official may think it contains a tape recorder and do not lie, double cross or make mistakes, do not lobby at a party until coffee is being served: eat where law makers eat; smile until your face aches'. Both lists, Greenwald says, stress pleasantness and competence, reflecting the reality that lobbyists have little with which to threaten legislators. One Canadian lobbyist we talked with argued that 'retreads from the bureaucracy' make the best lobbyists: 'It is easier to teach about the industry than to teach "life in the town" to the man who already knows the industrial background'.

'Success' is a function of limited goals and a bargaining mentality. A British lobbyist (NFU) has observed that 'Some lobbies do seem to have difficulty in judging the art of the possible; to see what is on and what is not. They tend to be rather plaintive about a compromise solution.' He stressed the contrary, the need to educate the membership on what is feasible. Inflated expectations would cause problems. He said [we] get the best deal going and then explain to the farmers . . .'

The professional view is

Political lobbying is not a smash and grab . . . You've got to cultivate them and it takes time. Like gardening some of your plants will come up nicely and others not at all . . . It's important that briefing should be accurate. There is no point in giving a politician something which doesn't tell the whole truth . . . In presenting a case to the Ministry and to politicians your case must be accurate, reasonable and politically attractive . . . The important thing is not to discredit the source by over-selling any particular argument.

The CBI advice to its members (in *Working with Politicians*, 1983, p. 14) similarly argues, 'Regular dialogue . . . makes it more likely that the MP will be attentive to *ad hoc* representations on issues . . .'

Grant (1984, p. 137) claims that to obtain access to senior civil servants the group has to show civil servants that it can (and is prepared to) 'talk their language', and that it knows how to present a case and how to bargain and accept the outcomes of the bargaining process. He quotes an editorial from *Association Management* (the professional journal for group officials): 'We have to learn the language and procedures of government and blend our work with it where necessary.' An official of the National Consumers' Council has also emphasized the importance of knowing civil servants and of being willing to bargain and compromise. Thus he argues that 'Most important is an acquaintance with key civil servants: departmental officials know better than anyone else which way things are moving', and 'Lobbying inevitably calls for bargaining at some stage, either directly with allies, officials or competitors, indirectly via the political process, or both. The jargon of the bargaining process—in lobbying as in other activities—speaks of "tradeoffs", "fall-back positions", and "sticking-points".' (Smith 1986, p. 10.) Interestingly, Smith (as a working lobbyist) also uses a rather broad definition of the term 'pressure group'. He argues that 'pressure group' is 'a phrase which should be construed more widely than it usually is . . . Politicians and civil servants are frequently heard to say "I (or we) are under pressure from x to do y . . .". Pressure is there to be absorbed, resisted, manipulated or responded to as appropriate: the rules of the game on the other side of the fence are well understood.' (Smith 1986, p. 2.)

2

The Development of the Modern Pluralist Approach

The thrust of our argument is that pressure group writing stems from empirical studies of the policy process. While it is natural to attempt to set the scene by defining 'a pressure group', and by establishing subsidiary types of group as is suggested in chapter 1, we would do better to define our interest as a process. The units which interest us are the actors in that process of pressure politics. Early group writers, such as Odegard (1928), set out to answer the question, 'How is policy made?' Odegard's book is a well-documented, blow-by-blow account of pressure politics about prohibition; for example:

A preliminary poll showed a majority of one in favour. Two days before the vote was to be taken, Senator Crook of Dayton, who had promised to support the [temperance] bill, announced that three committees of brewers distillers and saloon keepers of Dayton had visited him and that he had decided to vote against it. That afternoon, Mr. Russell [of the Temperance Alliance] went to Dayton. Letters, telegrams and petitions from citizens of the city poured in . . . The Senator did vote for it and the measure passed by a majority of one. (Odegard 1928, p. 3.)

One complication in the genealogy of the ideas is that the conclusions of the empiricists such as Odegard about how decisions *are* made are similar to (the largely) nineteenth-century pluralist view on how decisions *should be* made. It is therefore common to see group theory as the outgrowth of classical pluralism. Garson (1978, p. 15), for one, writes that Latham (1952) is absolutely correct in emphasizing the origin of modern group theory of politics in the pluralist critique of sovereignty. Connolly (1969, p. 4) places the intellectual roots of pluralist theory back with Aristotle, Madison, and de Toqueville. Against this assumption of continuity must be weighed the fact that the early 'sources'—save perhaps for Dahl's interest in Madison—are simply not quoted with frequency by contemporary pluralists.

We do not believe that Odegard or Herring—or more recent commentators—developed the group interpretation of modern policy-making while looking over their shoulder at nineteenth-century, or earlier, theory. It is possible and tempting to find passages in the classical thinkers which anticipate current concerns, but Odegard wrote about groups because they seemed to influence policy, not because of a theory about the state.

Indeed the remarkable feature of contemporary pluralism is not only its lack of continuity with earlier work but its lack of internal coherence and of definitional sophistication. Dahl (1984, p. 232) has observed how the concept of pluralism, which he had used in passing in *Politics, Economics and Welfare* (1953), took on a life of its own. He said

'Pluralist theory', came to designate a strange mélange of ideas. In fact, a good deal of the 'theory' consisted of interpretations by hostile critics who sometimes constructed a compound of straw men and inferences from the work of assorted writers who by no means held the same views. Frequently the result was a 'theory' that probably no competent theorist—pluralist or not—would find plausible.

Disarmingly, Dahl (1984, p. 240) says about his key work *Who Governs?* (1961), '*Pace* some interpretations, the book was not written to advance a general "pluralist theory of politics": in fact, "pluralism" and pluralist democracy are not included in the index. In hindsight, it might have been better to set out a more explicit theory. But perhaps not.'

Pluralism is often presented as the dominant political science creed, but there is a lack of a systematic, sympathetic, and authoritative account of pluralist features. *Polyarchy* is better-defined than pluralism. Polyarchy was used by Dahl and Lindblom (1953) as their term for the approximation to democracy of the Western political systems. They retain 'democracy' as an ideal type against which existing polyarchies can be measured. In Dahl and Lindblom's work pluralism is involved as a component in polyarchy because there was a deliberate contradiction (based on de Tocqueville) of the notion (associated with Rousseau) that societies had, or should aspire to, a common good and a common will. A dispersal of political power and political views was seen as an advantage. While polyarchy is better-defined, pluralism seems a more natural-sounding (and is certainly the more popular) term.

The latter term has more or less usurped the status and meaning of the former. When Dahl himself wrote *Who Governs?*, in using the term 'pluralism'—as in 'the need for a new pluralist theory of community power' (p. vi), or 'New Haven has gradually changed from oligarchy to pluralism' (p. 11), or 'does the way in which political resources are distributed encourage oligarchy or pluralism?' (p. 7)—he seems to have himself used the term interchangeably with 'polyarchy'.

Dahl argues (1985, p. 232) that, while aspirations aimed at discovering a common will in society were embodied in classical democratic theory, this was only (if at all) realizable in the small city-state rather than the large nation state. In the nation state, conflict and differentiation was inevitable, and Dahl argues that de Tocqueville saw varied associational life in the nation state as a means of countering tyranny—even a tyranny of the majority.

He argued (1984, p. 34) that

A monostic view like Rousseau's in the *Social Contract* arguably might be applicable to democracy on the smaller scale of the city state . . . In a small and intimate democratic association the presence of other associations that compete for loyalty and support, weaken cohesion and consensus, and stimulate conflict may be . . . downright undesirable . . . However that may be, whenever an effort has been made to realise the democratic idea on the scale of the nation state and the institutions of polyarchy have come to exist, relatively independent associations and organizations of considerable variety and number have also developed.

Therefore Dahl's argument is that organizational pluralism, while anathema to classical (city-state) democracy, is both inevitable and desirable in large-scale democracy. Suppression of such pluralism is generally recognized as the sort of behaviour pursued by authoritarian regimes (he cites Chile and Uruguay in 1973).

He goes on (1985, p. 235) to recognize that this—valued—pluralism may have undesirable consequences. Some interests might have more resources and better access to decision processes: the pattern of inequalities in society might be maintained. The pursuit of sectoral interests might be at the expense of minorities. Dahl says, 'organizational pluralism . . . may also distort the public agenda by focussing the political process on alternatives that promise visible short-run benefits to a small minority of well-organised citizens rather than on alternatives that would provide significant long run benefits to a large number of unorganized citizens.' (See Olson 1982, discussed in our concluding chapter.)

Dahl also expresses concern that the autonomous organizations can themselves take on public functions. The difficulty for democracy in these arrangements is that the organizations are not themselves, controlled by the public. While he concedes that a mixture of numerical democracy and corporate pluralism has advantages, he says 'it is also undeniable that they raise perplexing problems for democratic theory'.

Pluralism (or polyarchy) is then an ill-defined concept, but it seems to hold that policy is best made through a competition of viewpoints; that valid representation of the public is made through the leadership of interest groups; that the groups influential in one area will not necessarily be powerful elsewhere: that decisions are not all made centrally, but at different levels; that participants show a willingness to bargain and to compromise.

Although Garson (1978) is undoubtedly correct to argue that the point can be exaggerated, the classical pluralists were in reaction against a normative view that the state should be sovereign. They saw groups/associations as defences against the over-powerful state. We would argue that that state sovereignty literature and its criticism are arguably of only historical interest. Modern group and pluralist writers are more inclined to use the term 'government' than 'state'. As Wolfe has noted critically, 'political science became the study, not of the state, but of something at a less rarefied level called government' (1977, p. xii, quoted in Ham and Hill 1984, p. 29). Pluralists rarely need to invoke the concept of state as opposed to government, and may even use the terms as synonymous. Latham (1952, p. 380) usefully discriminates between the *philosophic* pluralists of the nineteenth century and the *analytical* pluralists (broadly) of the twentieth. The latter school is more empirical, less normative, than the former.

We see the contemporary interest in pluralism as stemming from the 'Who does what to influence outcomes?' sort of orientation of Odegard, rather than the anti-statist political philosophy of Laski, Maitland, and others. Odegard's book (above) is of course a description of the battle between alcohol prohibition groups such as the Anti-Saloon League and pro-drink interests such as the Civil Liberty League, the Liberty League, and the American Hotel Protective Association. The label group theory can be attached, though only in his preface does Odegard write about group theory rather than group action. Like many other 'pluralist' writers, Odegard was more intent on describing than theorizing. He notes that direct democracy is incompatible with large numbers, and that organized democracy is the consequence. He claims that political parties can reflect a very few cleavages of opinion, most especially in a two-party system. Accordingly he sees the pressure group as the organized response to the gap between the individual and the two-party system:

Without organization, in the modern state, the individual is lost and his influence is negligible. If he goes to Washington or Albany as a private citizen in an effort to influence legislation it is improbable that he will be so much as be given a hearing. If he goes as the agent of the United States Chamber of Commerce, the Association Against the Prohibition Amendment or the Ku Klux Klan, his influence will be considerable.

Odegard certainly implies that he sees this activity as legitimate: 'To say that the members of business organizations or religious groups shall not take an active part in politics is to say that they shall have no voice in the determination of the legal arrangements governing their own lives.' (p. ix.) He suggests that group activity does exist, and that it is no bad thing. This kind of 'group theory' is certainly consistent with pluralism or polyarchy, but it did not anticipate the explicit argument of Dahl's A Preface to Democratic Theory (1956).

E. P. Herring produced two main volumes of relevance to this discussion of the historical background to modern pluralism. The first was Group Representation Before Congress (1929). We have already cited Herring's assumption that most viewpoints were organized. He claimed that his was not a study of political theory, but rather a description of fact, an account of the number and power of groups in existence. But patently he sided with what he called the pluralistic conception of the state (p. 10). His most potent idea is perhaps his proposition that the seed of the growth of interest participation in government was complexity, as in 'the problems . . . in some cases have become so technical and complex that the legislator needs expert guidance' (p. 11).

His picture of American lobbyists in the 1920s does not look unfamiliar when held up against Britain in the 1980s. Herring describes the importance of mailing lists (p. 63), 'front' organizations

(p. 64), the value of organizing mass personal mail for Congressmen (p. 70), the importance of technical data (p. 72), and of gimmicks (p. 72).

One particular reason for reviewing the work of Herring is that he, as did other early group writers, recognized that the public interest was an issue. To defeat a given group, a counterweight representing a definite interest is needed. He commented: 'it is rare indeed that so general a concept as the "public interest" is sufficient to defeat the measure. The public has no lobby.' (p. 63.) But on the whole Herring was a sympathetic critic of the 'new lobby'. He suggested that it is impossible to suppress the lobby—''Twere easier to dam Niagra'—and instead he encouraged incorporation of special interests in the decision process.

The Public Interest?

Herring's second main book, *Public Administration and the Public Interest* (1936), again raised the concept of the 'public interest' as one of the key issues. Herring adopts a very different position from his—better-known—predecessor Bentley, who had in his bold style written off the public interest. Bentley queried whether government could (or should) attempt by detached reasoning to divine *the* public or national interest. (p. 447.) He claimed that it was group pressure which established the values 'that reason may claim to use as its guides'. We have deliberately not started off our discussion with Bentley's work. While his work is important, there is no direct connection between Bentley and later group writers. Bentley adopted an extreme position on the public interest, and had a specialist conception, unqualified, of 'group' that was simply not followed by later writers in the group tradition.

Bentley (1908, 1967 edn., p. 347) took the view that the so-called governmental view was the dominant group view. Thus he instanced that when Roosevelt took office he was known to have tariff reform sympathies. He explained Roosevelt's 'betrayal' as stemming from the fact that there was not an extensive enough set of groups to back the change: 'Government is then the prevailing balance of interests.' (p. 264.) He claimed that the balance of the group pressures *is* the existing state of society (p. 259).

It can be argued that Bentley's indifference as to who prevails gives 'academic absolution to the triumph of special interests over the common good' (Odegard in Bentley, p. xxxv).

There are three possible positions over this proposition:

(a) that what the Government does *is* the public interest—the Bentley line.

(b) that the Government 'holds the ring' between competing interests, adjudicating competing claims.

(c) that the Government can legitimately determine the public interest and that attempts to sway by pressure could be restricted.

Bentley, for most tastes, goes too far in appearing to say 'What is, is best.' For example, interviews at the Department of Transport in 1983 established that the department was pursuing a policy demanding a new type of dim–dip headlight even though major producer group pressures were against it. The manufacturer's lobby, which opposed the extra expense, was considered by the department to be better organized, with better parliamentary contacts than its road safety opponents. It was described as 'super-professional'. None the less the department wanted to go ahead, influenced by some kind of basic sense of public interest. This is not to say that on the other hand the Government has a technique of reliably establishing the public interest. The support of interested publics is more pressing than the 'public interest', but any civil servant would retain some idea of a broader interest than their immediate clientele, and on occasion the particular claims being made will not convince them.

Certainly not all group theorists follow Bentley and see no possible public interest, but nor would they favour option (c) and believe that government could decide without being informed by the interests to be affected by any particular policy.

In other words, the mainstream pluralist position appears to be judgemental, that normally the public interest is served by group pressures, but that sometimes government should act as referee rather than the arm of the majority. While we must beware this judgemental compromise as being a fudge of the issue, reservations by, say, Herring seem sensible.

Herring (1936, p. 388) does not, for example, believe in closed policy-making, and advocates consultation with groups and persons as a regular feature of administration. He claimed that 'Officials cannot properly set themselves up as the sole expounders as to just what constitutes the public interest.' But, at the same time, Herring denies that any (one) group can interpret the public interest with complete finality (p. 28). He claims that under democracy the public interest is based on a compounding of many group interests (p. vii). Lindblom (1959, p. 85) also suggests that the system works if 'every important interest or value has its watch dog'.) Herring's preface establishes that the issue for him is the fairness of the contest. He suggests that 'In theory our government should strike a balance among these conflicting forces so as to promote the welfare of all. In fact some groups are placed more advantageously than others within our governmental structure and under our industrial system.' (p. vii.) 'How can a balanced execution of law in the public interest result from an administrative service that is the product of fortunately situated economic groups?' When, in similar tone, Herring notes that 'the voice of the people' sometimes suggests 'the squeal of pigs at the trough,' it is clear that within the early group literature many of the later criticisms are anticipated. Herring asks, 'Is the scope and development of our administrative service to be determined by the urging of special groups . . .? How can interests that are socially important but politically weak be given a place in the federal administration?' (p. 5.) He labels US bureaucracy as a 'tangle of alphabetical monstrosities', but concludes that the modern democratic state is in business to reconcile group interests, and that this requires a 'great administrative machine' (p. 9).

In practice, the administrator begins to equate public interest with the interest of the special publics that lobby him. The current Permanent Secretary at the British Treasury has presented the willingness to talk to organizations which represent groups of people as a practical substitute for fuller public contact (in Young and Sloman 1984, p. 75). The articulated demands of groups across the table are more pressing than conjecture about the wishes of unorganized publics. Of course the public interest is a potent slogan and interest groups prefer to argue with it than against it. So the group contest is often conducted in terms of competing versions of the so-called public interest.

Group theorists have tended to see a competition among group interests as a realist approximation to public interest, but they have not at all times been complacent about the outcome of group interactions. This, in turn, lays them open to another criticism. It is not obvious where these values come from that allow them to judge 'fairness', but that has not been the usual criticism.

Dahl and Truman: The Pluralist Platform

The two major figures in the development of the modern literature are undoubtedly Truman (1951) and Dahl (e.g. 1967). As we have seen, Dahl's (1967, p. 386) main theme is perhaps the widespread distribution of political resources of a pluralist society: 'few groups in the United States who are determined to influence the government—certainly few if any who are organized, active and persistent—lack the capacity and opportunity to influence some officials somewhere in the political system in order to obtain at least some of their goals'. However, Dahl and Truman do have reservations on the desirability of group politics. Truman claims that righteous indignation is not a sufficient response to group abuse: what is needed 'are correctives, protections and controls' (p. 12). His concluding chapter discusses imperfections in group democracy. He acknowledges, for example, that certain interests could fail to mobilize in time to articulate and protect their viewpoint (p. 516). But the general tone in *The Governmental Process* is positive: a favourable gloss is given to group activity. His opening chapter addresses 'The *Alleged* Mischiefs of Faction', and is a defence of politics as competition of interests.

Truman's apparent complacency at this form of politics is perhaps based on a belief that the range of groups is so wide as to be, *de facto*, a realistic form of democratic expression. His image of society is 'a sort of mosaic' of groups; he sees 'a bewildering array of groups'. He uses a 1949 US Department of Commerce survey of national associations to give some crude idea of the scale of the group phenomenon: over 200,000 groups, with 4,000 at national level (p. 58). While many of these were business groups, others existed, and Truman notes that the business groups were often in competition with each other: for example, importers might want low tariffs while domestic industry might wish for barriers.

If one of the reasons for Truman's acceptance of group democracy is the range of groups in existence, the second is the possibility of the 'the potential group'. He believes that an interest can be identified whether or not it exists at a point in time. It is part of Truman's defence of group democracy that where an interest is neglected in the political system there will (generally) be mobilization of this new interest.

In developing the potential group concept Truman appears uneasy. While not following Bentley in all important regards—his definition of 'group' is much narrower—he was respectful enough of his pioneer's work to wish to avoid contradicting him. And Bentley had, of course, appeared to warn against belief in potential groups. He was for rigid empiricism: 'From the interest as a thing by itself no conclusion can be drawn.' Truman's *potential* group is not itself directly observable.

It was an article of faith for Truman that group pressures stimulate new group formation. Partly this is an argument based on logical prediction, partly it is developed from empirical observation; but we suspect that it is also partly wishful thinking. It avoids issues of justice in the system.

Truman is aware that he has to explain how harmony emerges from this image of conflict, in that organized interests more or less consistently reconcile their differences, adjust, and accept compromises. He accepts that some explanation is needed (p. 59), and appears to sneak in a concept of the state as part of his (not very clear) explanation, though he refuses to accept a national interest or public interest (pp. 50, 51). More emphasis is, however, placed on the mechanism of overlapping groups as a limit to conflict.

The overlapping membership idea is crucial. There is in Truman's terms a 'complex of criss-crossing membership' (p. 508). Although the example is almost trivial, he develops the point by stating, 'Thus the leaders of a Parent Teacher Association must take some of the fact that their proposals must also be acceptable to members who also belong to the local taxpayers league, to the local chamber of commerce, to the Catholic Church.' (p. 509.) He thus concludes (p. 520), 'Overlapping membership among organized interest groups and among these and potential groups is, as we have seen, the principal balancing force in the politics of a multigroup society such as the United States.' Schattschneider (1942) similarly makes the point that to assume that minorities will stop at nothing to get what they want is to postulate a degree of unanimity within these groups that does not often exist in real life. He claims that most people have many conflicting interests dispersing their drives: 'The result of the fact that every individual is torn by the diversity of his own interests, the fact that he is a member of many groups, is *the law of* the imperfect mobilization of interests.'

Another source of particular relevance in the development of the group approach is Earl Latham's 1952 study, which is in large part a case study of an attempt by the Federal Trade Commission to stop the Cement Institute (a manufacturer's organization) controlling the price of cement. There is also a general theoretical discussion of some significance, however. In particular Latham makes the important and necessary distinction between 'official' groups and others. By official he means (roughly) governmental. He notes that the Bureau of Internal Revenue can tax individuals and corporations, but not vice versa, and that the policeman on the corner can blow a whistle and stop a car driver, but the driver cannot stop the policeman. There is, then, no full reciprocity in the relationships. Latham notes the importance of the group in controlling member-ship: though this point was developed by the corporatists in the 1970s, it was a premiss of the earlier group analysts.

The Position in Britain

The major literature on pressure groups is thus American. There is no major British contributor to theory, despite a frequent claim that the British political science orthodoxy is pluralist. Indeed, one can extend this point to claim (with only a little less confidence) that there is nowhere a major British theoretical discussion from an explicitly pro-pluralist position. Cawson (1985, p. 3) has acknow-ledged the commitment to empirical research as a strength of pluralism, and presents theoretical self-consciousness as the virtue of neo-Marxism. Certainly pluralism's empirical focus has not been supported by theoretical introspection.

The major contribution of North American writers in describing British pressure groups has probably given the impression that British groups were discovered through the application of American theory in the 1950s. However, if one looks at a major book on Britain of this period—S. H. Beer's *Modern British Politics* (1965)—there is no explicit connection to the American pluralists, although Beer is American and although Truman and Dahl were well-established American texts.

Although Bernard Crick (1959, p. 118) quotes Fainsod claiming that the interest group is almost a unique characteristic of American

political science, and although Crick himself is so confident about
the unusual strength of American groups that he can casually claim,
'Now, of course, pressure groups are more important in the United
States . . . than in any other country' (p. 128), the assertion is at
least debatable. As early as 1956 Beer had made the point that, even
compared with American examples, 'pressure groups in Britain are
numerous, massive, well organized and highly effective' (1956,
p. 1). (By 1958 Beer was in fact claiming that 'If we had a way of
measuring political power, we could possibly demonstrate that at
the present time pressure groups are more powerful in Britain than
in the United States.')

The textual evidence indeed suggests that the early American
pressure group writers leant heavily on Britain as an example of
group prevalence. Truman himself had used Britain and its group
life as part of his argument about the importance of groups in the
USA. Drawing on Ivor Jenning's *Parliament*, Truman (1955 edn.,
p. 8) claimed that organized political groups were as extensive in
Britain as in the US. In *Parliament* Truman would have found
Jenning's claim that 'much legislation is derived from organized
interests . . . most of it is amended on the representation of such
interests, and that often parliamentary opposition is in truth the
opposition of interests' (1939, p. 527). In 1930 Herring had drawn
attention to British practice in a brief article, 'Great Britain has
Lobbies Too'.

The importance of British pressure groups was thus well
established before their rediscovery in the 1950s. Jenning's *Parliament* has a chapter, 'Who Makes the Laws', that stresses that 'the
national interest is an amalgam of hundreds of group interests'
(p. 190). He produces a list of the bodies with which the NFU
negotiated or co-operated—thirty bodies, running from the County
Landowners' Association to the National Cheese Council—and
comments 'Lists of this kind might be multiplied twenty-fold'
(p. 186.) His Appendix II, which sets out 'Who Made the Laws in
1936–37', very frequently gives the origin as group pressure.

Ramsay Muir's *How Britain is Governed*, (1930, p. 304) both
recorded and regretted the growth of groups, as is suggested by his
phrase 'organised interests outside the Constitution'. He observed
how pressure on Parliament through candidates (e.g. by the drink
trade) had been extended to pressure upon the Government. He
claimed, for example, that the development of associations of local

authorities meant there were powers which the Government could not ignore, as so large a part of the work of government had to be carried on through the authorities. He saw such outside groups as organs of criticism and even of control far more potent than Parliament itself. He argued that 'A Government which feels that—secure in the possession of a docile majority—it can afford to disregard the criticism of other parliamentary parties, will listen with respect to the representations of the combined local authorities.' He claimed that the real discussion on the Derating and Local Government Bill of 1928 took place outside Parliament, where the local authorities wrested from the minister large concessions and amendments which he would never have accepted in Parliament (p. 306).

The issue of group–government relations in Britain is thus long-standing. In 1931 the Institute of Public Administration organized a conference under the title 'Officials and the Public', with sessions on 'Consultation and Negotiation between Public Authorities and Organized Private Interests in the Industrial Sphere' and 'Consultation and Negotiation between Public Authorities and Organized Private Interests in the Sphere of Social Services'. In *Public Administration* (1931), G. D. H. Cole had an article which dwelt on consultation with outside bodies in the legislative process. Another article in the same issue (by a civil servant, E. J. Foley) argued that 'The methods of consultation with organised interests before action should now be pretty clear. For major questions advisory committees representing every interest in the industry should be freely used.' (p. 21.) And Herman Finer—looking mainly at France and Germany—found that 'The formal institutions [of consultation] have grown out of departmental recognition that official knowledge was seriously limited, and that the law would have the more authority and less the character of unjustified imposition if collaboration with expert and interested outsiders were established.' (p. 27.)

Another pre-war source which emphasized the role of British groups was Richard Crossman's *How Britain is Governed* (c. 1938). He described how public opinion was not a homogeneous mass but a complicated network of groups and interests, and how the real basis of political democracy was not in (electoral) politics, but below the surface in the organization of a whole network of popular interests into pressure groups.

In the British pre-war literature, then, there was recognition of pressure group activity, but the studies of the 1950s none the less, and paradoxically, began from the assumption that Britain had little group influence. Professor Robert McKenzie's article in 1958 recounted how a British information officer lecturing in America in 1954 had claimed that there was a complete absence of pressure groups and lobbies in Britain. Professor W. J. M. Mackenzie, in similar vein, cites a parliamentary exchange in 1954 (*Hansard*, 20 July, col. 1217), which included the indignant assertion, 'We do not have pressure groups on this side of the House.' The myth of weak groups was necessary to accommodate itself with the dominant myth, of representational (parliamentary) democracy. Strong groups threatened the picture-book version of British democracy that emphasized electoral competition, voter choice, and implementation of manifestos.

In comparison with the US—which is generally credited with powerful groups—the contemporary British group scene has certain features which are *more* impressive than in the US. American business has no single group to match the CBI, with 74 per cent of manufacturers with fifty or more employees affiliated to it (Grant in Marsh 1983, p. 113). The central trade union body in the United States, the AFL-CIO, has less than 21 per cent of the potential membership (Wilson 1981, p. 52): major unions such as the Teamsters, the National Education Association, United Mine Workers, and United Auto Workers are not affiliated. (In Britain almost 50 per cent of the workforce is unionized.) The American Medical Association has only 50 per cent of practising doctors in membership. In US agriculture, more than in Britain, groups compete for the same membership with about four notable national general agriculture groups—the American Farm Bureau Federation, the National Farmers' Union, the Grange, and the National Farmers' Organization—and important single-commodity groups, such as (for milk) Associated Milk Producers Inc., Mid-American Dairies, and Diarymen Inc. Wilson (1981, p. 31) concluded that *all the groups together* (our emphasis) organize a low percentage of farmers in the United States. No more than 35 per cent of American farmers belong to any interest group, a density of membership far lower than the British National Farmers' Union alone enjoys (over 80 per cent). Wilson also points out that the conflict and competition of American agriculture groups weakens their voice, and that the US agricultural interest groups have not achieved that reputation for non-partisan technical competence which successful British groups represent. The argument that American groups are the most powerful is not self-evidently convincing.

One feature where British practice is perhaps different from American is the focus of activity. Although we have no direct British evidence on this, a survey by Presthus among directors of interest groups in the US and Canada found that their primary targets were very different (see Table 2.1).

TABLE 2.1. *Major Cross-national Targets of Interest Groups*

Target	Proportion ranking each target first	
	US (%)	Canada (%)
Bureaucracy	21	40
Legislators	41	20
Legislative committees	19	7
Cabinet	4	19
Executive assistants	3	5
Judiciary	3	3
Other	9	6

Source: Presthus, *Elites in the Policy Process* (1974, p. 255).

Our view would be that Britain, with its strongly partisan legislature, would, if anything, encourage even more of an orientation on the bureacracy than is found in Canada.

The version of group politics that developed in Britain in the 1950s stressed a bipartisan acceptance of the broad outlines of societal arrangements. Beer (1955, p. 33) expressed the belief that 'the main lines of British policy at home would be much the same no matter which party was in power and that if Labour is returned to power in the next election we may expect as much continuity with present Tory policy as there has been with Labour policy under the present government.'

Despite the popularity of the concept of adversary politics, this bipartisanship arguably remains. Whiteley and Winyard (1983, p. 14) quote one senior civil servant claiming, 'The area of consensus is much larger than one thinks, there is little difference between the parties on poverty.' Elsewhere we have argued at some length that in major areas of economic policy and over a wide range of non-economic policy the adversarial thesis is greatly exaggerated (Jordan and Richardson 1987; see also Gamble and Walkland 1984).

Given the weakness of 'party' as a determinant of policy, attention was directed to the group–department connection. Beer (1955, p. 39) said he wanted to focus not on noisy threats and loud demanding claims or mass demonstrations but, 'The civil servants of the organised interest groups . . . countless trade unions, trade associations and professional organizations . . . [who] deal directly and continually with civil servants in government'. Other students of the period made the same priority: pressure politics was about on-going relationships between civil servants and professional group negotiators. Finer, for example, points to close, confidential, and, by and large, friendly contact with the Civil Service (1966 edn., p. 28). He saw this as being particularly true of interest groups representing trade, industry labour, the professions, and groups like the County Councils' Association. J. D. Stewart (1958, p. 30) pointed out that the consultation is welcomed by most group leaders, and 'especially by the permanent officials who over time have developed friendly relations with their opposite numbers in the ministries'. Indeed, Stewart concluded that 'the supremacy of consultation was the most useful weapon for the analysis of the behaviour of pressure groups in Great Britain'. Parliamentary efforts were presented as a subsidiary technique, most useful when consultation had left the group dissatisfied or when the group was attempting to establish a reputation leading to recognition of the group by the relevant department. Stewart presented the campaign as 'a risk. It has now become abnormal, an action that requires decision and explanation . . . the general rule (is) of consultation first and foremost.' (p. 42.)

Eckstein too observed that because there has been a broad consensus of general policy in Britain, 'shifting political conflict to matters of technique and detail', then group pressure is focused on to the executive, 'because the broad scope and technical character of contemporary social and economic policies has led to a considerable shift of functions to the executive' (1960, p. 19).

The Automobile Association handbook can be used to illustrate the emphasis on relations with the civil servants:

the influencing of public policy is a much longer-term consideration, since issues of greater complexity require research and evaluation ... The difficulties are further compounded by frequent changes among the ranks of the chief decision-makers, the Ministers of the Crown. The Association therefore looks mainly to the senior permanent Departmental officials to provide the necessary continuity in its dealings with government.

The handbook claims that the AA is continually being consulted 'behind the scenes' as issues progress through their formulative stages.

Criticisms: The Politics of Marginal Adjustment?

Politics, it was claimed, *had* become a matter of detail for negotiated 'professional' settlement: ideological confrontation was over. There have been several criticisms of this approach:

(*a*) that it neglects a class of pressure group activity (radical challenge, such as RAP and prison reform);
(*b*) that even if ideological convergence did take place, that the trend is now reversed;
(*c*) that the competitive group struggle is profoundly biased: this can be seen on the balance issue.

This third criticism appears to be based on a misreading of group interpreters. The misreading is made with varying degrees of subtlety: Philippe Schmitter (in Berger 1981, p. 286) states that supporters of the pluralist system believe it to be both self-equilibrating and self-legitimating. Otto Newman (1981, p. 200) not only thinks pluralism is about electoral competition 'free and untrammelled' and 'access to decisive critical judgment [*sic*] ... uniformly available', but that the pluralist case rests on public control via elections and that the interest group system has 'an ideal capacity for self-adjusting equilibrium and modification' (p. 203). Dunleavy (1983, p. 263) considers that the pluralists present a picture of a 'free wheeling, open and egalitarian interest group process'.

C. Wright Mills was perhaps the leader of those who attacked the theory of balance, which they first invented. Mills saw the automatic balance concept of government as dating back to the eighteenth century. He saw the dominant power model 'as an automatic balance, with its assumptions of a plurality of independent, relatively equal and conflicting groups of the balancing society' (1959, edn., p. 243).

Data compiled by Chubb (1983, p. 149) in his study of the changing politics of energy in the US rather neatly confirm that there *is* an inequality of access. Taking advantage of compulsory logging of meetings from 1974 onwards in the Federal Energy Administration (FEA), Chubb discovered that meetings with outside groups held by the official in charge of oil regulation leant heavily towards industrial rather than environmentalist interests (see Table 2.2).

TABLE 2.2   *Frequency of Meetings between Interest Groups and the FEA Assistant Administrator of Regulatory Programmes 1 July 1975–15 January 1977*

	%	(n)
Environmental/consumer/public interest	0	(0)
Petroleum & gas industry	76	(81)
Electric power	8	(8)
Labour unions	0	(0)
Commercial users	15	(16)
Financial institutions	1	(1)

Source: derived from Chubb 1983, p. 149.

Chubb observed that under a Carter appointee the pattern of interest group access 'grew decidedly more pluralistic', but the point remains that imbalances do occur.

However, the claims that pluralists, of whatever shade, believed that access was open and resources equal have been rebutted with some forcefulness by Polsby (1979) and Dahl (1982). Dahl notes, 'I have been puzzled by the assertions sometimes made by critics of "pluralist theory" that such a theory contends, or assumes, that all interest groups and so on are equal or substantially equal in organization capacities and access, or sources, or power, or influence, or the like.' Dahl quotes to the contrary from Truman and his own work and points out that critics who assert an equal power version of pluralism have failed to cite a single source. As Dahl says, since the proposition is on its face rather absurd, had the 'pluralists' believed such assertions they would have displayed an astonishing ignorance of ordinary social and political reality.

A reviewer of Dahl (Morriss 1984, p. 164) considers that Dahl's vigorous defence of liberal pluralism is 'irrelevant'. This is to fail to appreciate the frustration caused by repeated criticisms which were in fact anticipated by the pluralists themselves. Work such as Douglass Cater (1964), J. Leiper Freeman (1965), Davidson (1977), and Ripley and Franklin (1984) promotes ideas of whirlpools, cosy triangles, subgovernments, policy-making triads, policy subsystems, and—most classically—*iron triangles* that most certainly cannot encourage any belief in uncontroversial access and equal resources. The criticism by commentators such as Theodore Lowi attacking the complacency of the pluralists in the face of their picture of a structuring of the decision-making process to *exclude* interests only emphasizes that there was awareness that competition was not equally open to all. Pluralists perhaps invite misunderstanding because essentially they are arguing that there is an impressive volume of pressure group activity, as measured by number of groups, consultation invitations, etc. This seems to support the open competition idea, but pluralists, by and large, seem to go on to say that access is incomplete and that some interests are weighted more heavily than others.

The attack on the pluralists is then not totally unwarranted, but the specific target of 'belief in equal access' is poorly selected: who believes this? Arguably, where the pluralists divide from the anti-pluralists is in their reaction to the political system described. Apparently the anti-pluralists find the distribution of political resources more offensive than their colleagues: a different tone characterizes their descriptions. But even prominent pluralists such as Dahl (1985) turn, especially in their later work, to be far from uncritical about existing polyarchy. The modern pluralist approach is full of reservations and qualifications and means that sweeping criticisms and comments can rarely avoid being anticipated.

3

The Logic of Collective Action?

A major subliterature in the group field has been initiated by Mancur Olson's (1965) work on *collective goods*: this is perhaps the most powerful criticism of group theory. It is a criticism of the pluralist assumption that groups automatically emerge to reflect and defend common interests. If countervailing groups do not emerge, the criticism of bias in the system has more force. The notion of 'collective good' that is central to his argument applies to something *non-exclusive*. The 'collective good' idea has aroused controversy, but its central claim is that things such as national defence or a clean environment are inevitably produced for all. Olson argues that there is no rational basis for groups and individuals to pursue these desirable outcomes collectively. He does grant two major exceptions, in the circumstances of certain small groups (pp. 33–6) and philanthropic and religious lobbies (p. 160.) Pressure group cohesion is not achieved by 'lobbying', but lobbying is a *by-product* of other activities.

In *The Logic of Collective Action* Olson does not (directly) address the influence of groups in policy-making, but claims that the rational reaction of individuals is *not* to join a group, but is to 'free-ride' the costs of group membership and consume the collective product. Until Olson's major impact, the matter of group membership had been seen as non-problematic. Truman (1951, p. 87), for example, had claimed that agriculture groups 'emerged out of increased interactions of farmers in response to intense disturbances of their accustomed behaviour'. His key proposition was that groups would apparently emerge from a disturbance to expected patterns (say a fall in agriculture prices). Although Truman supported this with a range of references to psychological studies, the main appeal was to common sense. He claimed, 'The moving pattern of a complex society . . . is one of changes and disturbances in the habitual subpatterns of interaction, followed by a return to the previous state of equilibrium or if the disturbances are intense or prolonged by the emergence of new groups whose specialized function it is to facilitate the establishment of a new balance . . .' (p. 44.) With hindsight we can note that as a prophecy it is self-fulfilling. If new groups form, the disturbances must have been intense; if no group is formed the disturbances were less traumatic. One of the other elements in Truman's implicit theory is the fragmentation or proliferation idea, that groups develop because of increased specialization in society (1951, p. 57). Until Olson's work, it seemed that members joined interest groups because they shared group goals: it appeared a self-evident truth. Olson instead proposed that, for example, a consumer organization designed to counter a producer interest would not emerge automatically because the individual consumer would not, rationally, support the consumer organization, with its generalized benefits.

Olson's analysis was pegged on a rational actor model, and he pointed out that it was not enough to assume that group activity followed shared attitudes of potential members. The rational potential member would allow others to bear the financial and time costs involved. The simplest example is perhaps the pay increase after a strike, which is made to all employees whether or not they actually pay a membership levy to their union or take part in the strike. Thus Olson's book hinges on the key proposition,

If members of a large group rationally seek to maximise their personal welfare they will not act to advance their common or group objectives unless there is a coercion to force them to do so, or unless some separate incentive, distinct from the achievement of the common or group interest, is offered to the members of the group individually on the condition that they will help bear the costs or burdens involved in the achievement of the group objectives. (1968 edn., p. 2.)

According to Olson, then, members become active in groups *not* in pursuit of some collective good—which would be available to them irrespective of membership—but because of 'selective incentives' of immediate and personal benefit. At its simplest, Olson's model suggests that a member of a trade union joins not for salary increases—which he would get anyway when the union won it— but for other particular 'membership-only' incentives unions provide, such as shopping discounts or legal insurance. In some cases the service basis is transparent, for example the Automobile Association in Britain. While its handbook makes claims such as 'the Association is continually being consulted by Government

Departments, especially on controversial motoring issues. The authorities expect the AA to speak for its members and thus, by extension, for motorists generally', its recruitment literature is centrally in terms of a breakdown service. As we have noted, Olson sees collective lobbying by large economic groups as a *by-product*: such groups, he argues, exist for some other purpose.

The Olson challenge has been tackled in several ways. One approach, developed by Richard Kimber (1981, p. 192), addresses what Kimber sees as the new orthodoxy as developed by Olson and others, that rational individuals will not contribute to the provision of a collective good (that is, a good when provided is freely available to all, for example, national defence). Kimber's main proposition in this context is that the potential member's rational choice is not whether he should pay or be a free-rider, but whether he can afford to be a free-rider if he is uncertain that there is something to 'ride-free'. Kimber's rule is *if the supply of the good is uncertain, join; if it is certain, do not join*. Kimber points out that Olson's simple objection to Marx's theory of class action (namely, that the rational proletarian will not willingly support a proletarian revolution because he would get the benefit of a proletarian government anyway) does not hold because of the uncertainty of the establishment of proletarian government (p. 194). Kimber concludes that there is something intuitively odd with an explanation that joining a group in pursuit of a collective good is irrational. He suggests that there is something whimsical about the idea that the Council for the Protection of Rural England is really organized, not to protect rural England but to provide wine and cheese parties for its members. He concludes: 'If lobbying *is* merely a by-product of whatever function enables an organization to secure its membership as Olson maintains (p. 133), then one might ask, as David Marsh (1978) does, "Why any interest group continues to attempt to supply the collective good if potential members only join to obtain selective benefits. Why don't interest groups merely supply selective incentives?" ' In later work with Dowding (1984), Kimber also points to problems in the commonly accepted collective good/ selective incentive boundary. It is, in practice, often difficult to categorize in these terms. Moreover, Hardin (1982, p. 34) has pointed out that in most cases lobbying groups have grafted on selective services, and not vice versa.

Another kind of response to Olson was by Salisbury (1969), in which he distinguishes between the 'logic' as it applies to the group organizer (entrepreneur, in Salisbury's terms) and the customer/member. The group emergence/maintenance issue is regarded as an *exchange* situation in which entrepreneurs invest in a set of benefits which they offer to members at a price, namely membership (see also Frolich, Oppenheimer, and Young 1971).

In his 1969 article most of Salisbury's empirical material was drawn from a study (with Heinz) of agriculture groups. Initially Salisbury discusses the pattern of agricultural group formation in terms of (a) Truman's propositions about group proliferation to match a specialization in society and (b) in terms of the alternative suggestion of group formation as a response to disturbance in the environment. He finds problems for both approaches. He notes that for nearly half a century (after the Civil War) farm groups did *not* proliferate into more and more organizations, each with its specialized concerns (p. 6). He notes that while a specialized National Corn Growers Association appeared in the mid-1950s, corn growing had been differentiated as an activity for years, and recruitment was so low in any case that it was still unclear that growers could be considered organized. Thus there was no necessary or immediate connection between specialization and group development (p. 10). Even more persuasively, on the equilibrium theory he observes how groups seemed to expand in times of prosperity and decline in economic recession. This contradicted the assumption derived from the disequilibrium idea which suggested that groups might be organized in response to bargaining disadvantage (p. 8). He also notes how 'the empirical landscape is cluttered with abandoned farm group vehicles'. Theories about group success and maintenance are thus needed as well as those about group emergence.

The broad conclusion is that group members join for benefits other than collective and material benefits, notably solidarity feelings or the opportunity for expressive action. Presumably members of CND, for example, actually feel personal benefit in giving public expression to their values. Salisbury suggests that what we generally observe to be lobbying behaviour by group leaders may not result from membership demands but from the personal choice and values of the leaders (p. 28). Lobbying is one of the rewards sought by the entrepreneur, not a membership demand. Lobbying (and perhaps a salary) are the entrepreneur's 'profit'. The

Automobile Association is again an interesting case of high-level lobbying that is perhaps remote from the concerns of members. The AA recognizes this and takes the unusual step of conducting market research of its members to determine their views. It claims that all 50,000 members are contacted by postal questionnaires, in informal group discussions, and by personal interview. The AA claims that these surveys have a 'profound influence' upon AA public policy, but it also makes the implicit claim that the central expertise is perhaps superior to that of members: 'In all these respects, the Association is fortunate in having at its disposal information from various sources which is not normally available to individual members.' (*Handbook* 1982/3, p. 22.)

Walker (1983) conducted a survey of voluntary groups in the US—that is, deliberately excluding trade unions and business corporations—to explore the emergence of groups. His survey, and his summary of other studies, confirmed the widespread impression of a rapid growth in the number of groups. He comments (p. 396), 'The work of Olson largely undermined Truman's theory of the spontaneous generation of groups, and yet, despite the power of Olson's analysis, at first glance recent increases in the number of groups suggest that Truman has the data on his side.' Walker argues that Olson's theory can be rescued if these new groups were basing recruitment on selective benefits, and he produces two groups, the National Retired Teachers' Association and the American Association of Retired Persons, which did just that. However, he concludes that the reliance of the NRTA/AARP on selective benefits was quite unusual.

Walker's novel contribution is his emphasis on *patronage* (outside funding) as a means of maintaining the groups. Moon and Richardson show that public (i.e. governmental) patronage is an important source of funding for anti-unemployment groups in Britain. For example, groups such as Community Service Volunteers, Community Task Force, National Council for Voluntary Organizations, and the Community Projects Foundation have become an important part of the system for delivering anti-unemployment schemes, and receive Manpower Services Commission funding for that. A group like the National Association for the Care and Resettlement of Offenders (NACRO) provided some 3,000 Youth Training Scheme places in 1986, and provided up to 18,000 places on the Community Programme for long-term unemployed ex-offenders. NACRO's own Employment Development Unit (for YTS schemes) is financed by the Home Office, the MSC, and the DHSS. Some of the groups have adjusted their own activities and internal structures according to the nature of the public funding available. Thus, in the unemployment field, with its range of public funding opportunities, 'an entrepreneurial phenomenon is at work, with voluntary bodies being attracted to MSC programmes and the issues which surround them. Leaders of existing groups see the unemployment problem as not just a problem but also an *opportunity* for extending their own base.' (Moon and Richardson 1984, pp. 399–400.)

Linking back to the last chapter and the idea that groups perform useful functions for government, government itself can stimulate group formation, as well as give financial support to groups it 'needs'. Grant (1984, p. 128) notes, 'Although pressure groups are not actually set up by the state, their formation is often deliberately encouraged, for example, by seconding civil servants to staff the organisation or even by providing Crown premises at a low rent.' Two bodies we have examined recently—The Engineering Council and the Scottish Seed Promotion Association—share a technically non-governmental status, but they were initially largely staffed by civil servants.

Walker's arguments on sponsorship mesh with parts of Salisbury's discussion. For example, Salisbury (1969, p. 12) wrote of how an agriculture group—The Grange—was initiated by a entrepreneur, Oliver Hudson Kelly, who, by considerable personal sacrifice and *some generous friends* (our emphasis), managed to survive until his organization was established. Discussing Newton Gresham of the Farmers' Union, Salisbury showed how he fed his family on credit and neighbours' largesse until the union attracted enough dues-paying members to sustain him. He also discussed how other groups were supported by, variously, publishers trying to build newspaper circulation, parent groups, and even federal and state governments looking for supporting organizations.

Arguing that neither Truman nor Olson fully explain the growth of groups, Walker's data suggest the importance (at least in the US context) of patrons (by using tax deductions) funding organized groups. Walker's work, while not aimed as 'one big explanation' of group mobilization, is a supplement to other ideas. The patronage concept is empirically relevant and had been hitherto neglected.

(For more on the idea of subsidization see Hansen 1985.) In Britain the RSPCA provided initial secretarial services for the Committee for the Reform of Animal Experimentation, the Farm Animal Welfare Community Exectutive, and the Humane Education Council. One group can thus be the patron of many less-established interests (Hollands 1980, p. 147).

The best-known qualification of Olson is probably Terry Moe's *The Organization of Interests* (1980). His approach is frontal, to apply Olson's economically self-interested approach to economic interest groups. (Truman himself in his second edition, 1971, accepted that the economic type analysis fitted some groups.) Moe claims, though, that such economic groups are the most powerful in virtually all Western democracies. Olson's theory is most usefully applicable to that limited sector, as opposed to (say) groups of a religious, ideological, or social nature.

Moe points out that analysing individual behaviour (to join or not to join a group) by an assumption of rationality tells us only that the individual will select his preferred option from alternatives: but *what* he chooses will depend upon what information and values he brings to bear (p. 14). Different men behaving rationally can choose different options. In taking this view on rationality, Moe is much less deterministic than Olson about what an individual *should* do to behave logically.

Moe's empirical data are derived from a study of members of five economic groups. One of the features of his results is (with hindsight) obvious: the kinds of factors that are operational differ for different members and for different groups. Moe's questionnaire established the main reasons—seen by members—for their own membership, as shown in Table 3.1.

Table 3.1 shows the variety of the responses, but services were the main response in all but one case. The importance of services was confirmed by a table (p. 209) reporting a straight forced choice between service and lobbying as an explanation of the decision to join. Only members of the Farmers' Union (by 56 to 44 per cent) chose lobbying rather than services as the major reason.

There is certainly some encouragement here for the Olson approach, but at the same time individuals—even in the printing industry—join for other than services. Moe observes that the more restricted and specialized the nature of the group the more heavily economic services seem to count. Moe concludes that services have

TABLE 3.1. *Members' Main Reason for Joining*

	Printing Industries of the Twin Cities (89 companies) (%)	Minnesota Retail Federation (600 members) (%)	Minnesota Dakotas Hardware Association (900 chain stores) (%)	Minnesota Farm Bureau (35,000 members) (%)	Minnesota Farmers' Union (23,000 members) (%)
Services	86	44	56	54	34
Lobbying	—	27	14	25	37
Social	2	1	—	4	5
Responsi-bility	9	27	26	12	20
Expected to join by others	2	1	3	4	4

Source: Moe 1980, p. 208.

greater inducement value than lobbying, but he also notes that 'at the same time, the motivational roles of lobbying and feelings of responsibility are not at all insignificant; while they are hardly the crucial factors that pluralists make them out to be, they are certainly more prevalent than Olson's original analysis would lead us to expect' (p. 209).

With ingenuity, Moe also asked how members would react if the group stopped providing services or stopped lobbying. This confirmed that in all groups except the Farmers' Union most members would drop out if their economically relevant services were taken away. However, when Moe reanalysed to discover how many members considered lobbying as pivotal to their decision (some would want services *and* lobbying, others lobbying only or lobbying *or* services), he discovered that only for the printing association was politics pivotal for less than half the membership. The discovery of *the* source of membership is complicated by the concept of *jointness of supply*, which holds that consumers want a *mixture* of collective and selective benefits.

Moe's revised model of collective action, whereby the member gets personal satisfaction by *doing*, suggests that the satisfactions need not be the provision of collective goods, but the opportunity to express support (1981, p. 536). This takes us into territory at some distance from the economic calculus of Olson, but even Olson has to recognise erotic (*sic*), psychological, and moral incentives (see Dowding and Kimber 1984, p. 15). Olson saw *social* pressures as selective incentives, but he thought they operated only at local level. However, it is not the size of the organization that counts but its nature. It is possible to have 'at a distance' relations with small groups, but be in daily (e.g. work) contact with fellow members of large groups (e.g. unions). (see Dowding and Kimber 1984, p. 22.)

Marsh's 1976 work on the CBI concluded that there was social pressure on managers of some firms to join. Similarly, our interviews with the National Farmers' Union headquarters found that there they discussed membership in terms of 'a discernible spirit and community in farming . . . working together for the common good . . . unity needed more than ever when industry threatened'. Certainly there are services—like legal advice and representation over road schemes—but the view seemed to be that it was the social cohesion of the farming community that underpinned its 85 per cent or so of farmers in membership.

What Kind of Groups Predominate?

Robert Salisbury (1984) has made a further simple but fundamental amendment to the pressure group literature by arguing that interest representation is dominated by institutions, such as corporations or local governments. As he outlines (p. 64), the conventional mental picture of the pressure group omits, 'individual corporations, state and local governments, universities, think tanks and most other *institutions* of the private sector. Likewise unnoticed are the multitudes of Washington representatives, free standing and for hire, including lawyers, public relations firms and diverse other counsellors.' As Salisbury contends, recognizing the nature of these non-membership-based interest groups raises significantly different issues from those considered by Olson.

Salisbury points out how several thousand corporations maintain permanent Washington offices, essentially government affairs divisions (p. 70). And corporations (and Labour unions) also tie into politics in another way through the Political Action Committee, which is a device used by interest groups in the US to channel money into campaign support for political candidates. He cites a 1983 figure of 78 per cent of PACs being institutionally based.

Although some might balk at the liberalism of a definition of pressure group which includes individual companies (see Dunleavy 1983, p. 262), the following account by the Ford Motor Company in Britain of its relations with government shows that, quite apart from any dealings through intermediary trade associations, Ford has direct communication in pursuit of its goals:

It is virtually impossible to quantify the number of meetings between ourselves, the Government and the Civil Service, but they must run into thousands per annum.

As a major motor manufacturer, we have constant dealings with the Department of Transport and the Department of the Environment. As suppliers of vehicles, our sales staff are in touch with the purchasing sections of the Armed Forces, the Foreign Office and the Civil Service. As a major employer, we are in regular touch with the Department of Employment. As a major industrial company, we are in constant liaison with the Department of Industry. As a source of information we are regularly in touch with the Central Office of Information. These contacts, meetings and consultations take place at every conceivable level. Lastly, our senior executives have not infrequent meetings with Government Ministers, MPs and senior civil servants and have often given advice before House of Commons Select Committees. (Letter to authors.)

It would be hard to distinguish this, behaviourally, from (say) the activities of the National Farmers' Union.

The theory needed to explain why individuals join in voluntary associations to exert pressure is clearly different from that needed to explain why existing institutions attempt to alter the environment in their favour. Walker made the valid point (1983, p. 390) that 'It is not surprising that huge, concentrated industries such as the automobile manufacturers or the major aerospace contractors have successfully organized to advance their interests in Washington, but it is not obvious that the political system would inevitably have spawned groups like the American Alliance for Health, Physical Education and Dance.'

The Salisbury argument about the weight of institutionally based groups neatly cuts back the scale of the problem of the logic of individual membership, but, of course, it does not dispose of it altogether. The literature to date no more than introduces the kind of considerations that are relevant. For example, there is the remarkable version of the creation of the Automobile Association in Britain by its first secretary, Stenson Cooke. As noted earlier, the

AA is an example of a group where the selective benefit of emergency car repair is clearly (now) the inducement to join. None the less, the AA as a lobbying body talks for those members, who may have little concern about the matter. Reading Cooke's entirely untheoretical account written in the 1930s, one finds that many of the theoretical variables show through. For a start, he begins his account by describing his own personal (mis)fortunes in August 1905. He describes how his pre-AA job of selling and dealing 'was indeed an overrated amusement'. Cooke very frankly makes plain that his interest in motoring was negligible (he had only been in a car twice), and that the attraction of a successful organization was personal. Unless he recruited sixty members and found a hundred pounds in the bank, his new (and necessary) job disappeared.

From his account, the role of the entrepreneurs emerges: borrowed offices, borrowed typewriter, personal subventions from well-wishers. (His account uncovers some ambiguity over 'entrepreneur'. Was he an entrepreneur in the same sense as the committee?) His salary inducement was not the same as that of committee members. Cooke asks, 'What had inspired [the original committee] to give money, to lend office-room and requisites, to forgather . . . to get things done. There could be no personal profit for them.' It emerges that the founders were incensed by the speed traps instituted under the Motor Car Act of 1903. A letter to the press brought together various individuals, including some from the motor trade, which saw prosecutions as bad for business. The idea of the organization was to use cyclists to discover traps, and then to warn motorists.

While the AA has survived as the major motoring lobby, some opinion at the time saw 'too many organisations formed with similar objects'. Cooke noted, 'Two organizations already held the field . . . Feeling ran high at the instant progress of young upstart Number Three.' As some organizations flourished and others, equally promising, disappeared, it appears that pressure group development is another area where over-mechanistic explanations fail.

The participation and activity of key individuals seems to be a characteristic of the process of forming animal welfare societies— Revd. Arthur Broome and the RSPCA (1824); a Mrs Tealby and Mrs Major and the formation of the Home for Lost and Starving Dogs at Battersea (1860); Mrs Dickin and the Peoples' Dispensary for Sick Animals of the Poor (1927); Mrs Williamson and the Royal Society for the Protection of Birds (1889), and so on (see Hollands 1980).

Whiteley and Winyard's 1984 work on the emergence of the 40 or so groups in the poverty lobby in Britain shows the heterogeneity of group origins. On the entrepreneur aspect they find that groups in the income maintenance field divide roughly into two: this information is set out in Table 3.2

TABLE 3.2. *Political Entrepreneurship and the Origins of Groups*

		Group	Number in sample	Example
(1)	(a)	Groups organized by 1 or 2 entrepreneurs with personal involvement in issue area	9	Royal National Institute for the Blind
	(b)	Entrepreneurs with no personal involvement	8	Low Pay Unit
(2)	(a)	Groups with no clear entrepreneur, but run by individuals with personal involvement	6	British Association for the Hard of Hearing
	(b)	Arising from number of individuals (or organisations) with no personal involvement	13	Shelter
(3)		Arising as a result of government intervention.	3	MIND

Thus the detailed examination by Whiteley and Winyard disconcerts over-sweeping theoretical predictions: groups will emerge from a variety of circumstances. The same phenomenon of empirical complexity arises when they test Truman's disturbance idea on group generation. They conclude that the empirical evidence of disturbance, if anything, is a less satisfactory account of group formation than Salisbury's exchange idea: some twenty-five of the forty-three or forty-four groups considered did not originate from any identifiable disturbance. Some groups *did* fit the model; for example, Shelter rose out of the powerful television play *Cathy Come Home* about homelessness; but few cases were that specific in origin. Some groups did fit Salisbury's exchange model in that 'the entrepreneur supplies organizing talent and initiative in return for paid employment' (e.g. Gingerbread, CRUSE (national association for widows), MENCAP) but this was not true for RNIB, RNID, and other groups where no individual entrepreneur appeared to gain obvious material benefit.

Likewise, the general proposition that groups proliferated because of a growing complexity of society was unconfirmed. In one sense the proposition cannot be dismissed: a body like the American Electronics Association (AEA), which is the trade association of Silicon Valley, does reflect new specialist interests. However, Whiteley and Winyard argue that the dearth of groups in their study with their origins in the inter-war years is not consistent with the regularity of growth assumed in the growing complexity hypothesis. Their careful work—in setting out the diversity of group origins—is important in relating attractive broad hypotheses to the complex circumstances of *particular groups*.

The issue of *why* members participate is considered in King's recent work (1985) on why firms joined their local Chambers of Commerce. This is based on a study of the Leeds chamber in England, which has 1,600 members but represents only 17 per cent of companies in the area. It did not appear that selective benefits adequately explain why one in every six firms did join: 20 per cent did mention assistance with export documentation, but wanting to be included in the business community was equally often put forward as a membership reason. Bigger firms in particular (37.5 per cent) gave the sort of reason as 'being part of the business life of Leeds'. This sense of solidarity existed even though firms generally had very little actual contact with the chamber and its officers. Around 23 per cent of King's respondents did not know when the company joined and *over one quarter of members* did *not* feel that advantages outweighed the costs of joining. King concluded, '*the vast majority of respondents* (70.4 per cent) *chose neither services or collective goals as the major reason for joining but business involvement, status, and so on. Most of the respondents thought it was important just to be involved* . . .' (emphasis in original). As noted above, Hardin has demonstrated that pressure groups develop their lobbying/political side before their service side. Selective benefits are the real 'by-products'.

Groups do try to persuade members that they are 'successful': for example, *CBI News* of August 1985 claimed, 'Along the way [to passing the Finance Act 1985] the CBI has fought to introduce into its darker passages more rays of hope . . . there are many examples of successful CBI lobbying on subjects of vital concern to members.' The headline was 'Victory on points'. The NFU parliamentary director has described the need to 'get the best deal going and then explain to the farmers that this is the best deal in the circumstances'. In other words the NFU sees a problem in persuading the ministry of its case *and* in persuading the members that it has done a good deal. However, while groups are obviously sensible to attempt to impress members with results, King's work suggests that goal achievement is only part of the assessment made by members in joining or retaining membership.

The Rise of the Public Interest Lobby

The development of so-called public interest lobbying is of some interest *per se*, for its implication for the balance issue of the group contest, and for the implication for Olson's 'logic of collective action'. Berry (1977, p. 7) defined the public interest groups in a way which stressed their collective good orientation: 'a public interest group is one that seeks a collective good, the achievement of which will not selectively and materially benefit the membership of the organization'. American groups such as Common Cause, the Ralph Nader Network, the Consumers' Union (1.8 million subscribers), and the Sierra Club (153,000 members) were a feature of American politics in the 1970s.

McFarland (1976, p. 4) argued that some public interest groups were still 'explicable' in selective benefit terms: 'Anyone with an upper middle-class income will surely save many times the $11 price of membership in Consumers Union if he pays attention to the product information reported in that group's journal.' (He could get the information reading someone else's copy!). McFarland goes on, though,

> But why do 275,000 persons send $15 to $20 to Common Cause when they receive nothing in return but thank you letters and an eight-page monthly newsletter? The 100,000 persons who send an average of $11 a year to Nader's Public Citizen, Inc., get a five-page progress report and a pamphlet, but no thank-you letter . . . neither of the so called major political parties . . . [and] only a handful of presidential contenders could hope to match the result of Common Cause's solicitation of funds.

Gais *et al.* (1984) show that citizen groups have not been sustained entirely by membership subscriptions: 'most citizen groups are supported by a mixture of gifts from foundations, grants and contracts from government agencies, and gifts from a small number of wealthy individuals' (p. 164). (See also Walker, above.)

Some material on Britain also suggests the importance of financial patronage as a factor in group formation. Frank Field, former director of the Child Poverty Action Group, has outlined the importance of the Quakers in the creation of a number of British cause groups:

The Child Poverty Action Group was formed in 1965 and, if anybody believes there's not such a thing as political conspiracy in this country, they are wrong. The political conspiracy is really formed around the Quakers, in that here is a group, some of whom are highly professional and dedicated to bringing about change. The Child Poverty Action Group was formed by them, as was Shelter, and they were behind a number of interesting developments of the social pressure groups of the mid and late 1960s.

The above is quoted by Davies (1985, p. 4), who goes on to discuss the 'Hampstead worthies', wealthy liberals prepared to encourage a number of reform groups such as abortion law reform, cannabis liberalization, and homosexual law reform.

On the public interest front there are again definitional problems: for example, is the League of Women Voters in the United States (140,000 members) a public interest/'good government' group or a feminist group? (Barbrook 1979, p. 5.) The gist of the public interest (or people's interest) definition is, however, contained in one of the Common Cause's first advertisements in 1970. John Gardner, the founder, put out the message, 'Everybody is organized but the people . . . [We will create] a third force in American life, which will uphold the public interest against . . . the special interests that dominate our national life today.' (Quoted in Greenwald 1977, p. 33.)

The public interest characteristics have been set out by Barbrook (1979, p. 4) as a relative lack of self-interest by those proposing measures purporting to be in the public interest, and a sincere belief that the measures were in the interests of the public at large and were more in the public interest than any available alternative. The theoretical interest in such groups lies, of course, in the difficulty of mobilizing the membership. It had long been a clichéd criticism of pluralism that (largely) economic commercial producer interests were easier to activate. Olson proposed, 'Organized groups are among the largest groups in the nation, and they have some of the most vital common interests ... The consumers are at least as numerous as any other group in the society, but they have no aggregation to countervail the power of organized or monopolistic consumers.' (Quoted in Barbrook 1979, p. 6.)

However, McFarland (1976, p. 38) has used the work of Mitchell (1974) to show that the one versus one, public versus particular, contest is probably unusual and over-simplified. In a table Mitchell lists some (not all) of the possible 'winners' and 'losers' in an issue such as the deregulation of natural gas prices. He argues that the 'gainers' include owners of gasfields, producing state governments and taxpayers, consumers and importers of imported items (due to a higher exchange rate), and oil and coal consumers, while the 'losers' include gas consumers, exporters, and oil and coal producers. McFarland points out,

it is interesting to see that there are nine latent (not formally organised) groups involved—six on one side and three on the other. Also involved are seventeen particular interests—that is, the financial interests of particular industries or groups ... such complexity is typical of most policy-making situations ...

The public interest dissolves into a state-by-state, fuel-by-fuel patchwork.

Some apparently public interest lobbies are the 'fronts' for sectional interests: an example, the anti-litter group Keep America Beautiful (KAB), was supported by the beverage and packing industries fighting against returnable bottles (Greenwald 1977, p. 5). In Britain the Association for the Conservation of Energy contains insulation firms as members.

A practical problem for the public interest lobby is membership stability. Colby (1983) shows that half the Common Cause membership fails to renew its $15 subscription after the initial year's membership, requiring Common Cause to spend almost one-third of its membership budget on recruitment expenses. Berry (1977, p. 29) shows that Common Cause sent out 6.5 million pieces of mail in its first year. Nader spent $314,000 to raise £1.1m. in Public Citizen's first year. According to Colby, for the different main public interest groups the 'logic' of membership differs. The Sierra Club has selective incentives, the Nader groups have a charismatic leader, and Common Cause presses consensus issues coupled with enormous expenditures on membership building. He says, 'Membership does not arise *spontaneously* [our emphasis] out of consumer outrage, environmentalist dismay or political reformer zeal.' His main conclusion is that the financial contribution is so marginal to the mainly middle-class professionals who contribute that the act is not worth the weight of deliberation implied in the rational choice model: 'it is not a very expensive proposition and may simply make one feel good'. This observation, that some public interest subscriptions might be seen as trivial expenditures, might have broader significance. The fact that groups for the unemployed and poor are notoriously difficult to recruit might, in part, be because the allocation of that membership subscription might have to be made much more rigorously (and logically) than subscriptions to other kinds of bodies, where the decision can be entered into with a casualness which belies the economic–rational model of Olson. Even the subscription to the National Farmers' Union in England and Wales—while collectively yielding £8.7 million to fund a very effective organization—is the product of a levy of £30 basic subscription plus 44p per acre farmed, giving an average of £87 per member. In terms of the farm costs this might not appear worthy of too much close analysis. It is only a rather narrow slice of an average cow.

This line of explanation has recently been confirmed by King's 1985 study of Chambers of Commerce. He concluded that the chamber's main problem 'is less one of controlling demanding members than of resurrecting any interest at all from the bulk of membership in their representational activities'. He argued that firms paid the membership costs (£47–£345) with very little thought because they were so low: they joined because they felt they *ought* to join.

And as the subscription issue might loom smaller for the member than Olson's crisis in logic assumes, so the involvement by members can be more peripheral to organizations than he imagines. Mike Daube, who has been involved in a number of British groups (Shelter, Action on Smoking and Health, Action on Alcohol Abuse) has been quoted as follows: 'The most effective pressure groups tend to be those which one can run by a small, highly professional core: members can be useful (not least in paying subscriptions) but they can also be a hindrance and often fail to realise that time spent servicing them could have been spent more profitably.' (Davies

1985, p. 31.) Lowe and Goyder's study of environmental groups has also indicated the ambiguous nature of membership as an asset to a group. For example, some leaders, particularly from some of the historic preservation groups, expressed a preference for a small membership. Thus the general secretary of the Ancient Monuments Society asserted, 'We're a learned society, a repository of expertise. We don't want to be a popular society with a big membership.' A few groups had no subscription membership whatsoever, believing that individual subscriptions would be more trouble than they were worth (Lowe and Goyder 1983, p. 41).

The emergence of prominent public interest lobbies in the 1970s, did not contradict Olson in a literal sense. He had acknowledged (p. 160) 'philanthropic groups' which did not have as a goal the welfare of their exclusive membership, but the scale and importance of the public interest groups did seem unexpected from Olson's perspective. He saw the possibility of altruistic behaviour as so exceptional as to have 'little if any merit'. However, the boom of the public interest group is perhaps past: in the words of one American contact, 'The lustre in the 1980s is off', and perhaps—in the longer run—the difficulties predicted by Olson are prevailing. The public interest lobby, though, also perhaps underlines that for the individual the sort of benefits that he demands from different types of groups will vary. Some groups, such as trade unions, might be joined for selective benefit reasons; others might be joined for purely expressive reasons (e.g. CND or the Civic Trust).

4

The Power of Business

Lindblom's early work constitutes some of the pillars of contemporary pluralism, and therefore his *Politics and Markets* (1977) gratified critics of pluralism as apparently confirming that they had been right all along. Lindblom (1983, p. 384) has said plainly: 'I consider some of my amendments—specifically the arguments on the privileged position of business and on circularity through indoctrination—to be antagonistic to pluralism rather than resuscitating it.'

Lindblom's new position is, then, that because of the strength of business, politics is pluralist only on secondary issues. Therefore Lindblom says, in striking fashion, that he must consider himself only a 0.5 pluralist. And, further, he says that he has to reduce his commitment to 0.4 to acknowlege that among secondary issues many are settled by interchange greatly restricted to businessmen and government officials (1983, p. 385).

A major response to *Politics and Markets* is Wildavsky's 'Changing Forward versus Changing Back' (1978). One of Wildavsky's central points is that business is engaged in controlling government precisely because it is business that government primarily (attempts to) control: 'In a democracy one cannot have it both ways—government control over an industry and no effort by industry to exert control over government.' (p. 277.) For example, the chairman of one of Britain's biggest companies complained to us that his company now employed hundreds of lawyers to deal with governmental regulation of his industry, whereas forty years ago the company employed very few lawyers, reflecting a relatively unregulated business environment at that time. Wildavsky's major concern in the article is to argue that society needs a facility both to move forward *and* back. He raises 'terms seldom heard in the debate on capitalism and democracy: terms like diversity, reversibility, error recognition and error correction' (p. 218). He defines the priority of democracy as concerning correctable rather than correct decisions. He responds to Lindblom by questioning the radical alternative to pluralism now advanced by Lindblom.

There *is* a different rationality of political activity involved for (say) a large oil company as opposed to a middle-income citizen. For the oil company, activity is relatively cheap—employing lobbyists, maintaining relations with officials, gathering political intelligence—and is a low percentage of income, while at a level individuals cannot entertain. Likewise the impact of government regulation, tariff setting, or whatever is again likely to be a stronger incentive for a corporate activity than for the individual. Accordingly, we would not dissent from Lindblom's claims that the organized group world is dominated by business and professional bodies and, indeed, that 'every separate business enterprise is a financial organization that can . . . act as an interest group' (1977, p. 197).

It is undoubtedly true that 'Because public functions in the market system rest in the hands of businessmen, it follows that jobs, prices, production, growth, the standard of living and the economic security of everyone all rest in their hands. Consequently government officials cannot be indifferent to how well business performs its functions.' (p. 172.) Sir Douglas Wass, then Permanent Secretary at the British Treasury—and no shade of neo-radical—observed that 'If markets take the view that the policies pursued by a particular country are likely to damage assets held in that country or in that country's currency, they are likely to behave in ways which can actually enforce a policy change.' (See King 1985.) But it is one thing to admit that government wants prosperity and another to say that therefore it prefers business to public demands: it is the essential point of the phenomenon that no conflict is recognized between what is 'good for General Motors' and 'good for the country'.

OECD data (1977) quoted by Paloheimo (1984, pp. 26–8) indicate that in fourteen countries examined there was 'a tendency for the rate of (corporate) profit to fall from the 1960s onwards'. Not only does Lindblom not rebut *such* empirical material, he ignores it. Paloheimo argues that there was a very clear tendency for the rate of profit to fall in the UK and US, but not in countries such as Switzerland and Austria. In citing this material it is not necessary to accept OECD's verdict on how well corporations have been doing in the US. Moreover, although probably the particular

OECD data were published too late for Lindblom's use, the issue is whether Lindblom's assumptions about corporate power were really compatible with a US corporate economy that was in part in oil shock crises while he was writing. At least the business environment was such that he needed to support and reinforce his bland picture of powerful business.

Another development of the 1960s and 1970s, already noted, that also seemed to make Lindblom's case less persuasive was the increase in government regulations between (say) 1967 and 1976. According to Wilson (1985, p. 31), 'This entailed not only a five-fold increase in the number of staff employed in the regulatory agencies and a similar increase in their budgets, but also a dramatic increase in the impact of regulation on business.' Wilson cites four academic studies in making the point that it was possible to argue that governments in the US were more stringent in their regulation of business than the governments of supposedly more left-wing countries.

Des Wilson's study (1983) of the campaign against lead in petrol in Britain begins with an account of how one of the priorities of the new Reagan administration in 1980 was to scrap regulations such as the 'lead phase-down programme'. Wilson's chapter title summarizes subsequent events: 'How the environmentalists beat big business in the USA'.

This is not to argue conclusively that there is no privilege for business, but to argue that the empirical pattern is much patchier than Lindblom allows. As we noted in the previous chapter, on an issue such as the deregulation of natural gas prices, 'the business interest' is divided.

If the US system is still generally responsive to the wishes of capitalism, non-capitalist systems are also likely to be biased in favour of production arguments. One has no reason to doubt the potency of the prosperity argument in the Soviet Union, and certainly inspection of socialist governments in Britain and France shows that they have (even if reluctantly) been aware of the production-before-consumption necessity. Lindblom says, 'In the polyarchies, government responsibility for avoiding inflation and unemployment is a common issue in elections . . . in countless ways governments in these systems recognise that businessmen need to be encouraged to perform.' (p. 173.) This is not controversial. At some point in the argument there might be conflict between business and public interest, but not at the level pitched by Lindblom. Is inflation and unemployment a 'good' for the public or do they do benefit from business success?

An important case study in the argument about the power of business in Crenson's 1971 study of the cities of East Chicago and Gary in Indiana. He argues that while they both faced problems of air pollution, the industrialists of Gary (largely dominated by US Steel) were able to prevent (without having to exert themselves, but through a general appreciation of their importance to the local economy) or at least delay the arrival of the issue of pollution on the political agenda. One American academic of our acquaintance rebutted the Crenson analysis with the telling point that when he grew up in a similar town, the air pollution was termed (by employees) 'the smell of prosperity'. In other words, there is a difference between suppression by business and local consensus. (See Jones 1975, cited in Polsby 1979, p. 541.)

Lindblom's evidence is on occasion uncharacteristically weak. He *asserts*,

Any government official who understands the requirements of his position and the responsibilities that market-orientated systems will throw on businessmen will therefore grant them a privileged position. He does not have to be bribed, duped or pressured to do so. Nor does he have to be an uncritical admirer of businessmen to do so. He simply understands, as is plain to see, that public affairs in market-orientated systems are in the hands of two groups of leaders, government and business, who must collaborate and that, to make the system work government leadership must often defer to business leadership.

He then attempts to prove or at least illustrate this by a couple of quotations. A leader of a West German business association is recorded as claiming that politics 'is not an alien world to the entrepreneur: it is his own. At stake for him is the leadership of the state.' For one thing, the quote is trivial, and innumerable kindred examples could be found from pressure group leaders, trade unionists, religious leaders. In his review Wildavsky, for example, in passing neutralizes the point by citing a business group spokesman: 'Businessmen have to be radicals now, because they're the outsiders.' For another, it is a quote seeking to stimulate business action rather than stating that it happens: if anything, to seek to promote business activity suggests that it is not happening.

His next example is even less convincing. He says that a Du Pont employee writes, 'the strength of the position of business and the weakness of the position of government is that government needs a strong economy just as much as business does, *and the people need it and demand it even more*' (our emphasis). This quote makes precisely our point, that the claim of a conflict between business and wider public interests has yet to be made. Certainly there isn't *evidence* here to cause fundamental reconsideration of pluralism. Lindblom quotes widely but seems to avoid confronting some of the most telling material. For example, Carol Greenwald's (1977, p. 314) discussion of the work of Schattschneider shows that there is a well-known view which accepts that business is privileged but holds that the democratic system is *the* counterbalance to the economic system:

In Schattschneider's view, losers take their case to the government in order to enlarge the number of participants and alter the consequences . . . The SST [supersonic transport] provides such an example, since the research continued quietly for ten years as an in-house bureaucratic decision. Controversy arose when Congress, awakened to the problem by the environmentalist coalition of losers, challenged the Pentagon and reversed the power equation.

Nor is there justification for Lindblom's claim that pluralism is about secondary issues, whereas business is interested in certain other issues. But a self-fulfilling circularity follows. The issues that interest business are assumed to be the primary issues. *Ergo*, business dominates the primary issues . . .

And what of the standing criticism that there has to be evidence of unity of purpose within the business élite? Lindblom has only a trivial discussion as to how government squares the competing demands of business for low tariffs/high tariffs, a strong currency/a weak currency, and so on (1977, p. 178). When, in Britain in the early 1980s, the Society of Motor Manufacturers and Traders was campaigning against the equalization of car prices within the EEC, what was the British interest, and, even more difficult, what was the capitalist interest? Examples of conflict are explained away as secondary issues.

Lindblom has similar omissions in discussing union power. In one paragraph (p. 176) he says that governments must break general strikes and cites Britain in 1926, but then goes on to hazard a cross-national generalization that 'In short, the rules of market orientated systems, while granting a privileged position to business, so far appear to prohibit the organizational moves that would win a comparable position for labour.' Although he concedes 'special circumstances', he fails to address, in sustained fashion, Scandinavian and even British union experience. He cites Blank's 1973 study of the Federation of British Industries, which documents intimate contacts between the federation and government departments and which concludes, 'It looked and acted like a government department.' (p. 181.) The issue raised by that quote is why that particular example sums up Britain and not a host of other quotes which would show that government–group intimacy was *not* restricted to business: see work by Finer (1966 edn.), Beer (1965), Stewart (1958), and Potter (1961). Moreover, it does not coincide with Grant and Marsh's thorough analysis of the CBI, which concluded that the CBI is rather weak (Grant and Marsh 1977) or with the call, in 1981, by the then director general of the CBI for a 'bare knuckle' fight with the Conservative Government (see Chapter 7).

Later he admits that non-business leaders are admitted to 'circles of explicit negotiation, bargaining and reciprocal persuasion', but it is again merely asserted that in these consultations corporate executives occupy a privileged position since they and not the (other) interest group leaders are in attendance mainly in their capacity as 'public officials' (p. 179). No evidence is offered for this claim.

He further (p. 186) claims that in the United Kingdom hundreds of business advisory committees confer authority on corporate executives. These mysterious institutions are not, for example, described in Grant and Marsh's authoritative study (1977) of *The CBI* or Stephen Young's *Intervention in the Mixed Economy* (1974). These bodies are apparently 'in addition' to the more recognizable department committees and royal commissions. When he discusses these commissions, Lindblom quotes Blondel and presents them as means to allow businessmen and other participants 'active participation in administration, as if the administrators were no longer able to bear alone the burden of the administrative State and had to pass it along to private individuals'. Such an interpretation of groups and government is an important theme, but where is his evidence that this is a privilege limited to a homogenous business interest?

Lindblom's examples from the British system are introduced with what can only be described as reckless abandon. The wish is surely father of the 'fact' when he claims, 'Quietly and gradually, workplace committees have come to play an important role in British industry. Roughly half of British trade unionists are members of one. The authority of the groups is informal, but they have become important participants in the determination of wages and working conditions . . .' (p. 330.)

Notwithstanding Lindblom's apparent difficulty in this regard, material on conflict between government and industry is easily uncovered. In 1986, there was a major controversy in British politics over the future of the helicopter manufacturers, Westland; where was the national interest in these circumstances? In meeting such instances, Lindblom considers that

It follows that evidence, which is abundant, of conflict between business and government—and of business defeats—is not evidence of lack of privilege. Knowing that they must have some privileges . . . businessmen ask for a great deal . . . disputes between government and business are intense because of—not in spite of—their sharing the major leadership roles in the politico-economic order.

In other words, Lindblom finds even more comfort for his argument *because* the two are apparently at each other's throats.

He finds that urban renewal comes to the aid of retailers, banks, theatres, public utilities, brokers, and builders. Highway development promotes a long list of industries including cement, automobiles, construction, petroleum, construction equipment, and trucking. The benefit to the public as residents and consumers is not thought worthy of mention.

After a textual confusing of the political left with the political right, Lindblom sneaks in an admission that decade by decade the environment is slowly changing to one of loss and privilege for business, but before the reader can dwell on this Lindblom is asserting with conviction, but without convincing, some kind of iron law that there is at any time 'some minimum of privilege short of which inducements will fail to motivate business performance'. Then, accelerating away from his monetary concession, Lindblom is back to the constraints that giant multinational corporations can impose on small nations (p. 181).

British Conservative Governments, since Lindblom wrote, have had the stated aim of removing government interference with business. This is presumably popular with business and consistent with Lindblom's arguments. But had the reverse happened and extensive intervention been increased, Lindblom would as cheerfully have seen intervention as a means to satisfy industry . . . Likewise, the undoubted increase in lobbying activity by American business is a double-edged argument. When business was not organized it was a sign of strength, because its collective interests were little challenged. Heads it's proof of business power, tails it's conclusive proof of business power.

The privileged place of business is, as it were, a direct power of business. In a later chapter Lindblom suggests that business has power because it so indoctrinates citizens that 'citizen volitions serve not their own interests but the interests of business men' (p. 202). He admits that the European polyarchies are less constrained than in the US. He has to swallow the uncomfortable fact that left-wing governments are elected, but even when he has to face up to large communist parties, as in France, he has a ready answer: 'The communist party itself will often, as a practical matter, endorse not a distinctive grand alternative but policies within a narrow spectrum of alternatives. A communist party often has to pay that price for admission to parliamentary politics.' (p. 210.)

When he recognizes that the US has no widely circulating radical newspaper because no wide audience wants it, he again sees only confirmation. 'But that is our very point.' In other words, false consciousness . . . Indeed, Lindblom is often only a rather tardy echo of the neo-Marxist liturgy. We recognize echoes of Gramsci's 'ideological hegemony', whereby the dominant class defines the debate: Poulantzas (1973) argued, 'The dominance of this ideology is shown by the fact that the dominated classes live their conditions of political existence through the forms of dominant political discourse: this means that often they live even their revolt against the domination of the system within the frame of reference of the dominant ideology.' (Quoted in Birch 1984.)

Miliband (1969, p. 145) argued, 'business enters the [pluralist] competition on extremely favourable terms in comparison with labour or any other interest'. He claimed that businessmen and their representatives normally have a *rapport* with ministers, civil servants and other members of the state which is very different from that of labour and *its* representatives . . . The demands of business . . . are *always* claimed to be in the 'national interest' . . . business demands which are designed to strengthen the position of individual firms . . . or of the capitalist enterprise at large, can always be presented, with a high degree of plausibility, given the capitalist context in which they are made, as congruent with the 'national interest'.

Ironically, Miliband goes back to an American source—Schatt-schneider (1935, p. 287)—which had claimed that 'Businessmen collectively constitute the most class-conscious group in American society. As a class they are more highly organised, more easily mobilised, have more facilities for communication, are more like minded, and are more accustomed to stand together in defence of their privileges than any other group.'

Politics and Markets is unlikely to persuade anyone to adopt Lindblom's new approach, unless they are inclined to accept his new value positions and assumptions. It makes no attempt to engage competing propositions, such as the 'overload' approach, which would contend that one of the key problems of economic management for liberal democracies is that party competition leads to excessive expectations among the electorate. (See Brittan, in King *et al.* 1976, p. 97.)

One critique of the later work of Dahl and Lindblom was made by Manley (1983), who identified two variants, Pluralism I and Pluralism II. (The pluralist material certainly needs organization and sub-division: see also David Marsh's (1983, p. 10) categories of classical pluralism and élite pluralism, and Kelso (1978), Kvavik (1976), and Hayward (1966).) Manley portrays Pluralism I as a political system reasonably open to multiple interests. Pluralism II is seen as a major revision by Dahl and Lindblom in (*a*) their introduction to the 1976 edition to *Politics, Economics and Welfare* (first published in 1953), (*b*) Lindblom's *Politics and Markets* (1977), and (*c*) Dahl's *Dilemmas of Pluralist Democracy* (1982). Dahl, in a comment on Manley's article, stresses that Lindblom and he are not an undifferentiated mind, but Manley does substantiate that both Dahl and Lindblom have shifted ground to be critical of the complacent, best-of-all-worlds image of American society of Pluralism I.

Some of the Dahl and Lindblom comments in their 1976

introduction to *Politics, Economics and Welfare* are clear trailers to Lindblom (1977), for example: 'Businessmen play a distinctive role in polyarchal politics that is qualitatively different from that of any interest group. It is also much more powerful than an interest-group role.' (p. xxxvi.) It also presages Dahl's less explicit reservations about the health of American democracy. Both Dahl and Lindblom are greatly interested in Yugoslav attempts at socialist decentralization.

While criticizing pluralism, neither Dahl nor Lindblom embrace non-pluralist alternatives: indeed, it is the lack of a tenable alternative that is striking. For example, Dahl in *Dilemmas of Pluralist Democracy* points out that if a socialist economic order were to be democratic, it would necessarily have to contain such organizationally pluralist features that many of the standard problems of pluralist democracy would remain (see also 1983, p. 387). Lindblom is equally pessimistic about alternatives: with 'unobscured view, no society looks defensible' (1977, p. 247).

In fact, reading *Politics and Markets* in conjunction with Lindblom's 'Another State of Mind' (his presidential address to the American Political Science Association, 1981 (published 1982)), we can perhaps see that it is the complacency of (US) political science about the nature of the political system that seems to be prompting Lindblom's new interests. He presents the work of his peers as vulnerable to radical critique. He admits that there might be disqualifying weaknesses in the radical model: 'I do not want to argue that the radical model is better than the conventional. I only want to show that the conventional model is extremely weak . . . How comparative study of and experimentation with the two models, sustained and dispassionate, could turn out, I would not guess.' (1982, p. 14). He later explains that one reason for the non-pursuit of the radical literature by mainstream political science is that we feel 'rebuffed by what we are fairly confident are serious short comings in much radical writing . . . Its terms sometimes defy association with any observable real-world process. It begs questions. And its authors . . . sometimes make no attempt to communicate beyond a privileged radical circle with its private language—thus also excusing themselves from the demands for evidence.' (p. 20.) Clearly for Lindblom, pluralism fails, if it fails, because of internal tensions, not by comparison with a superior model.

Though Lindblom's argument is suspect, there might well, none the less, be an important truth. It is true from a European perspective that there is a singular and crippling lack of breadth to the American political (and political science) agenda. Dahl and Lindblom (1976, p. xxxviii) observed, 'The fact that the dominant form of business enterprise in the United States is the privately owned and controlled corporation is not a product of even a moderately rational public calculation of relative advantages. In fact, no such public inquiry has taken place.'

Lindblom complained that we have failed to imagine mutual adjustment or a pluralistic polyarchy free of business privilege: 'None of the market-orientated polyarchies has ever practiced pluralism without the lop sided participation of businessmen . . . a pluralism without business vetoes . . . has hardly been explored.' (p. 347.) That kind of discussion might still be too strong for some tastes, but at least bias and lop-sidedness are more likely than the claims that all primary issues are resolved in favour of business. The major weaknesses in his 'pin everything on business' attempt are the apparently incompatible divisions within business and the level of generality he often uses. If policy is good for all business it is not self-evident that for everyone else it is bad. Moreover, governments like to win elections and must satisfy voters: that the voters adopt the volitions of business argument would need much stronger sustenance than is given in *Politics and Markets*.

Finally, one needs to note that business interests are as much as prisoner of the political culture as are the rest of us. For example, Vogel's comparative study (1983, p. 102) of environmental regulation in the USA and Britain suggests that British businessmen are much more compliant, when faced with the authority of the state, than their American counterparts. He emphasizes the mutual trust between firms and the regulators in the UK and the importance of political culture in socializing British businessmen to act 'responsibly'.

5

The Revival of Corporatist Interest

Iron Triangles and Subgovernments

This chapter concerns not groups themselves but the literature discussing how groups relate to government and policy-making. So far we have seen that the idea of a mutually rewarding relationship between groups and government departments is an important dimension of political science in the US, the UK, and elsewhere in the twentieth century. A clear picture of American conventional wisdom comes from Chubb's (1983, p. 249) study on the making of US energy policy. He describes the traditional pattern of policy formulation and implementation as being in political *subsystems* 'that more often than not promoted or generously accommodated the interests of major energy producers. Each subsystem was organized around an independent administrative agency with political support from a few major interest groups and, usually, a committee in each house of Congress.'

This is the image of the US 'iron triangle' or group subgovernment (McConnell, 1966). E. S. Griffiths is quoted in Freeman (1965) as follows:

It is my opinion that ordinarily the relationship among these non-legislators, administrators, lobbyists, scholars—who are interested in a common problem—is a much more real relationship than the relationship between congressmen generally or between administrators generally. In other words, he who would understand the prevailing pattern of our present governmental behavior, instead of studying the formal institutions . . . may possibly obtain a better picture of the way things really happen if he would study the 'whirlpools' of special social interest and problems.

Polsby (1981, p. 9) has, in passing, noted US "issue-networks", "sub-governments", "iron triangles", and similarly described groups of variously situated people who do business with one another because of their common focus on a particular subject matter'.

Harmon Zeigler's classic study (1964, p. 191) of US interest groups described how the 'tightly drawn web' between the Farm Bureau Federation (interest group) and the federal agencies had become 'a coalition of monopolistic proportions'. He described how the Farm Bureau actually helped administer the Agricultural Adjustment Administration, and how as the Farm Bureau representatives delivered the benefit cheques to farmers, the interest group took on the appearance of the source of the relief.

A final example of this sort of discussion can be drawn from Ripley and Franklin (1984 edn., p. 10):

Subgovernments are clusters of individuals that effectively make most of the routine decisions in a given substantive area of policy . . . a typical [US] subgovernment is composed of members of the House and/or Senate, members of congressional staffs, a few bureaucrats, and representatives of private groups and organizations interested in the policy area . . . Most of the policy making in which subgovernments engage consists of routine matters. 'Routine' policy is simply policy that is not currently involved in a high degree of controversy. The substance of routine policy changes only slowly over time, and the participants most interested in it are also thoroughly familiar with it and quietly efficient in both its implementation and minor operations . . .

. . . If the members of a subgovernment can reach compromises among themselves on any disagreements about policy, they can reduce the chances of calling a broader audience together that might become involved in their activities and output. When more participants enter, the chances of basic policy realignments increase . . . [and] such realignments might not be perceived to be in the best interests of the members of the subgovernment. Thus, there is a strong incentive for them to reach compromises and avoid broadening the number of participants.

The two main elements of this conception of policy-making are the identification of segmentation of policy-making in specialized policy communities and an expectation that regularized relations emerge between interests and officials. This kind of politics is different from the open, adversarial, party-dominated, Parliament-based politics often presented as *the* British policy process. None the less, the picture of British politics as being about insider group relations with departments was signalled in the first chapter through discussion of the work of Finer and others. As Ashford (1981, p. 57) put it, 'British administration mastered the principles of co-operation and mutual self-interest long before the "corporate state" became a political science buzzword'. Finer described the 'ever-closer interdependency of the interest groups and Whitehall. Each *needs* the other' (1966 edn., p. 30.) He described formal contacts such as representation on royal commissions and formal invitations to comment on policy proposals, but went on, 'Yet, numerous as they are, the official channels do not nearly suffice to convey the swelling tide of the Lobby's problems, notions and grievances. Beyond and around them flows a veritable Atlantic of informal to-ings and fro-ings. This contact is close, pervasive and continuous. In some cases it is even intimate.' (1966 edn., p. 33.)

This has very much the same flavour as Wildavsky's (1976, pp. 55–6) observations on staff-level contacts between Congressional and bureaucratic officials: 'Many agencies choose to keep sub committee staff informed months and sometimes years ahead . . . Mutual dependence is the order of the day and both sides generally regard their contacts as prerequisites to doing their best work.' Ripley and Franklin (1984, p. 11), citing Lowi, also describe the interest group–bureaucracy relations in intimate terms:

The 'rules of the game' of American politics . . . minimize the distinction between governmental and nongovernmental institutions . . . This results in a general belief on the part of those involved that individuals and groups that are most affected by governmental actions should have almost continual access to governmental officials during the policy-making process.

Interviews by observers in Britain such as Whiteley and Winyard (1983) found confirmation of this trait of segmentation: 'There is very much a feeling that each is in his own corner fighting his own cause . . . there is no feeling that we are part of central government.' The Whiteley and Winyard material is unusual in that the stress on regularized group access often associated with producer groups, is extended to the social policy groups of their sample. As discussed in chapter 8, this institutionalization of access is found in reports on most Western political systems.

A number of factors underpin policy-making by group integration:

1. If groups don't get involved, most have political connections with the media or legislature and thus have a potential for noise and nuisance, so it is better for policy-makers (political and bureaucratic) to pre-empt the overt politicization of the issue through co-option.

2. Lack of expertise within the bureaucracy means that it is

sensible to draw on the resources of the group. This helps problem definition and improves the match of problem and policy.

3. There has been a growing recognition in the past decade of the importance of policy implementation and the importance of co-operation at the implementation stage.

4. In attempting to reduce uncertainty, government has been using the *small number strategy* (see Daintith 1985, p. 185) to find 'viable interlocutors, discussion partners and agents through which it may evolve, test and operate its policies'. Daintith defines the strategy as follows: 'If such numbers can only be sufficiently reduced, not only may the operation of measures be more effectively policed, but government can obtain the knowledge it needs in advance, by asking those affected by its measures what their reactions will be or, even better, obtaining commitments from them about their future behaviour.'

5. There is often a legal requirement for consultation. Even in policy sectors without statutory compulsion there may have been a 'spill over' of custom.

6. There is a cultural bias to consensus. It is a 'rule of the game' to consult.

7. Participation, itself, has been a 'good thing' in Western democracies.

The above portrait of a drift to subgovernment, policy communities, and consultation is no more than the conventional wisdom of political science in Europe and the UK by the 1970s. The discovery of corporatism in the late 1970s therefore appears to have been unnecessarily dramatic: the themes were well established.

Corporatism

This rediscovered corporatism (or neo-corporatism) was precise in its formulation. Ross Martin (1983, p. 86) has noted how in the 1950s and 1960s writers on British politics such as Andrew Shonfield, Harry Eckstein, and Samuel Beer used the term, but he continues that they had used it, 'loosely, without troubling to define it closely, and without making any large claims for its heuristic capacity'. Not so the corporatists of the past decade.

One sympathetic commentator on the literature on corporatism that has developed in recent years acknowledged it to contain 'some of the most indigestible material in political science . . . a bewildering, and often intrinsically tedious, body of material . . .' (Coates in Harrison 1984, p. 122). Yet whatever deficiencies and complexities exist in this corporatist literature, its importance in the past decade is clear: interest group writing has taken place under the umbrella of, or in reaction against, the neo-corporatist approach.

However, it can be argued that the mainspring of the corporatist attack, Philippe Schmitter, created a divisive debate where none need have existed. His rationale for devising the corporatist model was to offer a new theoretical paradigm to replace the studies of pressure groups, lobbies, and interest associations which, he claimed, had long been an area of, 'conceptual torpor and theoretical orthodoxy in the discipline of political science' (1979, p. 5). He saw the corporatist definition as 'a sort of paradigmatic revolution when juxtaposed to the long predominant, "pluralist", way of describing and analysing the role of organised interests' (1982, p. 260).

The corporatist approach thus stands as a putative corrective to the pluralist literature. It is argued that it underlines features which characterize empirical Western societies better than the pluralist alternative. Schmitter's vital definition is:

Corporatism can be defined as a system of interest representation in which the constituent units are organised into a limited number of singular, compulsory, non-competitive, hierarchically ordered and functionally differentiated categories, recognised or licensed (if not created) by the state and granted a deliberate representational monopoly within their respective categories in exchange for observing certain controls on their selection of leaders and articulation of demands and supports. (1979, p. 13.)

The corporatist literature is then one kind of model of interest group–government (or state) relations which attempts to capture reality better than pluralism does. The term 'intermediation' is used by the corporatist theorists (rather than representation by interest groups) to make the important point that groups act as instruments of government as well as instruments of their members: Schmitter (1979, p. 93) does not make much of an issue of this, but a footnote does describe groups acting as agents of 'social control' and displaying 'private governmental functions'. Relationships with groups are seen as ordered and controlled. Government recognizes (even creates) a limited number of 'group partners' with effective representational monopoly in their policy area. In exchange for monopoly the groups discipline and control members, enforce policy, and make a more manageable environment for the government (see Crouch 1983, p. 453).

While the literature on corporatism has become keenly disputed, Marsh (1983, p. 2) has offered a reasonably neutral account of the difference between corporatist and pluralist features. Interpreting Schmitter's definition of pluralism, he says:

The crucial elements of a pluralist system of interest group representation are therefore clear. There are a large number of groups, in which the leadership is responsive to its membership, which compete with one another for the allocation of scarce resources. In [this] model of government—the 'state', despite what Schmitter's definition might imply, is not a concept used by pluralists—is given a minimal passive role, merely authoritatively allocating scarce resources, with its decisions reflecting the balance between the interest groups within society at a given time. As such, while interest groups may make continuing representations to government, which may even become institutionalised, the government remains independent of, and opposed to, too close contact with the interest groups.

Marsh contrasts this image with one of corporatism, in which the emphasis is on a *limited number* of interest groups, primarily representing capital and labour. The groups can 'deliver' their membership. In addition, the links between the corporations (that is, business *and* labour corporations) and government would be very close.

It is a main theme of this chapter that the clearer the definition of corporatism, the less contact it has with empirical practice. However, Schmitter (1979, p. 15) in fact qualified his comparison between corporatism and pluralism by acknowledging that:

Pluralism and corporatism share a number of basic assumptions, as would almost any realistic model of modern interest politics:

1. the growing importance of formal associational units of representation;
2. the persistence and expansion of functionally differentiated and potentially conflicting interests;
3. the burgeoning role of permanent administrative staffs, of specialised information, of technical expertise and, consequently, of entrenched oligarchy;
4. the decline in the importance of territorial and partisan representation; and

5. the secular trend towards expansion in the scope of public policy and
6. the interpenetration of private and public decision areas.

The Problem of Empirical Application

Despite Schmitter's observations on the similarity of pluralism and corporatism, the central corporatist purpose was to *replace* the pluralist model, as Marsh showed above. The debate of the past decade began with Schmitter's full-blooded and forceful rejection of the pluralist approach: corporatism was put up 'as an explicit alternative to the paradigm of interest politics which has until now completely dominated the discipline of North American political science: *pluralism*' (Schmitter 1979, p. 14).

Williamson (1985, p. 145) has reasonably charged an inconsistency in the attacks (Jordan 1981, 1984) on Schmitter's corporatism that seem to complain that Schmitter should be dismissed both as providing a model too rigid and restricted to match empirical disorder *and* as providing a model that has been so revised as to be difficult to distinguish from pluralism. The apparent contradiction stems from the gulf within Schmitter's work. Since Schmitter's corporatism (unqualified) and his state corporatism (1979, pp. 13, 29) differ so dramatically from the societal corporatism (1979, p. 21), very different complaints can legitimately be made about them.

Any approach which covers such a broad range and both attempts to present itself as in fundamental disagreement with pluralism and also as 'sharing a number of basic assumptions with pluralism' is inviting some apparently contradictory criticisms.

Neo-corporatist theory has appeared to concern a well-structured and relatively simple set of relationships between a powerful state and a limited number of privileged interest groups. It is quite possible to see value in this corporatist ideal type, even though it is seldom—or even never—found in practice: the contrast can clarify analysis of empirical situations. However, it must be said that this was not the original role of the Schmitter tool. It was not to be used as a contrast with reality but as a shorthand for reality. When Schmitter himself saw forms of corporatism as applicable to Sweden, Switzerland, Netherlands, Portugal, Spain, Brazil, Chile, Peru, Fascist Italy, he was attempting to provide descriptive criteria, not highlighting features not found (see Schmitter 1979, pp. 21–2).

TABLE 5.1. *Subtypes of Corporatism*

Dimension	Societal corporatism	State corporatism
Limited number	Arrived at by inter-associational arrangement	Arrived at by deliberate government restriction
Singular	Spontaneous co-optation or competitive elimination by surviving associations	State-imposed eradication of multiple associations
Compulsory	*De facto*	*De jure*
Non-competitive	Product of oligarchical tendencies	State-enforced
Hierarchically ordered	Product of intrinsic processes of bureaucracy	Product of state-decreed centralization
Functionally differentiated	Voluntary agreements of mutual non-interference by groups	State-established
Recognition by state	Necessity forced from below	Granted from above
Representational monopoly	Secured *from* state	Conceded by state
Control on leadership selection and interest articulation	Reciprocal consensus	Imposition

Source: based upon Schmitter 1979, pp. 20–1.

Schmitter used phrases such as 'Empirically, it is best exemplified . . .' (1979, p. 21), or 'defining corporatism in terms of its praxis . . .'. He talked about a 'specific concrete set of institutional practices . . . of empirically observable group interests' (1979, p. 9).

Therefore corporatism (or neo-corporatism, as it is often labelled) appears to have been devised to underline empirically observable traits (Schmitter 1979, p. 13). In the original use, neo-corporatism replaced pluralism as an effective summary description of political systems, as for example implied in Schmitter's portrayal of 'the decay of pluralism and its gradual displacement by societal corporatism' (1979, p. 24). In the early Schmitter, societal corporatism is 'found' (1979, p. 22). He argued (1979, p. 65) that while no empirically extant system of interest intermediation may perfectly reproduce or replicate corporatism, sets of observable, institutionally descriptive traits tend to cohere, making it possible to categorize historically specific systems (or parts of systems). Again this is broadly stating that it was thought that there were corporatist systems largely extant.

This section of the chapter advances the criticism that it is difficult to make use of the list of corporatist criteria. Whereas Schmitter confidently states that the postulated components of corporatism 'can be easily assessed, if not immediately quantified' (p. 14) and sets out to provide 'an operational definition' (p. 8), operationalization is difficult. Ambiguity on many of the key features is the necessity of practical politics. Even if it was decided to introduce a corporatist political system, the likelihood would be that there would be a fudging of features, such as licensing by the state or a representational monopoly. A new institution, the Engineering Council, has been set up in Britain in the field of representing (and regulating) the engineering profession. The (then) Social Science Research Council Research Panel in Corporatism and Accountability identified the development as a promising case for corporatist research, but the essence of the Engineering Council solution is its chameleon nature, allowing different interpretations to different protagonists (see Jordan and Richardson 1984). Everyone's favourite example of a corporatist nation is Austria, but in a study of the actual Austrian practice, Marin (1985, p. 110–12) discusses the importance of *indeterminacy, informality,* and *institutional ambiguity.* He dismisses the significance of 'formal agreements' and instead dwells on 'long chains and complex networks of generalised political exchanges'. He notes that 'conflict regulation between adversary interest associations will be more stable the more it is simultaneously *underdetermined formally but overdetermined informally.* Indeterminacy is able to create more mutual trust and binding obligations than formal coercive norms or written contracts, parts or treaties . . .'

As we have seen, Crouch (1983) has made out the crucial distinction between pluralism and (neo-) corporatism to be that interest organizations constrain and discipline their own members for the sake of some presumed 'general' interest as well as (or even instead of) representing them. The difficulty with that kind of criterion is that in order to maintain membership satisfaction the public motivation might differ from the private; the negotiators might even have convinced themselves that the public interest *is* their members' interest or that their members' interests are best served *in the long* term by the public interest.

In terms of 'discipline', it might be that bodies such as the TUC and CBI in Britain have little *formal* capacity to secure compliance, but the verdict of a well-placed observer (the director-general of NEDO) was that while an expression of commitment by the CBI did not mean that every company in the land would be willing to run a Work Experience Programme, any more than the support of the TUC meant that every shop steward in the land was in its favour, it did commit the CBI and TUC to bring their powers of persuasion to bear on those of their constituents who doubted or even opposed the running of WEP schemes. 'This . . . commitment is no light thing. It is a commitment which has been loyally honoured . . .' (Cassels 1985, p. 16). How do we weigh 'commitment' in the scale of corporatist compliance?

Williamson (1985, p. 144) notes that Jordan has claimed that Schmitter-type 'pure' corporatism can be separated from pluralism in the emphasis on bargaining in the latter and the neglect in the former. He points out that bargaining cannot be regarded as the exclusive property of pluralism, and certainly to define pluralism as about bargaining and corporatism in terms of its absence is to weigh (not to say bias) the argument about usefulness in favour of pluralism. However, while *bargaining* is obviously a vital dimension in all group–government relations, it is not a theme of the seminal Schmitter article. The words which Schmitter does not use are control, limitation, compulsory, ordered, granted . . .

It has been said that if Bertrand Russell met God, he intended to complain about the lack of evidence God had allowed him of His existence. If Schmitter's corporatism is about bargaining, we agnostics can similarly complain about a lack of evidence on that front. The nearest to a discussion of bargaining is perhaps: 'Corporatist systems may manage to acquire and sustain similar [to pluralist systems] outcomes of demand moderation, negotiated solutions . . .' (1979, p. 19). Schmitter went on to make some opaque point about 'political culture stressing formalism, consensus and continuous bargaining', but whether this was seen as a feature unique to corporatism or another of the similarities between corporatism and pluralism is simply not clear.

Arguably, Schmitter's cryptic observations on bargaining are not a matter of oversight, but arise because opening the issue up at any length reinforces the links to pluralism and destroys the 'revolutionary' nature of his paradigm. Thus when Williamson (1985, pp. 158–66) turns to discuss bargaining within corporatism, he repeatedly concludes that corporatist authors blur the line: 'Lehmbruch's approach is, however, full of pitfalls'; the ideas of Offe and Wiesenthal are 'too abstract'; Panitch's argument on the subordination of trade unions in the bargaining 'is not, unfortunately, fully elaborated'. He sees Crouch's answer to the problem 'is to redefine the concept to a marked degree . . . distinguishing traits from established models of pluralism is unclear'. On Cawson's contribution, he judges that 'the dividing-line between corporatism and pluralism remains too blurred'.

Of course the lack of a perspective on bargaining is not serious if corporatism is conceived of as a system of state domination and imposition. Notwithstanding Williamson (1985, p. 144), bargaining is not considered to be exclusively the property of pluralism, but if bargaining *is* a feature, then any new paradigm would surely be wise to consider the corpus of late pluralist and counter-pluralist work in the US in the 1960s and 1970s.

Ross Martin (1983, p. 96) is also uneasy about this bargaining dimension: 'The puzzle about this is that bargaining, in the normal meaning of the term necessarily implies an element of competition . . . what is required is an explanation of the distinction the new corporatists postulate between corporatist bargaining (which they equate with "collaboration") and pluralist bargaining (which they equate with "competition").'

Martin (p. 102) concludes that under societal corporatism governments and groups are in a bargaining relationship, varying only in degree from pluralist forms of group–government dealing. In his rejoinder, Crouch claims that 'unlike the pluralist case, corporatist interest organizations are Janus-faced; part of their structure and activity faces outwards towards the polity and other interest groups; but part faces inwards towards the makers, regulating and disciplining them'. In fact, it is difficult to imagine pluralist bargaining if the pluralist groups cannot control their membership and 'deliver' compliance. Grant (1985, p. 4), following Crouch, does note that 'the negotiation of understandings, with no obligation on the part of interest organisations to secure the compliance of their members does not constitute a corporatist arrangement . . .'. At first sight this might appear a reasonable distinction; but, in fact, is there a set of negotiations where there is no 'attempt to secure compliance'? What is being traded? The formula offers no successful basis of distinguishing pluralism and corporatism, particularly if indeterminacy is a feature of corporatist practice.

Perhaps as a consequence of this operationalization problem, a remarkable transformation has occurred in the presentation of the value of corporatist theory. The title of the second volume by Lehmbruch and Schmitter (1982) suggests an intention to advance to empirical application of the theory, but by 1982 it is conspicuous that Schmitter labels no particular and specific country as corporatist (in this, the volume which he claims is about an empirical focus on corporatism). Corporatism has retreated (in the size of claims made) as it has advanced (in terms of widespread adoption). In this more guarded version, corporatism no longer *is*, but, 'For definitional purposes it may be preferable to define concepts in terms of polar opposites . . . but the real world is almost always located somewhere in between' (Schmitter 1982, p. 265). He argues, 'Corporatism, however defined and however preceded by adjectives, is clearly not something a polity has or does not have' (1982, pp. 264–5). Where now the confident categorization in the 1979 volume, which found, by and large, corporatism from Sweden to Yugoslavia to Peru?

Now corporatism is not presented as descriptive, but the ideal type end of some continuum; this is more realistic, but if it was only ever intended as some ideal type unrelated to the somewhere-in-betweens of the real world, the concept would not have generated so much excitement.

Dilution

A related issue with the corporatist conundrum concerns the dilution of the technical content of the concept, both by its advocates and their acolytes. In his seminal chapter, Schmitter no sooner defines corporatism than he plunges into subtypes of *state* and *societal* form which were set out earlier.

The elements of societal corporatism make it even more difficult to distinguish from pluralism than the original version. The details of societal corporatism demonstrate that as it is essentially a voluntary, bargained system, it will be difficult to disentangle from some form of pluralism: where is the distinctive role of the state in this pattern? Relaxing the rigidity of the corporatist formula does make corporatism more plausible (we know few Western systems have formal imposed corporatism), but the cost in making corporatism more relevant is again to make it less distinctive.

The practice of concept dilution is not peculiar to Schmitter. Many find it necessary to weaken the concept of corporatism so much to find it applicable that it is difficult to believe that it is anything more than chic pluralism. Although Lehmbruch (1979, p. 150) warned that '[liberal] corporatism should not be confounded with simply more consultation and co-operation of government with organised interest groups', this seems to have happened when many authors have taken up the term 'corporatism' to describe their particular case study. One example is Simmie's 1981 study of physical planning in Oxford, which is presented in corporatist terms, but a sympathetic reviewer felt obliged to point out that 'The post war planning process in Oxford can only be said to have been corporatist, if the concept of corporation is employed in its lowest sense' (Saunders 1982, p. 69). Indeed, even in the 1982 Lehmbruch and Schmitter volume several of the chapters seem to have so relaxed the definition of corporatism that they are using it to discuss no more than consultation and co-operation. Streeck, for example (1982, p. 32), presents the transformation of the pluralist mode of interest representation into 'a liberal corporatist one, as well as the conceptual distinction between pluralism and liberal-corporatism, as largely matters of emphasis and degree . . .'.

One leading corporatist analyst, Colin Crouch (1984, p. 114), has himself drawn attention to a particular example of over-stretching the corporatist banner. In reviewing Lehmbruch and Schmitter (1982), he rebukes one pair of contributors: 'Johansen and Kristensen . . . in their careful and detailed study of corporatist traits in Denmark, seem to take interest-group involvement in policy administration as *ipso facto* evidence of corporatism. Surely that must be complemented by evidence that the behaviour of memberships of the groups concerned has been constrained by that involvement, otherwise all we are observing is an advanced state of pluralism.' Schmitter also (1985, p. 46) felt obliged to distance himself from some of his over-enthusiastic followers (such as King 1983 and Cawson 1985a) when he commented that scholars have been 'particularly inventive in discovering "local corporatisms" although they seem little more than mechanisms for the direct consultation of functional interests . . .'.

McBride (1985, p. 456) argues that 'Some [corporatist] writers may escape [problems] . . . by diluting the role the state is said to play in "societal" corporatism and lowering the threshold of formality with which that role is supposedly played. But this drastically reduces the concept's distinctiveness from pluralism and lays the writers open to precisely the same criticisms as are directed against the pluralists . . .'.

Reinventing the Wheel

The reason why it is important to note the drift in corporatist theory from a descriptive to an analytical tool and from a rigorous to a less clear-cut concept is concerned with the relationship of this new corpus of study to the foregoing academic analysis. Wyn Grant, for example, defends the new approach, citing Middlemas: 'Pluralist explanations could not capture the process whereby what had been merely interest groups crossed the political threshold and became part of the extended state.' (Middlemas 1979, p. 373.) The introduction to this chapter sought to make the point that it is the erosion of that line that has, in fact, been of interest to students of groups for fifty years. For Schmitter (1979, p. 73) to consider that pluralism in the US was said to exhibit spontaneous, overlapping, chaotic, and competitive properties means that he was ignoring the work on sectorization, subgovernment, and iron triangles with which this chapter began. If this judgement is considered abrasive, two points can be mentioned in mitigation: (a) if corporatism is a profound turning-point in our analysis it deserves searching analysis and it should deal with the accounts it seeks to supplant; (b) there is something unsatifactory in Schmitter's original articles, in which he attempts to replace the dominant discipline in North American political science, but in seventy-one footnotes the only modern discussions of the US he mentions are Kariel, McConnell, and Lowi (in three footnotes). The issue is that the corporatist approach so cavalierly dismisses previous work. What, for example, about the work of Schattschneider (1960, p. 36), who managed to criticize the 'somnambulatory quality of thinking in the field' and the tendency of group research to deal only with successful pressure compaigns, or 'the willingness of scholars to be satisfied with having placed pressure groups on the scene of the crime without following through to see if the effect can really be attributed to the crime'. It is because the pressure group literature is so self-criticial that it lays itself open to the corporatist charge that it is inconsistent. Schattschneider (1960, p. 71), for example, goes on, 'If we must talk about politics in terms of conflict of interests, the least we might do is stop talking about interests as if they were free and equal. We need to discover the hierarchies of unequal interests, of dominant and subordinate interests.' As Almond (1983, p. 202) put it in his review of Berger's 1981 edited collection on corporatism, 'The casualness of the search of the earlier literature and the distortion of its contents are serious weaknesses in an otherwise important contribution to the interest group literature.'

Williamson (1985, p. 142) has made the point that pluralist writers, in making their criticisms of corporatism, have acknowledged 'no reference to the major criticisms laid against pluralism in the past 25 years'. This charge of selectivity might be more pointedly directed against others. Surely any paradigm revolution replacing pluralism needs to be put in the context of existing dissent to pluralism?

Our primary objection to the Schmitter innovation is its overdramatic claims for novelty. In presenting corporatism as a 'paradigmatic shift' Schmitter neglects the work of that earlier contribution which considered the integration of groups in the policy process. Lehmbruch (in Schmitter and Lehmbruch 1979, p. 150) claims that it is precisely because of the intimate mutual penetration of state bureaux and large interest organizations that the traditional concept of 'interest representation becomes quite inappropriate for a theoretical understanding of corporatism'. But what were the pluralists (and their critics) doing if not tracking intimate mutual penetration? The thrust of writing in the pluralist debate was about the regularization and structuring of group–government contacts. If the corporatists mean no more than this they are reinventing the wheel.

As Ross Martin has argued, there is no school of self-professed pluralists expressly committed to staking out pluralism's claim, and (quoting Wolfinger) he claimed that the term has become almost exclusively the property of scholars who employ it as a weapon of attack (1983, p. 92). Martin's main line is that Schmitter misrepresents the group writers by insisting that they saw a passive, non-active state. Martin documents case after case to the contrary. It therefore follows that not only do the corporatists disagree among themselves about the concept of the state under pluralism, they manage to find an agreement among pluralists that does not exist.

Our own position is that in the portmanteau of the pluralist argument there can be discerned at least two main variants—there is a version which dwells on open competition between groups. This is more widely criticized than advanced, and most writers in the group tradition have recognized practices of privileged access, regular group–department relations, and, often indeed, participation in implementation. Thus, for different—if compatible—reasons, we would conclude with Martin (1983, p. 102) that, 'despite the new corporatists and their terminology the affinity between [liberal and state] corporatism is, in a decisive sense, slighter than the affinity between liberal corporatism and pluralism'.

Corporate Pluralism

The introductory section of this chapter signposted some of the extensive non-corporatist material on regularized group relations with government departments. In an earlier article Jordan (1984) attempted to establish that much 'corporatist' writing in fact only accords with a looser concept of *corporate pluralism*. The *corporate pluralist* term was used by Kvavik (1976, p. 20) in contradistinction to *competitive pluralism* of the free-wheeling competition between groups, or to *statist pluralism*, in which the state essentially determines and imposes 'the public interest'. Kvavik notes a similar discussion by Hayward (1966), in his *Private Interests and Public Policy*. Heisler and Kvavik (1974, p. 42) identify 'a scheme of sectoral representation akin to neo-corporatism, or perhaps more accurately, corporate pluralism'. Schmitter cites this work, only to dismiss it. This seems to lack vision as to what the various sources on corporate pluralism have to offer. The corporate pluralist model is profoundly different from competitive pluralism.

Heisler and Kvavik (1974, p. 43) discuss group participation in the decision-making process on a continuing basis. Access is established and structured:

In Scandinavian politics we find economic *sectors* [our emphasis] . . . that are highly organised and enjoy substantial self-government. Within each sector, a centralised and bureaucratized network of interest groups serves as the principal means for the advancement and co-ordination of sector interests. Most groups are in a position to develop and implement policy, etc. (1974, p. 47.)

The Heisler–Kvavik discussion of 'structured co-optation' (a recurrent phrase) is manifestly relevant for a discussion of realistic models of modern interest politics and clearly fits a segmented pluralism/sectorized corporation version of politics.

As is argued elsewhere (Jordan 1984), much of the apparent literature on corporatism in recent years fails to match up to any rigorous corporatist definitions. As Williamson (1985, p. 3) expressed it, this kind of corporatism has been no more than a 'handy label that will stick to almost any surface'. He observes that corporatism has been very much in vogue, gaining at least an honourable mention in a wide range of contexts: 'Many such contexts are seemingly dubious, but corporatism has a quality akin to celebrities who have walk-on parts in other people's shows: they don't contribute to the shows but they increase the audience and status.'

In Martin Heisler's 'Corporate Pluralism Revisited: Where is the Theory?' (1979), he starts from the position (also adopted here) that there is an issue which had originally been given insufficient prominence in earlier pluralist writings, but had been brought out by Beer (1966), McConnell (1966), and Lowi (1969): the *structured, regularized* participation of organized interests in policy-making (p. 277). Heisler (1979, pp. 184–5) effectively argues that whatever precise model is necessary it won't look much like corporatism (as used by Schmitter). He argues, for example,

when their work [of empirical scholars] is viewed as a whole [it has] . . . shown that corporate pluralism—at least in the Nordic countries, for which large bodies of data have been accumulated—is immensely complex, multifarious and polycentric; its norms are characterised by heterodoxy; the actor's motives are often unarticulated (and sometimes perhaps inarticulable), as well as *ad hoc* or opportunistic . . . Thus while it would be an exaggeration to say that empirical studies of corporate pluralism in the aggregate depict a system near chaos, it is difficult to escape the conclusion that the relatively parsimonious model of societal corporatism provided by Schmitter et al. imputes a degree of order far greater than that uncovered at least by those who have intensively studied the Nordic cases in the past few years.

Corporate pluralism is, then, a description of the problem rather than a theory of causation. It is a statement to the effect that there are patterns of regularity, although there is a growing number of active groups which introduce uncertainty and disorder to the system. But a mere statement of the problem is more useful than a theory which fails to connect to observable reality.

In his restatement of pluralism in the US, William Kelso (1978, pp. 5–6), writing outside the Nordic tradition, independently develops the corporate pluralism idea. As two of his varieties of pluralism, he neatly contrasts *laissez-faire pluralism*, which 'posits a self-regulating political system made up of a multitude of private interests that bargain among themselves and check one another's advances', with *corporate pluralism*, which

> minimizes the benefits that accrue from the clash of interests and instead stresses the importance of cooperation between interest groups and government agencies ... This model ... envisions a political system broken down into a series of autonomous fiefdoms presided over by small coteries of interest groups. In each separate domain, government authorities have conferred the ability to make public decisions upon private groups, thereby blurring the boundaries between private interests and public power.

The weakness in pluralism identified by Kelso—the failure to elucidate the different types of political process masked by the term 'pluralism'—is much more convincing than the pro-corporatist belief that pluralists were of one mind; that they believed in equality of group resources, or that Bentley could be regarded as a satisfactory statement of contemporary pluralist thought, etc.

As Kelso points out, the *laissez-faire* version of politics was largely based on empirical work on urban politics (Dahl, Banfield, Sayre, and Kaufman), whereas the American corporate pluralists (Lowi, McConnell) developed their ideas from studies of federal agencies and their clientele groups. The debate between groups is in part about differences of policy sectors: both models are needed to describe different policy areas.

Corporatism and Pluralism: The Common Ground?

Arguably the most convincing contribution to this field in recent years is by Johan Olsen (1981, 1983), who eschews the corporatist debate and instead focuses on the underlying phenomenon. He examines the variables that affect the likelihood that organizations become integrated into government, with their representatives assuming the role of policy-makers. He addresses 'the extensive and complicated interpenetration of governmental agencies and organized interests' (1981, p. 442). He starts from a frame of reference in which participation by groups is voluntary (not mandatory) and issues are dealt with 'by rules and routines for problem solving and conflict resolution'.

The kind of activity discussed by Olsen is both complicated and specialist, so specialist that he believes that the practices could be overlooked. Unlike the orientation of some of the corporatists, he is interested in the myriad of committees and boards rather than national councils and legislatures.

Olsen also draws the important line between the conception of interest activity as fluctuating, competitive, and *ad hoc* and the idea of 'stable, intimate relationships, a symbiosis of governmental authority and organized interests'. Picking up the clientele idea from La Palombora (1964), he suggests that 'An organization succeeds in becoming accepted by a governmental agency as the primary expression and representation of a given interest; the organization, in turn, views the governmental agency as the primary partner or point of reference. Public officials give organizations influence over governmental policies; organizations supply information, political support, and control over their members' (1981, p. 493.)

As discussed further in chapter 8, Olsen displays the costs and benefits of participation by groups. He recognizes that government agencies and organized interests may *both* benefit from integrated participation: 'so integration and symbiosis are prevalent'. He describes 'functional segments that become largely autonomous structures of power . . . They insulate themselves from control by voters, parties, legislatures, or the judiciary; from competition among organizations; from regulation of bureaucratic hierarchies; from control by rank-and-file members of the organizations; as well as from influence by public opinion in general.' (p. 495.) Olsen captures well the sense of sectoral autonomy implicit in many case studies.

The most important part of Olsen's discussion is probably where he uses the language of organizational behaviour to explore the interactions in these policy communities. He describes how both governmental and group participants can reduce risk and uncertainty by creating stable relationships: 'Participation in a well defined interorganizational structure offers security and protection because the reciprocal acceptance of organizational domains—a distinct area of competence, a clearly demarcated and exclusively served clientele, membership, or undisputed jurisdiction over a function, service, goal or cause—reduces rivalry to an exceptional thing.' (p. 497.) Therefore, following Olsen, it is possible to predict the emergence of sectorized policy-making without invoking a state-centric policy system, state domination, or even basic imperatives or needs of capitalism. Both corporatist and non-corporatist authors can find common cause in the sort of discussion put forward by Olsen, and, indeed, the corporate pluralist/corporatist approaches appear to have converged.

Agriculture: The Marginality of Corporatist Analysis

It is a cliché to suggest that we need to remedy our theoretical complaints, but a preliminary sketch of agriculture in the UK only confirms that the empirical pattern is likely to defeat elegant theoretical attempts to capture its essence. Certainly the British case of the Ministry of Agriculture, Fisheries, and Food–National Farmers' Union of England and Wales relationship is renowned as being close: the front-runner of the possible corporatist cases. There is indeed evidence—though perhaps of a fragmentary nature—of corporatist features. For example, Self and Storing (1971 edn.), in discussing the Government's powers to discipline farmers who were judged inefficient (see chapter 5, 'The Birch in the Cupboard'), cite farmers who discovered that the NFU, far from being their protection, could easily be the prosecution. One was advised by his solicitor that 'we might as well have put our heads in a lion's mouth as go to the NFU for help'.

The Conservative Government, however, rescinded the disciplinary proceedings, though mainly because of the political embarrassment of the Crichel Down affair, 'when the Conservatives decided to take the State out of the business of farming as quickly as possible' (Self and Storing 1971 edn., p. 119). The removal of the disciplinary powers was not apparently favoured by the NFU, but only by the small 'libertarian' Farmers' and Smallholders' Association.

A more contemporary example that might lean towards the corporatist interpretation is the arrangement for the eradication of Aujeszky's (pig) disease. In the case of foot-and-mouth disease for cattle, the ministry had operated a policy of slaughter of affected herds with compensation at market value from public funds. For Aujeszky's disease the ministry could not provide funds, and instead provided legislation by which a compulsory levy was applied (after a referendum) to all pig farmers, from which farmers of affected animals were compensated. While the industry and the NFU see it as 'their' scheme, since it is industry-funded, the administration of the scheme is still done by MAFF. This is a case of the group performing for government what the department itself cannot deliver.

While individuals at the NFU are in daily contact with MAFF—and the organization as a whole is probably in hourly contact (Wilson 1977, p. 45)—the NFU does find resistance. For example, in the 1980s the NFU had to fight a very long campaign on compensation for land affected by mining. It had last been looked at in 1949. The National Coal Board was not interested and MAFF gave the matter low priority. Other interested Whitehall departments (Environment and Energy) were unenthusiastic. Eventually, after the NFU stirring up matters via a Private Member's Bill, a departmental advisory committee was set up—to which no NFU nominees were appointed. A similar rather particular matter was the call for an increase in compensation to landowners for crop fires started by railway engines, a problem which was re-emerging with the growth in the number of light and hobby railways. The NFU managed to have an amendment to a Transport Bill accepted at the third time of asking, only because the Government was too busy on more profound aspects to swat down the very narrow amendment. While the NFU might be the textbook example of the influential group, it is worth noting that from the NFU's perspective its achievements are incomplete and unpredictable. Wilson claims acceptance of a form of neo-pluralism within MAFF and quotes one civil servant, 'We cannot worry about everything, so we leave some factors to other Ministries to worry about.' He records another, 'The duty of MAFF is to present the arguments for help for farming. Other Ministries will soon bring forth criticism based on trade policy implications for public expenditure.' (Wilson 1977, p. 45.)

Wyn Grant sees the NFU in 'an effective neo-corporatist relationship' (in March 1983, p. 132), and the 'closest to an effective working corporatist arrangement' (p. 130). He mentions the appointment of a chief economic policy adviser from MAFF. Grant's point is perhaps underscored by David Evans subsequently becoming deputy director general and then director general of the NFU. But that recruitment is still unusual enough to be noteworthy, and NFU staff could not think of absorption in the other direction. Grant himself admits that 'farmers have enjoyed a high level of subsidy *without* any sacrifice of decision-making autonomy on the part of the individual producer'. Grant fails to give much evidence in his claim (in March 1983, p. 131) that the 'corporatist arrangement' works because the 'NFU is able to discipline its own members'.

Even if we go along with Grant and see the NFU case as more corporatist than most, there are also profoundly non-corporatist features. The relationship between lobbyist and civil servant is often close; but the NFU is often glad to see individually unsympathetic civil servants move on. MAFF does 'carry the NFU ball' on many occasions; but the position is not automatic. Farmers cannot really be disciplined by the NFU: it is the farmer with his threat of a withdrawn subscription who has the power. The NFU representational monopoly is being challenged by a scattering of specialist interest groups.

The ministry is not always the best port of call and the NFU has to be ready to use political channels to the minister, or to mobilize back-bench pressure or enter 'common causes' with other interests. The relations are in the art of politics, not in the hierarchically ordered world of corporatism.

Naturally, a reliable observer such as Grant presents some convincing points. He writes (Marsh 1983, p. 134), 'Policy making in advanced industrial societies is increasingly conducted in a series of specialist policy areas with their own special assumptions, bodies of knowledge and jargon, but agriculture seems to have a higher perimeter fence around it than most such policy arenas.' But this segmentation can be reconciled with corporate pluralism and even Heclo's issue network (discussed below). If anything, the growth of specialist agricultural groups and the challenge of conservationist and other groups makes a strong corporatist interpretation less tenable than before.

This discussion of the politics of agriculture questions as its primary purpose the 'fit' of corporatism, but a second point is that an exaggerated picture of the 'insiderness' of the NFU is often a preamble to a complaint about the exclusion of a promotional group from the decision process. Our point is that the NFU too often also has this sense of powerlessness, although there is sense for a membership-based organization in not complaining too openly about this.

An example of the outsider group using the NFU as a model of a powerful group is the following quotation from Des Wilson:

you've got a Ministry that has been working with the NFU for so long that they talk the same language; they go to the same clubs and eat in the same restaurants. They know each other on first-name terms. At this moment Friends of the Earth has done all the research on pesticides . . . the Government is talking to farmers and the chemical industry in formulating legislative plans. They're not talking to us, we are not on the inside there, we are not part of the club. (In Davies 1985, p. 42.)

From the inside, the NFU would not recognize this picture of its influence: it sees the countervailing pressure of the food processing lobby—such as the Food and Drink Industries Council—and the strength of consumers in the electoral (if not the group) channel of democracy.

The agriculture case gives little confirmation to a rigorous corporatist model, but in fact the sort of language used latterly by corporatist authors better captures the practice—at some cost to the theory. A major step made by Lehmbruch (1984, 1985) in distinguishing between sectoral corporatism and corporatist concertation has allowed a common ground to develop between the corporatist and pluralist approaches. Segmented pluralism, policy subgovernment, policy communities, policy circuits, policy sectorization—all these sorts of labels seem to be attempts to capture the same phenomenon as is now labelled sectorized corporatism.

This major amendment by Lehmbruch (in Goldthorpe 1984 pp. 105 ff. and in Lehmbruch 1985) finds him less insistent on the novelty of corporatism than earlier corporatist authorities. In distinguishing between *sectoral corporatism* and *corporatist concertation* he concedes that 'sectoral corporatism . . . is a relatively old phenomenon . . . Agriculture provides an obvious example. In countries such as Germany, the pluralist competition of different agricultural associations gradually gave way to a representational monopoly on the part of associations.'

He makes the vital distinction between what he also calls the 'robbers coalition' between departments and groups in sectoral corporatism, and corporatist concertation. The latter concept is distinguished by two essential features:

(a) it involves not just a single organized interest with privileged access to government but rather a plurality of organizations usually representing antagonistic interests; and

(b) these organizations manage their conflicts and co-ordinate their action with that of government expressly in regard to the systemic (*gesamtwirtschaftliche*) requirement of the national economy (p. 62).

Arguably (see Jordan 1985), two further distinguishing features of corporatist concertation could be extracted from Lehmbruch's current position:

(c) 'government intervention is no longer limited to mere sector protectionism but takes the form of deliberate attempts at co-ordinating macro-economic parameters' (Lehmbruch 1985, p. 13).

(d) 'the large organizations are consulted in all important legislative matters (for example, labour and business organizations have a quite important voice in educational policy) and they are represented in advisory committees for the most important policy sectors' (Lehmbruch 1985, p. 12). Some groups are thus *generalist* in character for the operation of macro-level corporatist concertation. (Lehmbruch cites Bjurulf and Swahn 1980 as the source of the term.)

This (late) distinction relieves the corporatist theory proponents of much of the criticism (by Martin, Almond, and others) of their neglect of the 'iron triangle' type of literature. That is quite compatible with the sectoral corporatism of Lehmbruch, but whether sectoral corporatism is still distinctively corporatist is unresolved. It is, in Lehmbruch's terms, within corporatist concertation that any distinctive development of political economy has taken place.

Wyn Grant has given a good illustration of a department–group relationship which is of considerable interest, but which at most fits the sectoral corporatism and not corporatist concertation idea. He points out (in Borthwick and Spence 1984, p. 132) that the Chemical Industries Association (CIA) is an insider group, but not a group involved in CBI-type relations with government. He quotes a CIA report as follows:

Over the years, . . . CIA has welcomed the opportunity of consultation with various branches of government. This has been helped by monitoring and anticipating trends in public opinion; through informing politicians, civil servants and commissions; through trying to influence the course of legislation from early principles to final drafts; through cooperating with government departments and bodies in the detailed implementation of legislation . . .

Such a relationship is important, but different from the concertation option described by Lehmbruch (though, to complicate analysis further, the CIA is itself a prominent participant in the CBI). Corporatism as concertation is distinguished by its orientation to problems of economic and unemployment management, industrial policy, and industrial relations. It requires the participation of *generalist* groups interested in the national interest and not simply single sector groups. This latter kind of corporatism is fundamentally different from policy subgovernment or any of the other quasi-pluralist labels which attempted to capture Lehmruch's sectoral corporatism point.

Schmitter too can be seen in recent work to be writing in a vein which—intentionally or not—is far less unattractive to pluralist thought. The anti-pluralist character of early Schmitter corporatism attracted much opinion—mainly neo-Marxist—that had a strong attachment to theories of the state. Schmitter (1984), in attempting to rescue the corporatist term from over-enthusiastic state-centred supporters, acknowledges that the modern state lacks the simple unity of purpose or effective sovereignty, to allow much utility to the term 'state'. He presents the state (1985, p. 33) as 'an amorphous complex of agencies with ill-defined boundaries, performing a great variety of not very distinctive functions'.

In this mood Schmitter sees neo-corporatism as a political exchange between organized interests and state agencies: this conception of exchange seems to be voluntary. On the one hand interest groups seek their goals, but the state agencies attempt to secure 'public regarding' concessions. While not seeing this pattern of interest group institutionalization as the product of a dominant state, Schmitter does attempt to argue that it is more than—as we would tend to argue—the outcome of preferences of civil servants. (We very much see the practices in terms of what sort of management of the policy arena makes sense from the desk of the relevant civil servant.)

Schmitter does observe that one of the explanations of corporatist-like arrangements stems not from the relatively autonomous state, but from the relatively autonomous bureaux or agencies (or departments, in our terminology) looking for information, compliance, legitimacy, and support. Certainly Schmitter doesn't see this as a full account of sectorized relationships, but he does concede 'many instances' where such co-optive strategies would be the preference of civil servants. Elsewhere (Jordan and Richardson 1982, pp. 81–2), we described the British practices of bureaucratic accommodation as follows:

What we identify as the *dominant* style is a procedural ambition. There is a preferred type of machinery, reflecting normative values—which is to avoid electoral politics and public conflict in order to reach consensus or 'accommodation' in the labyrinth of consultative machinery which has developed. These *preferred* operating procedures tend also to be the *standard* operating procedures.

Schmitter thinks that the co-optive explanation is particularly weak in explaining the trans-sectoral arrangements (which Lehmbruch terms 'corporatist concertation'). While the genesis of such broad arrangements is perhaps more political than administrative, the same recognition of need for interest group co-operation and consent seems present. And while Schmitter does not accept the administrative logic argument of the sort we have advanced, he does appear to accept that it has a place in sectoral corporatist/corporate pluralist explanations. The Schmitter (1984) argument is an attempt to develop a zone of interest group–state/government relations between the hegemonic-state-type discussion and the micro-behavioural preferences of civil servants. The defining characteristics of these relationships appear to be bargaining, ambiguity.

More original perhaps than the discussion of exchanges between interests and government is Schmitter's discussion of the difference between 'sectoral corporatism' and 'comprehensive concertation'. Here he does more than acknowledge their differences, he notes their incompatibility. He argues that such sectorized arrangements well lead to a pattern of sectorized subsidy and resource allocations in excess of any 'state interests', which might produce negative externalities for society as a whole. He claims (1985, p. 46) that 'The net result of "sectoral" . . . corporatisms is a pattern of entrenched policy segmentation . . . which renders more difficult . . . efforts at . . . comprehensive concertation . . .'.

We would still wish to argue that these sorts of points can be satisfactorily accommodated as extensions to the work on modern pluralism. However, we would readily recognize that there is not *one* pluralist explanation or description. As mentioned above, three broad schools seem worth identifying. There is Kelso's *laissez-faire* pluralism, which owes its intellectual roots to the 1950s. There is corporatist concertation, which is distinguished by its trans-sectoral qualities. The method of operation of such an arrangement will vary from being a voluntary exchange of views to a set of arrangements where the groups act as instruments on behalf of government in exchange for influence. As a subsidiary type of corporatism, and most prevalently, there are sectoral arrangements which may be based on very different origins from system-wide corporatism (Jordan 1984, p. 151). In surprising contrast with the anti-pluralist tone of 1979, a reasonable degree of common ground has emerged between corporatists writing of sectoral corporatism and the mainstream field of corporate pluralism.

Rusty Triangles: The Erosion of Subgovernment?

Another (fourth) kind of image dissenting from the comparatively orderly pattern of corporate pluralism has been made, however, in Hugh Heclo's concept of *issue networks*. This has certainly not been the centre of a corporatist-like bandwagon, but in many respects it better captures trends in contemporary politics. In reaction against the *iron triangle* type of American literature, which emphasizes the stability and predictability of group–department–legislative committee relations, Heclo describes political administration as 'fragmented' rather than 'segmented'. The 'set' of participants is unlimited and unpredictable and complex: decision-making tends towards atomization (1978, p. 105). Heclo argues that American politics are no longer dominated by an old Washington community; 'Social security, which for a generation had been quietly managed by a small circle of insiders becomes controversial and politicized. The Army Corps of Engineers, once the picture-book example of control by subgovernments, is dragged into the brawl on environmental politics. The once quiet "traffic safety establishment" finds its own safety permanently endangered by the consumer movement.' A similar phenomenon is noted in A. L. Fritschler's *Smoking and Politics* (1975, p. 215), which states that 'The tobacco sub-system was changed completely in eight years. The small group of people in Congress, in the agencies, and in the tobacco groups lost control of the policy-making processes. As they did very remarkable changes in public policy occurred.' The image of politics which covers the British Medical Association's relations with the DHSS on salaries or patient care is naturally unlikely to be the same as that when the BMA engages in cross-sectoral disputes with (say) the tobacco industry. The latter activity demands public campaigning, as when the BMA distributed black-edged postcards to doctors to be sent to constituency MPs notifying them when one of their constituents died from a smoking-related disease (*The Times*, 17 October 1984).

Another recent analysis from the United States, by Gais *et al.* (1984, p. 162), has also argued that 'just as [the] vision of the American system as a frustrating maze of autonomous and impermeable iron triangles has become popular . . . several scholars have begun, to question its utility as a guide to the policy-making process'. In supporting Heclo's image of the 'new political system' as a 'conflictual, permeable, unpredictable system' they provide data on the rapid expansion of the number and variety of interests represented in the contemporary US polity. This stress on the increase in the number of competing pressure groups brings to mind Wilson's earlier argument (1981, pp. 130–46) that the claim by Dahl and Truman in the 1950s and 1960s of widely dispersed power and numerous interests was *more valid* in the 1970s than it had been earlier. His conclusion was 'Towards Pluralism'. He said (1981, p. 145), 'Interest groups have come closer, in short, to playing the role they were always supposed to—but did not—in American politics.'

It is perhaps easy to *underestimate* the number of groups active in policy areas. Thus it is one thing to assert casually that there are a number of competing groups in the field of environmentalism in Britain, but it is still quite startling when Lowe and Goyder's work

(1983) produces a survey of seventy-seven national organizations. Dudley's study (in Marsh 1983) of the road lobby is another example where working through a particular topic reveals a far more elaborate group network than might be first suspected. Following Hamer (1974), he divides the road lobby into six component categories: (1) the motor industry; (2) the bus operators; (3) road haulage firms; (4) the motorists' organizations; (5) the road construction industry; (6) the oil industry. Dudley observes that the road lobby label could be extended to almost all British industry, as nearly all companies are affected by transport, but even using a more restricted sense he includes groups such as the British Road Foundation, the Road Haulage Association, the Freight Transport Association, the Society of Motor Manufacturers and Traders, the Motor Agents' Association, the Automobile Association, the Royal Automobile Association, and the Confederation of British Road Passenger Transport.

Very relevantly for Heclo's argument of the fragmentation of policy structures, Dudley describes how environmental groups in the 1970s attempted to penetrate the close relationship between the Transport Ministry and the road lobby, and how they resorted to attempting to use the public inquiry stages to delay or deter implementation when influence at the centre appeared unlikely. Wardroper's study (1981, p. 13) of heavy lorries claims that, as Secretary of State for Transport, William Rodgers had 'ordained that people from leading amenity associations should occasionally be admitted to the department in Marsham Street, Westminster, to put their views to civil servants whose chief callers until then had been lorry lobbyists'.

Coleman and Grant's 1984 study on business associations in the industrial sectors—chemical and food processing—in Canada and the UK found the UK associations better able to implement public policy than the Canadian. The work is introduced at this point, however, simply to record the complexity of associational life uncovered by Coleman and Grant. Clive Hollands' 1980 study of the animal rights lobby lists sixty-seven bodies as active in Animal Welfare Year in 1976. Even this is not a complete map of the field, as some bodies, like the National Anti-vivisection Society, the World Wildlife Fund, the PDSA, and the RSPB, declined to participate. The most spectacular US 'universe' of groups is possibly the appendix in Guither's *The Food Lobbyists* (1980), which lists the bodies in the US which testified before Congressional committees on food and agriculture matters, or otherwise attempted to influence federal policy decision: this is set out in Table 5.2.

TABLE 5.2.   *Organizations and Firms with Legislative Interests in Food and Agriculture*

General farm organizations	5
Producer commodity organizations	24
Producer co-operatives	20
Farm wives	2
Other producer advocates	21
Business and industry	229
Citizens or consumers	65
Conservation or environmental	15
Organized Labour	5
Public employees/institutions	20
Professional, research, or information	20
Indian tribes	23
Total	449

Source: Guither 1980

Guither (1980, p. 4) cites Ogden (1977) in ascribing the making of public policy to segmented and decentralized 'power clusters'. He suggests that with the mobilization of consumer and conservation interests the food and agriculture 'power cluster' has expanded, and produced a new political agenda.

Similarly, in line with these examples of more complex policy environments. Chubb's case study on US energy policy observed how the fuel shortage of the early 1970s mobilized environmentalists, consumers, commercial users, and organized labour. He continued (1983, p. 250), 'These developments made the life of subsystems most difficult in Congress . . . the subsystem approach to policy making became politically infeasible.'

The shift towards issue networks from iron triangles as an appropriate image requires a different view of power. While McConnell (1966, p. 339) recognized 'narrow interest-centred *power structures* within the open framework of American political life', Heclo observed no fixed, identifiable power structure. He claimed (1978, p. 88), 'Looking for the closed triangles of control we tend to miss the fairly open networks of people that increasingly impinge upon government.'

One kind of British development that might fit with and confirm the Heclo image of boundary confusion is the practice of civil servants moving into industry, trade associations, or groups. Considerable attention has been given in recent years to the recruitment by firms and interests of civil servants in mid-career or on retirement. (See Treasury and Civil Service Select Committee 8th Report, HC302, 1984.) In 1985 this concern was extended to the fence-hopping of military personnel. When Lord Lewin, former chief of defence staff, joined the warship builders Brooke Marine he was the latest of about forty admirals, generals, and air marshals to join the defence industry in five years. Ministry of Defence figures also cited in the *Sunday Times* (19 May 1985) showed that 141 applications from civil servants and officers to join industrial companies had leapt by 1984 to 680. (See Jordan and Richardson 1979.) This is again a striking parallel with US concerns. Ripley and Franklin (1984 edn., pp. 11–12) observe that

Not only are the lines between governmental and non-governmental institutions blurred by the open, continual access during policy making, but there is also a constant flow of personnel between governmental and non-governmental institutions that further blurs distinctions . . . This flow of personnel enhances the importance and stability of subgovernments, and the magnitude of this type of personnel interchange is so large that subgovernments have also been called [by Lewis 1977] 'incest groups'.

Issue networks, then, suggest a reversion to basic competitive pluralist premises about power. As Polsby (1963, p. 113) claimed, there is an unspoken notion in pluralist research that at bottom *nobody* dominates. Heclo (1978, p. 102) claims, 'questions of power are still important. But for a host of policy initiatives undertaken in the last twenty years it is all but impossible to identify clearly who the dominant actors are.' He presents the older notions of iron triangles and subgovernments as small circles of participants who have succeeded in becoming largely autonomous, but he goes on to suggest that while iron triangles and subgovernments suggest a stable set of participants coalesced to control fairly narrow public programmes which are in the direct economic interest of each party to the alliance, issue networks are almost the reverse image. He says (p. 102), 'Rather than groups united in dominance over a program, no-one, as far as one can tell, is in control of the policy and issues.'

Issue networks are thus presented as far more unpredictable and imprecise than the iron triangle idea. The issue network idea rejects the portrayal of decision-making authority as being held by the state, by major economic interest, or whatever. Obviously, if one subscribes to any particular theory of domination, the issue network idea will be regarded as misperception of reality. But Heclo is consciously challenging these 'domination ideas': he argues, 'Unfortunately our standard political conceptions of power and control are not very well suited to the loose-joined play of influence that is emerging in political administration.'

Decision-making by issue networks has consequences for policy outputs. Heclo (1978, p. 121) suggests that there is a bias against agreement and a reward for intransigence:

All incentives in the policy technocracy work against closure of debate . . . The biggest rewards in these highly intellectual groups go to those who successfully challenge accepted wisdom. The networks thrive by continuously weighing alternative courses of action on particular policies, not by suspending disbelief and accepting that something must be done.

The Heclo image of disintegration, confusion, overcrowding seems to fit actual tendencies better than a corporatist pattern of a limited number of groups in highly ordered relations with the state. The new technology might act as a dimension to develop and emphasize the fragmentation of power and decision-making within society. This is certainly the argument of Mrs Thatcher's former Secretary of State for Transport David Howell (1985, p. 77). He sees the consequences of information technology as:

One: amazing dispersal of power, knowledge and information which modern technology has allowed and the weakening effect this is having on centralised administration . . . Networks take over from hierarchies, making nonsense of many of the assumptions upon which the traditional methods of government have been based.

Two: the information over-load at the governing centre, combined with a huge deterioration in the quality of that information, as activities in the society and the economy become more dispersed, less susceptible to organisation and documentation and generally harder to track (the opposite of what Orwell, Huxley and the other warning voices feared).

Three: the intellectual failure of 'aggregation' . . .

Four: the quite extraordinary speed at which communications technology . . . have established the global information network and have 'globalised' the world's financial system leaving national governments floundering in their unsuccessful efforts to retain local control and influence . . .

Howell (p. 85) thus concludes that, in a paradoxical manner, information technology is turning out to be the agent not of uniformity and control but of variety and disorder. Therefore, while the corporate pluralist idea is challenged by corporatist ideas, the challenge of distintegration explicit in Heclo, Gais *et al.*, and others is perhaps more in accord with the evidence. While the critics of pluralism of the 1960s thought that the political system would be improved by more participation, currently the concern appears to be that decision-making is increasingly difficult due to the proliferation of interest groups. Beer (1982, p. 26) suggests 'a third sort of pluralist stagnation which results not from the aggressiveness or the defensiveness of the interests involved but simply from their large number'.

Part Two

BRITISH PRACTICES

6

Managing Participation

We here make an assumption that probably seems exaggerated to civil servants as they go about their business. It is that the operational principles underlying their work constitute a 'revealed constitution'. It is assumed that in making decisions to consult or not, and whom to consult or not, constitutional issues on the appropriate relationship between interest groups and government are being raised, and, through the activities of the civil servants, resolved. It is perhaps worthwhile to start from the view that the bureaucracy is accustomed to *expect* direct contacts with groups. Data from Eldersveld *et al* (in Dogan 1975, p. 149) show that few (4 per cent) of the British higher civil servants in their sample felt that relations of close collaboration between a ministry and groups or sectors most affected by its activity were improper and unnecessary.

Walkland's *The Legislative Process in Great Britain* (1968, p. 11) emphasizes that in practice there is consultation before and after parliamentary involvement in policy-making:

The governing procedures associated with the modern [legislative] process are those of consultation by the executive with organised interest groups, followed by Parliamentary investigation . . . There is usually also a later 'administrative' stage where Statutory Instruments [delegated legislation] are promulgated. This stage makes use of a number of developed procedures, of which consultation with affected parties and with expert advisory agencies is again most marked.

Again comparison with Norway is useful. Olsen (1983, pp. 111–15) underlines the importance of 'anticipated reaction' and 'sounding out', that is, how policies are made taking into account the likely reactions of others. He says, 'If actors do not know what is politically possible, they know how to find out. They use a lot of energy to find acceptable solutions through careful discussions, adjustments, and negotiations . . .'. Olsen thus points out that in executive policy-making a major commandment is, 'Do not announce a position; do not commit yourself at an early stage.' He emphasizes that the process is quite different from the planning mentality of first establishing goals and then searching for means: goals are formed as part of the decision-making process. He accepts that there are costs for this technique: substantive benefits can be lost in compromises, time spent on one issue means other issues are neglected, etc. Olsen thus asks why a majority uses a great deal of energy to establish general acceptance. His answer is to the effect that political decision-making is not simply about substantive alternatives, but about gaining legitimacy for policies. Sounding-out is thus used to husband legitimacy, loyalty, trust, friendship. Where resources and sanctions are distributed in a sector, negotiated environments avoid uncertainty. Olsen (1983, p. 146) here observes a paradox similar to that in our conclusions on Britain. Whatever formal rights government possesses, 'policy making is characterized more by compromise than by confrontation. Analysis, anticipated reaction, persuasion and bargaining are more frequent than force, commands, and rules.'

Whatever the constitutional nostrums of the 'Queen in Parliament' and the mandate theory of government, it appears that over the broad range of policy, governments attempt to secure the consent of interested parties in processes outside Westminster. As Walkland argues, there has been—*de facto*—an unofficial reappraisal of the theory of liberal–democratic political representation to grant groups an important role in securing consent to government policy. In the midst of the furore over education in 1985, the White Paper *Better Schools* (Cmnd. 9469) concluded, 'the Government cannot act alone. Their success depends on the ready co-operation and mutual support of all the partners in education and of the customers of the schools. The Government intends to work closely with all of these . . .'.

It is possible that there is a difference in significance in consulting on primary and secondary legislation. This is the difference between two rather similar sounding quotations. The Minister of Agriculture, defending his 1947 Agriculture Bill, said, 'In translating these principles into detailed legislation, the Government have been wise enough to keep in close consultation with the main represen-tational bodies of the industry . . . We sought, and we used, their collective wisdom.' (In Stewart 1958, p. 18.) This voluntary consultation over the form of legislation differs from the mandatory consultation requirement contained *in* the Act, which (in S2 (3)) states that in its operation the ministers 'shall consult with such bodies of persons as appear to them to represent the interests of producers in the agricultural industry'.

The issue of legitimacy is perhaps more acute with delegated legislation. All legislation is subject to the argument that the consent of affected parties is preferable, but delegated legislation further lacks the defence of electoral legitimation. Griffith (1949) commended delegated legislation precisely because 'to the interests affected or their representatives is left the examination of particular, specialized and technical details'. Bevan wrote of 'legislation by negotiation' (see Miers and Page 1982, p. 12). The business of statutory instruments is often relegated to footnote-level discussion, but Walkland (1968, p. 17) has argued convincingly that in the twentieth century subordinate legislation 'has become the character-istic regulating device of a society which has developed politically to the stage where it needs comparatively few major adjustments to its organisation, but much by way of minute and technical oversight of its activities'. The chairman of the Joint Committee for Statutory Instruments, Andrew Bennett MP, has complained, 'the trouble is that a lot of statutory instruments today no longer deal with means but with principles' (H of C, 257–i, 25 Feb. 1986).

As in the 1947 Agriculture Act above, the Government is sometimes specifically enjoined in statute to consult while making regulations under delegated powers. Another example is the Building Scotland Act 1959 (c. 24, S3 (6)), which stipulates that before making regulations the Secretary of State shall 'consult the Buildings Standards Advisory Committee . . .'.

With the co-operation of the academic liaison officer, we contacted twenty-seven divisions of the Departments of Industry and Trade in 1981 to examine the frequency of such mandatory consultation. This produced replies indicating about sixty Acts under which statutory instruments were made. In around twenty of these cases mandatory consultation is required, but relatively few instances are of the formula 'consult such persons or organisations as appear to them to be representative of interests likely to be affected' (more usual is reference to a specific advisory body).

The most interesting finding of the small survey was, however, the respondents' readiness to consult *even where the legislation did not make it mandatory.* This was confirmed yet again by replies from the Scottish Development Department in 1985. In the previous twelve months, five separate proposals on pollution had been circulated for consultation: only in one case was consultation in fact mandatory. Divisions in departments thus normally maintain lists of 'their clients'. As one civil servant said about their lists, 'When you do it ad hoc, you get it wrong, so it is better to systematise and add on when you find it inadequate.'

A civil servant, Dudley Coates (1984, p. 157), has recently noted that, in his field of food standards,

Possible changes are widely canvassed, thoroughly discussed, considered in detail and, if broadly acceptable to all who show an interest, put into effect. If implications of possible changes are missed, the policy-makers can point out that they consulted fully at the formative stage. *This continuous process of consultation tends to commit the whole policy community not only to the policy process, but also the decisions it brings forth* . . . [our emphasis] . . . the interest in food standards is confined to relatively small parts of certain central government departments and of local authorities and to 26 or 30 interest groups, and even within that group the degree of practical interest shown varies from subject to subject. Not only do almost all members of the policy community *have a clear interest in the smooth functioning of the system* [our emphasis], but in this mature policy system most of the potential repercussions of any policy shifts are foreseen and taken into account in advance of any statement of policy.

Most but not all departments maintain lists of bodies to be consulted: some proceed in a more *ad hoc* fashion. The Department of Employment list for working papers (1981) contained fifty names, including, of course, the CBI and TUC, but also smaller organizations such as the National Federation of the Self-Employed, the Federation of Medium and Small Employers, and others.

One of the planning divisions of the DoE had a standard list of over two hundred bodies, and when we had contact with it in December 1983 it had, in the previous few months, consulted on planning fees, industry, good design, and planning conditions. The Health and Safety Executive, in 1981, maintained a directory of sixty pages with more than 1,500 entries. The Vehicle Safety Division of the Department of Transport (in 1980) maintained a list of over 620 recipients for notification of statutory instrument charges—consumer interests, manufacturers, and similar.

Some of these 'set menus' of consultation are maintained for the specific purpose of consulting in relation to statutory instrument charges, but are utilized for broader purposes. The Scottish Home and Health Department maintains a master list of forty-six bodies *re* the Food and Drugs (Scotland) Act 1956, but no all-purpose departmental list. Each is 'tailored' to fit the topic.

Standard lists are usually the starting point for the construction of lists for specific exercises: thus the DHSS noted, 'Depending on the precise topic we would also consult all pressure/interest groups known to be interested in the subject. The list for, say, mental handicap would be very different from, for example, surgical waiting lists.' There seems to be a low threshold of accessibility: civil servants seem prepared to admit on to the consultation lists readily, but of course *access is different from influence.* The DHSS comment went on, 'In terms of sending out papers we err on the generous side. Naturally some bodies carry greater weight, and this would be taken into account when considering comments.'

A range of documents can be used to gather views, with no very clear distinctions between them. At one end of the spectrum there are targeted letters to specific groups on specific points; there are consultative documents/consultation papers (the terminology apparently interchangeable) which will be distributed widely, and may even be the subject of a press release to attract wide attention. There are also Green Papers, which are statements that the Government is considering a change in a substantial policy area. These are published more formally than consultation papers, but the line between them is blurred. A White Paper is a statement of settled governmental policy, and such statements often have a pre-history of consultation: for example, the 1980 White Paper *Farming and the Nation* was the follow-on to a review document, *Food from our own Resources*, which had produced ninety-two responses from bodies as varied as the Consumers' Association, the Cocoa, Chocolate and Confectioners' Alliance, the Food Manufacturers' Federation, and the National Farmers' Union. Some 300 responses were generated to a consultative paper in 1978 from the DoE on touring, caravanning, and tent camping.

Views, written and oral, can also be gathered in response to the establishment of an inquiry by a committee of inquiry: for example, the *Report of the Committee of Inquiry into the Acquisition and Occupancy of Agricultural Land* (Cmnd. 7544) produced over 400 comments. The *Committee of Inquiry into the UK Prison Service*

(Cmnd. 7673), which reported in 1979, had evidence from eighty-six organizations (and a number of individuals). They ranged from the Association of Chief Police Officers, the British Association of Prison Governors, and the Prison Officers' Association to Radical Alternatives to Prison and the Salvation Army.

The *Royal Commission on Legal Services in Scotland* (Cmnd. 7846) received evidence from 135 groups and individuals. The *Royal Commission on Legal Services* (Cmnd. 7648) received evidence from 410 organizations and almost as many individuals. 4,000 copies of a consultative document *Patient First* were sent out by the DHSS in 1979: it received 3,500 comments. In the Department of Employment's review of manpower training services in 1980–1, over 2,100 groups were on the register of interested groups. The *Review of Investor Protection* (Cmnd. 9125) was based on comments by over 150 groups and individuals. Dorothy Johnstone's study (1975) of the introduction of VAT indicates that consultation is widespread and repetitive. The Customs and Excise Department sent out over 400 consultation papers and received the views of 800 different trade and professional organizations. Meetings were held with over 200 groups. *Social Assistance*, a consultative document published by the DHSS in 1978, attracted 1,100 responses. An unusual feature of that exercise was that civil servants directly addressed the public on that issue in a series of public meetings.

As Schwartz and Wade (1972, p. 89) described in the *Legal Control of Government*, similarities in practice exist between the US and UK. They point out, 'These run the gamut from correspondence, consultations, and conferences, to the Gallup Poll technique of questionnaires and interviews. Sometimes the requirement of consultation of interests is imposed by statute, though it is more usual for the consultative technique to be used without any statutory command.' However, Schwartz and Wade also describe how in the realm of delegated legislation Britain and the US have moved in opposite directions in their attempts to find satisfactory legitimizing procedures. In principle, the US and British systems differ, with the UK, superficially at least, *moving away* from mandatory consultation.

Schwartz and Wade point out that while under the original British Rules Publication Act of 1893 rules and regulations had to be published in advance and consideration given to objections submitted in writing within forty days, the Statutory Instrument Act of 1946 did *not* insist on formal consultation.

The deviation from mandatory consultation was not founded on distrust of consultation, however, but on a preference for informal consultation.

Schwartz and Wade contend that experience had led to a preference for *informal* consultation, and that 'The statutory procedure was too inflexible to suit many cases, and the practice of government by consultation was so habitual that there was no complaint about failure to consult.' A recent interview at the Department of Transport found this same belief that policy was better made without formal relationships. 'The good relationship [is] when it is informal . . . when things go public, hard positions are taken. The [informal] relationship is in both our interests: makes lives easier. If we said we won't talk on on this issue then things would go cold and we *want to trade again tomorrow on something else.*' This is one reason why quantification in this area is difficult. It is by no means the case that the most rewarding relationships for the groups are formalized, say through advisory committees. The same Department of Transport civil servant said, 'We would hope to know the views of the constituency out there. *There was no need for preconsultation.*'

The important consultation need not be the large-scale, but the sort where the civil servant says, 'We ring up the chief engineer of the [trade association] and say, "What is the line?" . . . Often it is not controversial—purely between us and the manufacturers or only a few clear views.'

The Government's arguments in 1945 for abandoning formal 'antecedent publicity' of the kind demanded in the 1893 Act were essentially twofold. It was argued that the provisions of the 1893 Act—which had a very chequered origin as a Private Member's Bill—were deficient and failed to cover many kinds of rule. (It did not, for example, apply to Scotland.) Dr Rosamund Thomas (1978, p. 208) quotes Lord Hewart's objections in his *New Despotism* to six loopholes in the 1893 Act. In many legislative cases (60 of the 200 then in force) its operation was specifically excluded, such as in the Livestock Industry Act 1937, the Army and Air Force (Annual) Act 1937, and the Agriculture Act 1937.

The second argument for non-retention of the statutory consultation principle was that the practice was so ingrained that the rule was unnecessary. The Solicitor-General claimed (*Hansard*, vol. 415, col. 1112) that

> normally, when Ministers or Departments have laid a statutory instrument, they have always discussed the thing in considerable detail with all parties affected . . . In substance, what would happen if you retained it is this. You would get the Department discussing the matter with interested parties . . . Then 40 days have to elapse during which nothing takes place . . . because the discussions with interested persons have already been completed . . .

These arguments were generally accepted, except for the reservation expressed by Eric Fletcher (MP). He confirmed that as a matter of 'wise administration' government departments did consult with trade and other interests, but he warned (col. 1112) that 'some interests are tolerably well organised while other interests are not so well organised. One cannot always assume that a combination of trade interests in reality represents any more than particular vested interests . . .'. Against conventional wisdom, but with good reason, Fletcher was drawing attention to the conflict between consultation as a manifestation of desirable open government and consultation as a practice leading to closed and biased systems.

Examination of the legislation passed in 1979 which is indexed in the Public General Statutes as involving orders or statutory instruments emphasizes that mandatory consultation is still exceptional. In the thirty-three measures listed, consultation using the formula (or a near variant) 'consult such persons or organisations as appear to them to be representative of interests likely to be affected' appeared only in the Estate Agents Act, the Forestry Act, and the Weights and Measures Act. In other instances there was consultation on the composition of consultative councils (Electricity (Scotland) Act) or with the Council of Tribunals on appeal procedures (Banking Act), but mandatory consultation is still the exception. We might have been surprised to find consultation in such areas as the Zimbabwe Act, but nor did it appear in policy areas where well-organized interests exist, for example the Agricultural Statistics Act or the Land Registration (Scotland) Act. The small experiment of examining the 1979 legislation confirms the more authoritative opinion of a helpful officer of the Office of the Parliamentary Counsel who suggested to us that 'statutory provisions which require some form of prior consultation before a statutory instrument is made . . . form a small percentage of the total number of provisions . . .'.

Jergesen (1978, p. 290) could therefore be misrepresented when he starts his study of consultation in Britain with 'The duty to consult makes its appearance frequently in administrative law . . .'. In fact, non-mandatory consultation is the dominant British practice. Harold Laski's comment of 1941 (*A Grammar of Politics*, p. 375, quoted in Self and Storing 1962, p. 218) that 'the making of policy . . . is the more successful the larger the number of affected interests consulted in its construction' is still the dominant recipe— but without *mandatory* consultation being seen to be necessary. A Home Office civil servant observed, 'consultation occurs because the expertise is needed; because the policy outputs need to be implemented, and because the "right" outputs need to be achieved.'

A DoE civil servant commented 'consultation is now part of the scene and is unlikely to go away'. Elsewhere (Jordan and Richardson 1982, p. 88) we recorded similar comments:

You are quite right to stress its [consultation] importance. Sounding out opinion in advance of potential changes in policy of subjecting possible proposals to informed comment is something which is done in this country whenever possible. Consultation between Departments with a common interest in a particular policy area takes place as a matter of course, both formally and informally, at meetings or on the telephone. The ways in which interested public opinion is tested can range in formality from Royal Commission and Departmental Committees of Inquiry through Green Papers to individual groups and general invitations to express views. (Ministry of Agriculture, Fisheries and Food.)

You are correct in assuming that consultation between Government Departments is an essential part of arriving at decisions . . . consultation between Government Departments and groups outside Government is also an important part of arriving at decisions although the scale and way in which this is done will depend on the type of decision being made. (Scottish Development Department)

Certainly . . . [one must] attach importance to the process of consultation both within the Civil Service and between Whitehall and other organisations. This is clearly an intrinsic part of the democratic government process. (Department of the Environment.)

If you don't consult them [the groups] they will only try and block the proposal in Parliament. Not consulting them is not worth the risk. (Health and Safety Executive.)

A paper by one (DHSS) assistant secretary to a Public Administration Committee conference has also established that

In order to manage the policy concerns of the Department it is often necessary to establish working parties or committees which include representatives of other Government Departments, local or health authorities, professional organisations and so forth. Sometimes a committee of legal commission may be established consisting entirely of non-departmental members, but serviced by the Department; such a measure may be particularly appropriate where Ministers wish to establish a public or professional view on a particularly intractable area of policy . . . Many of the most difficult issues involve a wide range of interests within society as a whole, so that if a satisfactory resolution is to be reached a broad public consent must be established before action is taken. In such situations, neither officials, nor Ministers, nor Parliaments can safely presume to act until the ground has been prepared; hence the use of such bodies to produce reports before major legislation.

The paper concluded,

Government in a democracy is by consent. But how is that consent obtained? The most persuasive means seems to be consultation—generally, however, with expert groups rather than individual members of the public. There is no sinister reason for this—it is just that most of the issues facing Government require technical or professional judgement of one form or another and those with the greatest expertise must be drawn into the consultative process if sensible decisions are to emerge.

Consultation in the US: The Legal Approach

While *de facto* both British and American systems might involve a considerable amount of participation, in Britain this is not as a rule based on statutory rights. As Schwartz and Wade concluded (1972, p. 98),

The difference is that in Britain [compared with the USA] it has been found preferable not to prescribe the procedure by law. A great many British regulations are made with the prior agreement, or at any rate with the full prior knowledge, of interests affected, and many of them are the outcome of lengthy negotiations . . . industries, professions and occupations of all kinds have their representative bodies which are consulted as a matter of course . . .

Mandatory consultation is not a frequent feature of statute, but to complicate the comparison, the courts in Britain—on the basis of the principle of 'natural justice'—do seem to favour the practice even where it is not specifically demanded. Jergesen, for example, cites Lord Denning indicating in 1972 that organizations should be heard regardless of any undertaking. This precedent was used by an officer of the British Legal Association in *Bates* v. *Lord Hailsham* when it was argued that a committee headed by the Lord Chancellor had no right to abolish fixed fees for solicitors by statutory order without consultation. Although the Bates injunction failed, this was partly on the judgement that the provision was made for consultation with the Council of the Law Society. It was thus considered that consultation with the British Legal Association was implicitly denied.

The courts, on the basis of Jergesen's review, do not seem to have reached strict criteria ensuring consultation, but there is evidence that under some circumstances the courts are prepared to back extensions to limit complete executive freedom. For example, the verdict on the trade union rights at the Government Communications Headquarters in Britain was that the unilateral action of the Government was only justifiable because national security was at issue. The Government's defence, entered by Sir Robert Armstrong (Secretary to the Cabinet), was that *normally the Government would have felt obliged to consult*, except that in this particular case this would have signalled areas of vulnerability in security arrangements to those who had shown themselves prepared to organise disruption. Lord Scarman said that he dismissed the union's appeal for one reason only. He was satisfied that the respondent had made out a case on the ground of national security (*The Times*, 23 November 1984). The DHSS was criticized by the High Court in May 1985 for failing to consult adequately over the amendment of the housing benefit scheme.

The chairman of the Association of Metropolitan Authorities claimed after its successful court case, 'Time and time again we have warned the Government that a cursory nod in the direction of consultation is not enough.' (*Municipal Review*, June 1985.)

While there is no general legal obligation in the UK for government to consult, specific laws might require it, as we have seen: for example, under the Local Government, Planning and Land Act 1980 the Secretary of State for the Environment, when setting rate support grant, 'has to take positive steps to inform the local authorities of how he is proposing to exercise his powers and to listen to any representations' (*Financial Times*, 24 March 1986).

As we have shown, the British courts are prepared to 'read into' relationships between the Government and groups a 'legitimate expectation' that past practice or natural justice would suggest that consultation will take place. The grounds for the case in which the Lord Chancellor, Lord Hailsham, was taken to court by the Bar Association in 1986 were not that Section 39(1) of the Legal Aid Act 1974 demanded consultation, but that Lord Hailsham had given the impression of serious negotiations, whereas expectations on that front had been unfulfilled. The *Financial Times* (24 March 1986) noted, 'The supreme advantage of the concept of prior consultation is to recognise that those outside government should be allowed to play some role in shaping government policy in a wide range of administrative action. The Lord Chancellor rendered himself exposed to just such a process, and any failure to comply with the process of negotiation over legal aid fees invited intervention from the courts.'

In connection with the same case, the *Sunday Times* (30 March 1986) noted that applications by individuals and lobby groups for 'judicial review' of governmental decision processes had increased from 375 cases in 1981 to over 1,000 in 1985. The American experience of a legal approach to government–group relations has a reinforced relevance.

While Britain was moving to deformalize consultation in 1946, the US Federal Administrative Procedure Act was making US processes both more formal and juridicial. In his detailed and lengthy discussion of American practices, R. B. Stewart (1975) establishes that between 1880 and 1960 a set of principles evolved which attempted to curtail administrative discretion. Stewart argues that from Hobbes and Locke the assumption was made that consent is the only legitimate basis for the exercise of coercive power. Accordingly, the major principles were that administratively determined sanctions on private individuals (and groups) must be subject to procedures (at, say, a public hearing) which allow the affected interest to present evidence and challenge the agency's facts and interpretations. These decision processes are subject to juridicial review.

Stewart outlines how the traditional American model has been so extended as to be transformed by efforts of federal judges to ensure more adequate representation for all interests. The formal procedure was adopted to counter deficiencies associated with informal processes (preferred in Britain). These formal procedures were, however, themselves considered to neglect poorly organized interests, and judges have, according to Stewart (1975, p. 1620),

greatly extended the machinery of the traditional model to protect new classes of interests. In the space of a few years the Supreme Court has largely eliminated the doctrine of standing as a barrier to challenging agency action in court, and judges have accorded a wide variety of affected interests the right not only to participate in, but to force the initiation of, formal proceedings ... Indeed, this process has gone beyond the mere extension of participation and standing rights ... Increasingly, the function of administrative law is not the protection of private autonomy but the provision of a surrogate political process to ensure the fair representation of a wide range of affected interests.

(This version of the American process is largely confirmed by Mermin in Pennock and Chapman 1975.)

The US system, as presented by Stewart, has developed beyond traditional rights to allow even wider access to interests which would once have been denied 'standing'. These developments are explicitly connected by Stewart to the widespread pluralistic conception of American society within legal circles. The traditional model was itself concerned to curb the interference of government in private interests, but the transformed version is more alert to the need to represent the poorly organized in the decision process. The traditional model was based on an assumption that in taking decisions agencies were no more than neutral transmission-belts of the legislature's intentions, but once agencies are conceptualized as adjusting competing pluralist interests, the problem of their legitimacy is accentuated. Even more disturbing for the traditional US model are interpretations of group–department relations which see the system as permanently biased. Stewart (p. 1685) discusses the crude 'capture' scenario, in which administrations are systematically controlled by particular interests.

Stewart argues (p. 1687) that the traditional model was also deficient in not applying to important areas of modern life: 'Many of the policy decisions most strongly attacked by agency critics— the failure to prosecute vigorously, the working out of agency policy by negotiation with regulated firms, the quiet settlement of litigation once initiated—take place through informal procedures where the traditional controls have not normally applied.' The extension of formal consideration and, ultimately, juridicial review to these areas are part of the expansion and transformation of the traditional model.

Collins (1980) has argued that the increase in the number of judicially recognized interests was intended to ensure 'an approximately equitable outcome'. He saw the issue of the public good to be resolved by an appeal to a judicial version of interest group theory, and that 'In short, discretionary, agency action, as it impacts upon a variety of interests, is to be viewed as legitimate to the degree that all affected interests have been permitted to participate and have a voice in the formulation of the decision. Legitimacy, and with it the concomitant of consent is associated with the relevant dimensions of the group struggle.'

He goes on (p. 469) to make the connection that interest group theory makes use of the market-place as an analogy of political society: 'If every relevant interest is heard, i.e. in the market, and if all significant information is employed, then the adoption of procedures insuring the existence of these factors will lead to substantively better response on the part of government.'

He quotes a former US Federal Communications Commissioner who argued that the only way a commission can be insulated from concentrated influence is to increase the informational inputs into the agency by expanding the number of affected interests which can be heard. Collins says,

The proper decision will be a result of the application of proper procedures to the variety of affected interests. The agency here acts as a surrogate market place to which consumers/citizens are permitted entry, and whose demands are met by the action of a neutral aggregation of the relevant information. Should such a market-like process result in an inferior product, the solution is to expand the level of participation . . . the problem of agency discretion, and the fusion of constitutional powers it represents is overcome because, by analogy to the market place, appropriate participatory procedures . . . insure the effective aggregation of all relevant interest. (p. 471.)

The development of public interest groups in the US in the 1960s and 1970s was the response to the pluralist conception of society, and was recognition that as things stood they were biased in favour of economic interests. This belief that democracy would be improved if the countervailing interests were stimulated was expressed in the Ford Foundation's sponsorship of public interest law firms in the 1970s: 'A central assumption of our democratic society is that the general interest or the common good will emerge out of the conflict of special interests. The public law firm seeks to improve this process by giving better representation to certain interests.' (Quoted in Berry 1984, p. 30.)

The fundamental weakness in this reasoning, as identified by Collins, is not a problem of effective entry (access to the system) but the problem of the weights being aggregated (i.e. the lack of equality of the interests): 'the problem is not so much who is participating but with what resources one is participating' (p. 472). To compound this problem we can add that, even if agencies and departments are neutral on the day of that creation, prejudices are later built up.

This discussion of US developments is of relevance as an explicitly alternative model to British practice. It does suggest that quantity of consultation, and calls for wider consultation, can be beside the point. It also suggests that the focus in the British literature on access or the lack of it potentially confuses the issue of who can be heard, and whose views count. Stewart considers Professor Joseph Sax too extreme in arguing, 'I know of no solid evidence to support the belief that requiring articulation, detailed findings or reasoned opinions enhances the integrity or propriety of administrative decisions. I think the emphasis on the redemptive quality of procedural reform is about nine parts myth and one part coconut oil.' But Stewart's dissent from that bleak verdict is only marginal. In connection with the expansion of citizen participation programmes under federal and state law, Berry (1984, p. 32) has pointed out that critics on the right feared the overload of the system and liberal critics argued that the programmes worked in favour of the middle-class élite.

Unlike the American procedures, the British practice is seldom formally based, but the weight of our evidence is that departments go to considerable lengths to receive views. It is possible that in some circumstances, particularly over matters of partisan import-ance, the consultation may be cynical and merely cosmetic. For example, the twelve-week consultation period with the unions, announced in April 1985, over the privatization of naval dockyards was unlikely to change government opinion. There is also depart-mental discretion over the subjects of consultation and the recipients of documents, but the thrust of our findings is that departments would rather, self-consciously, over-consult than be open to the criticism that significant interests had been ignored. These consultations are, in practice, not derived from statutory requirements or even the possibility of court intervention, but from the desire for a climate of co-operation and risk avoidance. Consultation is the partner of participation, both 'good things'.

If consultation is on the whole token—not a view we endorse—it can none the less be important. It is possible to contend that the unsuccessful participants in consultation will become frustrated. Our instinct is that consultation is a significant and expressive action, even without affecting policy outcomes. Though fault can be found in consultative practices, Schubert (1957, pp. 348–9) has made a distinction between the administrative realists who accept and defend the imperfect system and the administrative Platonists who have found fault with this form of pluralism.

The Remiss Alternative

While recent developments in the courts in Britain suggest some comparison with the US legal approach to giving a guarantee of group participation in policy-making, the more important comparison is, to our mind, with informal American practices, what we have documented as policy clusters, iron triangles, group sub-governments, and so on. Such an emphasis suggests that British practice can profitably be compared with the *remiss procedures* in Scandinavia, whereby the participation of groups in the policy process is regularized. Importantly, the remiss—and analogous British—practice is about participation in policy at the draft proposal stage. Legal challenges tend to be after-the-event appeals about unsatisfactory outcomes. The Scandinavian consultative practices are described in chapter 8. But the Swedish system of remiss, in particular, has a constitutional basis, unlike the informal basis we identify in Britain. The 1974 constitution states, 'To the extent necessary associations or private subjects shall be given an opportunity to express their views.'

Forms of Consultation

A variety of forms of consultation need to be identified. Civil servants acknowledge distinctions: for example, 'The Division believes it is using consultation within two broad categories—the first to test the wind on issues of policy; the second to ask for the views of experts on detailed matters which the Department may not get right on its own.' There is the *policy search* type where the Government has no very clear idea, and needs to be convinced that there is a worthwhile solution available. The Finniston Inquiry on the Engineering Profession perhaps fits this type. Another example cropped up in the transport area, where we were told that 'A conference can give up a feel of the balance [of views]. The Government has no interest of its own.' This is different from the *insurance policy* sort of consultation that typically takes place towards the implementation stage of the policy process. This essentially says that the Government has an idea, but is open to being convinced why it should not proceed. (For example, in 1985 the DTI proposed to cut back on trade missions because of Treasury cost restraints. The DTI wrote to 200 'sponsors', and as a result of protests, concessions were made.)

Yet another kind of example better fits the theoretical notions of *competitive* consultation—more realistically reflects the market analogy. An example here is from the very specialist area of Section 123(b) of the Food and Drugs Act 1955. However abstruse this sounds though, there is, as we have repeatedly discovered, a politics of the particular. From 1980 onwards there was conflict in the area over new meat products and the water content of meat. The outstanding quality in this example was the existence of well-developed conflict. The department has stressed to us that the consultation procedures here 'do not constitute a typical example of our normal consultation procedure, strongly conflicting views, and the complicated nature of the subject here led to a longer and more elaborate process than normal'.

The process of formal consultation—as opposed to informal 'soundings'—began with the publication in 1980 of the Food Standards Committee (an advisory committee set up under the 1955 Act) *Report on Meat Products*, which included recommendations for the declaration of the quantity of added water in cured meats. Comments on the report were received from over 100 bodies and individuals, and meetings were held between MAFF and the major organizations for manufacturing, trade, enforcement, and consumer interests. A major split in view emerged between manufacturing and enforcement interests over the ability of producers to comply with proposed controls. (The argument that 'We would like to help, but it is impractical' is common at this level of negotiation.)

It was agreed that draft meat product regulations should be published, but a working group consisting of MAFF, the manufacturers, and the enforcement representatives was set up to have a 'dry run' of testing procedures for ham. Samples were taken at six different processing plants. (A more limited study without MAFF involvement was also undertaken on bacon.) The draft regulations including controls on water content of cured meat were published in July 1981.

Our argument is that most grand issues eventually decompose to esoteric discussions in professional communities. That the draft proposals on meat product regulations were controversial within their policy field is beyond doubt. Over 118 written comments were received and meetings were held with all the major interests; some meetings were essentially for the department to explain its intentions, while others were by way of representations to the department from interests. In particular, two major meetings with representatives from a large number of trade and enforcement groups were held in February and March 1982. The ministry accepted that the working group studies showed a problem of variability which made testing procedures unsound. In 1983 revised statutory instrument proposals were issued to several hundred interested parties, and a new cycle of written observations and meetings set under way. The large scale of responses and the degree of conflict in this example make it unusual, but the constant attempts to find a consensus (however improbable) is symptomatic.

Consultation versus Negotiation

Although the usual word to describe the exchange of views between government and groups is 'consultation', the term, while convenient, in fact fudges the nature of the exchange. In Eckstein's words (1960, p. 23), 'Negotiations take place when a governmental body makes a decision hinge upon the actual approval of organizations interested in it, giving the organizations a veto over the decision, consultations occur when the views of the organizations are solicited and taken into account but not considered to be in any case decisive.' Clearly in exercises—which are now common—involving hundreds (and even thousands) of groups, most consultation is of the latter, 'courtesy' type. (Some civil servants also mentioned the *educative* aspects, allowing them to inform and persuade opinion likely to be hostile.) The difficulty arises at the other end of the spectrum because the formal status of the Government makes it difficult to acknowledge that it is ever engaged in negotiation.

The factors that lead to negotiation will clearly include the strategic importance of the groups in administering the policy. One civil servant we interviewed in 1985 said that he usually needed a customer group (his phrase) or professional group to make a policy in his field (education) happen: 'I need to take them along with the policy . . . We can't *make* them do anything.' In a literal sense the civil servant was perhaps wrong: government could make things happen, but he was pointing to the fact that in day to day business of tending to the needs of the department, co-operation is the practical way forward. At any one time the agenda of public business is so broad that simple political muscle is an impractical means to secure ends.

Unadmitted negotiations are more likely where the consent (or at least enthusiasm) of the group is necessary in policy implementation, and also where the expertise and data of the group are required in policy formulation. Thus groups active in the administration of policy, such as the BMA or the Association of Chief Police Officers, or in the implementation of desired goals, such as the oil companies in the area of oil exploitation in the North Sea, will naturally have more weight in discussion than purely supplicant groups.

Wilson's work on the NFU's relations with the Ministry of Agriculture, Fisheries, and Food shows that an organizational requirement for successful negotiation is the evolution within the group of the leadership discretion to allow the leaders to commit its membership (1977, p. 38). Negotiation is also probably simpler if there are effective broad umbrella groups (such as the NFU) rather than smaller competing groups. Where a number of groups exist, requirements like secrecy are more difficult, and out-bidding by groups could, a priori, make compromise difficult.

Eckstein (1960, pp. 25–6) suggests that J. D. Stewart (1958, p. 22) thought that departments could not negotiate because a minister, subject to Parliament, could not enter binding agreements.

Eckstein says that this is taking constitutional myths too seriously, and that, ordinarily, once a minister has made a decision it is final:

> Parliament reviews few departmental decisions . . . and those it reviews it generally rubber stamps. The Cabinet reviews few . . . departmental policies, unless important interdepartmental disputes are involved . . . [then] Ministers when negotiating with pressure groups, will also be negotiating with other interested departments, so that agreements reached with the pressure groups will be cleared in advance.

Our reservation about Eckstein's presentation is his dismissal of Stewart. In fact, Stewart presents the fullest discussion of consultative practice that we have, and the point picked up by Eckstein is against the drift of Stewart's presentation.

Stewart (1985, p. 5) begins with the perhaps now contentious point that there has been a falling away of major group demands compared with (say) the beginning of the century: 'Most groups are concerned with the administration by the government of a general framework which they accept. They require minor modifications to acts, alterations to administrative procedure, readjustments of licence provisions, and redrafting of regulations. These claims are important, but they do not appear as a challenge to the system of government.' Stewart suggests that, over time, as primary group goals are satisfied, major demands are replaced by matters for 'administrative adjustment'. He gives as an example the National Association of Local Government Officers, which campaigned for adequate superannuation provisions for local government officers. Once this was achieved the group was left with no more than a watching brief.

He sets out how the difficulties in actually consulting public opinion lead the Government to the easier substitute practice of consulting various representative organizations. He quotes Sir Norman Kipping, then director-general of the FBI, as follows:

> The justification for trade associations acting in a representative capacity is that, on the whole, it works. It is a physical impossibility for Ministers or their departments to test the opinions or seeks the advice of thousands of individuals . . . if the leaders misinterpret their members' views they will soon lead nobody but themselves.

He points out that the Government consults not just because it is interested in hearing views, but because it needs facts: 'The statistical and records departments of trade associations and trade unions may be able to supply information. Certainly they will have a technical know-how and an expertise which provide government proposals with a sound test.' In support he quotes the president of the Motor Agents' Association on the growth of trade associations:

Government will be in the future take a far greater interest and wield a far greater influence in industry than in the past, and they cannot hope to have an intelligent understanding of industry and trade except through Trade Associations, whether they be organisations of employer or worker . . .

Stewart then describes how consultation is not merely at ministerial level or even permanent secretary level, but how 'The whole administrative system of government is involved . . . There has been created a widespread machinery which is difficult to describe because so little formal expression is given . . .'.

Stewart's examples of consultation as the departmental routine can be updated, but the essential argument is still valid. The problem lies not in documenting the practice but in its impact: where and when does cosmetic consultation turn into negotiation? One problem is that the Government, conscious of its formal status, is reluctant to concede that the interactions are in fact negotiations. For example, in the process of evolving the Engineering Council, the Permanent Secretary at the Department of Industry told the engineering chartered bodies which specifically made the point that certain issues were 'non-negotiable' (see Jordan and Richardson 1984, p. 397). In the event the issues were not only negotiable but were conceded. The claim of being non-negotiable was part of the negotiating stance.

This discussion of consultation and negotiation only serves to emphasize that the label 'consultation' is an umbrella term diplomatically covering a range of processes. On the whole, though consultation fits in with Christoph's (in Dogan 1975, p. 45) perception that civil servants are

to a remarkable degree . . . engaged as brokers bringing group representatives into contact with the political élite machinery, and pressing on them primarily views of 'administrative realism'. These officials are seldom influential enough to head off persistent, large-scale conflict, such as major industrial strikes or disputes emanating from fundamental party policy. But at only a slightly lower level, they are active in ways which seldom catch the headlines. Those who welcome the muting or defusing of conflict, who are impressed with incremental change, rate this as a positive contribution of the higher bureaucracy.

To make explicit that so-called consultation does in fact cover a range of activities, it is perhaps worth 'breaking out' some of the different types of departmental activity often covered by the one term. Some of the terms are suggested by interview responses. For example, a Welsh Office civil servant distinguished between 'open' consultation where the list of consultees will consist of anyone who would appear to have an interest, or had shown an interest in the past, and 'closed' consultation, where the department wished specific assistance from a small range of interested bodies: (see Table 6.1.).

TABLE 6.1. *Modes of Group–Department Consultation*

Consultation is:	Nature of consultation	Departmental activity	Place of interest groups in process
Strong	Functional	Negotiation on principles with non-clients	Direct negotiation on principles
		Negotiation on principles with clients	Direct negotiation on principles with sponsor department
			Meeting and negotiation via sponsor department on principles
		Negotiation on detail with non-clients	Meeting and negotiation via sponsor department on detail
		Negotiation on principle with clients	Written invited representations via sponsor department
		Statutory consultation— meaningful ritual	Direct invited written representations
	Symbolic	Open consultation	Unsolicited comments
		Policy dissemination/ education	
Weak	Non-existent	Insulated bureaucratic policy-making	Signalling via parent department
		Insulated departmental policy-making	Non-involvement

That there is a range of consultations is clear. The honorary secretary of the Scottish District of the Institution of Building Control Officers—one of the very bodies claiming in the next section to enjoy regularized access—wrote to the *Scotsman* in November (13th) 1984 that the consultation process on the deletion of housing space standards from the Building Standard Regulations meant that 'the consultation process appears to have been reduced to a worthless imposture'. He claimed that the proposals had virtually no support among the broad spectrum of organizations consulted and that the department proceeded against the views of the overwhelming majority of the 150 bodies consulted (and the department's own Building Standards Advisory Committee). In this case the department was under three important pieces of counter-pressure. There was pressure in favour by developers, especially those who were able to use certain designs in England, but not in Scotland with its stricter controls; there was thus the national homogeneity argument. There was also some need by Scottish Conservative politicians to deliver in the Thatcher style in *some* area.

Scottish Office Experience

Interviews at the Scottish Office with civil servants responsible for a range of policy areas broadly confirmed—but with important reservations—the image we have depicted of policy-making through close group–department relations.

The matters of building control are perhaps of minimal political importance, except that there is an almost iron law that the politics of detail have the capacity to arouse unexpected controversy. In the case of building control, the wider public attention has stemmed from Part Q (Housing Standards section) of the Building Standards (Scotland) Regulations 1981 and 1982. This apparently esoteric provision most importantly covers minimum space standards in building. This has been pushed by developers, particularly for 'first home' and single occupation dwellings.

Section 3(6) of the Building (Scotland) Act (as amended 1970) states that before any amendment to the building standards regulations is made, the Secretary of State 'shall consult the Building Standards Advisory Committee and such other bodies as appear to be representative of the interests concerned.'

In the case of Part Q, the statutory consultation was initiated in June 1984, when 139 bodies were invited to comment. Sixty-nine did so but this included twenty-five not specifically invited to do so. Ninety-five of the 139 did not reply. However, this mandatory exercise was preceded by two consultation documents, 'Removal of Space Standards' and 'The Future of Building Control in Scotland'. The former paper went to 148 bodies while the latter paper went to 228 consultees, with 128 replies, nine from bodies not originally consulted and three from Building Standards Advisory Committee (BSAC) members. While most of the bodies were from the construction side of the issue, Shelter and the Consumer's Association were also included.

Even in less controversial policy areas, what appear as un-expectedly large numbers of consultees appear. On 'Access to Buildings for Disabled People', issued in February 1983, twenty-one bodies were consulted (fifteen replies), and on 'Access and Facilities in Buildings for the Benefit of the Disabled' (17 October 1983), twenty-seven bodies were consulted, with thirteen comments.

Another form of the consultation process is this circulation of documents. The building control division maintains its own master list of bodies, which contains names. Admittedly some of these names appear to be 'for information only', but the remarkable thing about the list is the specialization of the group world: for example, the Bituminous Roofing Council is followed by the Boiler and Radiator Manufacturers' Association, the Brick Development Association, the British Board of Agreement, British Combustion Equipment Manufacturers' Association, British Constructional Steelwork Association, British Electrical and Allied Manufacturers' Association, and many others.

The department stresses that 'we are careful to ensure that our consultations take in a wide range of bodies representative of "customers [sic] of the system" '. There is minimal selectivity: virtually any body which asks will be included for consultation in its area of interest, but there were attempts to keep individual companies out of the system. This would give too many problems of precedent, and trade associations were deliberately used to 'get coverage'. In so far as there is selection from the list, the term 'horses for courses' often arises. Even then the department would tend to 'play safe', but for the sake of economy not every group is approached. However, there would be little point in attempting to omit hostile opinion from the consultation, as it would merely use the lack of consultation as an extra stick with which to attack the department. But certainly in a world such as had evolved in building control, there was a need 'to clear the clutter', and the term *focused* consultation was used to describe the aim to excise the peripheral bodies with no history of significant interest. Rolling back the list, though, had risks: bodies *like* to be asked and groups get upset when left out. Thus the safest procedure was 'to shoot a little widely'. Consultation was presented as a matter of personal protection for the civil servant. The temptation was to use 'belt and braces', but it depended on past experience. The comments gathered in such a consultation exercise will usually be summarized into 'for' and 'against' statements for submission to ministers, together with a recommendation for action.

The second leg of consultation is through the advisory committee, in this case the BSAC. As is common in this type of body, the members of BSAC sit as individuals, though many of the participants will have a background which will allow them to speak informally for interests. Thus the current committee (1985–7) has representatives of local authorities (administration and building control side), consulting engineers, an architect, building contractors, academics, an assistant firemaster, and a couple of lay representatives. BSAC meets 2–3 times per year. The DOE, its Building and Fire Research Stations, and DOE(NI) sit in on meetings as observers.

A third area of consultation is formed by the Secretary of State giving class relaxation directions: generally these are where a manufacturer puts forward a new type of product not already sanctioned. Again these go to BSAC and other such bodies as the Secretary of State determines. In the seven cases between September 1983 and November 1984, for each submission an average of forty-two bodies were consulted.

The final form of consultation is the least formal, and takes the form of regular meetings with the Scottish Association of Chief Building Control Officers (SABCO). While the policy field is heavily populated, it was with this body and its members that contact was closest: 'We know some of these chaps quite well and it is a useful body to bounce ideas off.' However, we are not here talking of daily contact, but of less than once a month, although the technical side of the department might have far more frequent dealings. This forum was judged so useful that the Scottish Office has built on meetings with the chief building control officers and invited.participation from trade associations and professional bodies. To control numbers, other interests will only be invited to attend when their topics feature on the agenda. The extended forum is chaired and serviced by the Scottish Development Department.

The Building Control Forum's functions are to:

(a) foster common interpretation and administration of the building regulations;
(b) pool and disseminate information for use and reference;
(c) provide a collective liaison channel between building control authorities and the SDD; and
(d) furnish an advisory service for building control authorities on interpretative and other issues.

While there is emphasis on harmonization of interpretation, in fact a role of providing feedback on the success of policy also exists for the current SABCO meetings. The widened net is hoped to 'get more input from the customers of the system'.

Of course the test of consultation is in how much impact it has. The extended SABCO proposal is itself an amendment to the original SDD proposal, made after an earlier consultative paper. But several reasons exist to make it difficult to advance dramatic examples of effective influence. For one thing, there is the matter of anticipated reactions: proposals which were wildly out of favour with the client groups would mean that the informal communication system was faulty. One civil servant acknowledged that he *could* do most of the consultation 'in his head'. Reactions were generally predictable. Secondly, there is a political judgement. One civil servant put his position as: 'In considering the comments of consultees, the object is not to slavishly adopt whatever the consensus view might be: it is rather to reach informed decisions of good quality which sit well in the framework of Government policy as a whole.' But that statement is in turn to be put in perspective by the fact that in an area such as building control technical arguments can often be influential, whatever the political flavour.

The same civil servant, who claimed that consultation is not slavishly to adopt the consensus view, gave comments which had a rather different flavour:

We do have policy objectives that require cooperation . . . Local authorities might not be able to refuse but they could make it difficult. Cooperation is, in practice, essential. We might have legal authority but, hypothetically, they could (say) turn down every planning application and we would have to field them all as appeals.

At the end of the day people have to live with each other and get the business done. If things depended on legal rights and bits of paper, what would work? We need good will . . . Fortunately it isn't a question of sanctions. In developing new proposals it is very important to be seen as relevant, not ivory tower. It is important to get feedback in the field. Sometimes we can be persuaded of difficulties not in view from New St Andrews House . . .

A bridge between the discussions in the area of building control and discussions in educational provision was the unprompted suggestion that consultation was shaped by the fact that co-operation is necessary. Though a priori we suspected that the circumstances where there were groups with this strategic importance were perhaps few, again when we made the suggestion it was firmly rebuffed; '[we] have had to work with people; persuade people that cooperation is the way forward . . . "Mandarin" style is not on'. Of the local authorities, a civil servant observed (in 1985) that 'We can't *make* them do anything . . . They are their own masters over how they spend their allocation—though the Scottish Office does issue regulations in pursuit of overall policy, it prefers to give advice [rather] than coerce.' This civil servant's usual technique was to get a group in the 'customer area' (that phrase again) 'to make it happen . . . I need to take them along with the policy'.

Several other points crop up in several interviews. For example, the spirit of a comment on education is very similar to one on building noted earlier: 'The problem is simple—falling school rolls and per capita grants. Obviously unless schools close they will run half empty—with no money for books and other equipment. We don't need to convince officials about this: they can see the solution. It is the councillors who are the difficulty. Whenever a school is due to close an action group springs up and the councillors cave in . . .'. In other words, it was felt that professionals *could*, if left to their own devices, manage the policy area. Similarly, on health matters we recorded the comment, 'Relationships can be facilitated because it is a question of professionals talking to fellow professionals.' Even so, great care is taken to ensure that all potentially relevant groups are included. The civil servant dealing with a particular problem draws up a list of possible consultees based upon his experience of the policy area. He then sends the preliminary list round the division (and possibly to other divisions in the department), which adds names of groups and individuals who have been missed off. In practice, each civil servant knows the interest group map of his policy area like the back of his hand, but the consultation list grows as there is a 'directed trawl' around the Scottish Office generally.

The close professional relationship can, sometimes, be difficult to manage when a particularly contentious issue gets on to the political agenda. For example, the BMA was initially very reluctant to sit down and bargain over the proposal in 1985 to limit the range of drugs which GPs could prescribe, although eventually there was a bargained outcome. New groups do emerge and do become part of the consultative network. For example, the National Association for the Welfare of Children in Hospitals (NAWCH) has suggested useful improvements to the running of hospitals as it effects children, and the group's advice has been 'accepted'.

Differences between divisional practice do exist, but whether this is a product of different types of policy or the personal style of individual civil servants is unclear (as is whether some civil servants feel an obligation to report what they think are desirably 'pure' administrative practices, unsullied by group influences). Certainly one division felt that business groups had no place in the scheme of things: 'They write every six months or so and we reply that the limitation on finance makes it unlikely that the Minister can accommodate their wishes . . .'. The question of MAFF and the NFU cropped up, to be dismissed as 'a closed conspiracy'. Again a national transport organization was effectively dismissed as sending in 'a shopping list so enormous as to lose credibility'. Another point of difference is the frequency and intimacy of the contact with regular committees: we found that *administrators* would have little need for the famous daily contact of the NFU/MAFF, but technical specialists are far more likely to be in daily contact.

Other civil servants were quite prepared to identify cases of 'sham consultation' where the policy was not really amenable to change. Therefore the generalizations we form on consultative practices cannot cover every circumstance. Even within a division there may be very different types of consultation, with national bodies such as the road transport lobbies, perhaps, and with residents' groups about specific lines for bypass schemes.

Another major dimension with differences is the degree of integration. We have seen an increasing degree of formalization in building control, whereas, in contrast, the trunk road division had no comparable body. The most fully developed system we encountered was in health service planning, which has at its peak the Scottish Health Service Planning Council. This is based on the chairman of the various Scottish Health Boards, but also has representation from the Home and Health Department (administrators and medical specialists) and individual medical experts from Scottish universities. A complex system of related *ad hoc* committees also exists. For example, in the report for 1984 by the Planning Council the following bodies were mentioned: Working Group of the Mental Disorder Programme Planning Group, Working Group of the Prosthetics and Orthotics Committee, Radiology Sub-committee of the National Medical Consultative Committee, Working Group of the Geriatric Medicine Sub-committee of the National Medical Consultative Committee, National Nursing and Midwifery Consultative Committee, National Pharmaceutical Consultative Committee, Occupational Therapy Sub-committee of the National Paramedical Consultative Committee, Physiotherapy Sub-committee of above, Scottish Health Education Co-ordinating Committee, Working Group on NHS Supplies, Medical Physics and Bio-engineering Sub-committee of the National Consultative Committee for Scientists, In-patient Care Working Group of the National Medical Consultative Committee, Working Party on Patients' Funds, Committee on Child Health Records, Working Group on Out-of-Hours and Emergency Health Care, Information and Computer Services Advisory Group, Scientific Services Advisory Group, Advisory Group on New Developments in Health Care, Working Party on Obstetrical Anaesthesia, Advisory Group on Epidemiological and Other Aspects of Infection, and so on. Such subcommittees are specialized, but they are not necessarily unimportant. Each of these areas has a potential for high-profile attention.

A variant of consultation might in fact be the very close

relationship which *executive* civil servants develop with their 'clients'. For example, civil servants in the Exports Division of the Industry Department for Scotland are in daily contact with exporters from a wide range of industries. In essence the civil servants are executing policy and are not directly concerned with policy formulation. But feedback from clients can, itself, produce policy change. An example occurred when exporters informed civil servants that they needed help when they first wished to establish a permanent presence in an export market. The outcome was the Market Entry Guarantee Scheme for small and medium-sized companies. This covers, *inter alia*, the cost of employing salesmen to handle your goods and set up your own offices in export markets. Similarly, the direct experience of exporters in the Export Licensing Control System in the electronics field produces feedback which can in turn produce policy change (it is now easier, for example, to export some computers and (non-strategic) electronics equipment to the USSR). The civil servant as implementer is, perhaps without knowing it, often an important channel of consultation with affected interests.

Consultation (and negotiation) will, of course, vary from issue to issue (and may vary from department to department). It seems likely that the education sector is more liable to be involved in very wide consultation exercises than, say, the Scottish Development Department (SDD), in part because education as a policy area has higher political salience than many of the technical issues handled by the SDD. One of our respondents usefully suggested that consultation processes might be classified into three types. The first is consultation as a means of *informing* those outside government of what the Government is intending to do, such as in the implementation of certain provisions of the Pollution Control Act. The second is consultation to find out what is actually happening in a problem area. For example, the SDD carried out a consultation exercise on acid rain, in order to assess the extent of the problem, that is to get information from groups. One 'spin-off' from this particular consultation exercise was the identification of the relevant research community in Scotland. The third form of consultation is designed to discover what should happen in response to a policy problem. For example, the relevant groups concerned with coastal oil spillages were brought together to do a forecasting exercise, and they identified several possible methods of dealing with oil pollution on beaches. In some policy areas the group network will be very stable over time, as in groups concerned with noise regulations. In others, particularly with new issues such as acid rain, the group network may be less well established and departments less certain about who to consult and about who really counts.

While the routine business of such specialized worlds may be of little party political interest, if problems occur, almost any subject has, as we have claimed, a potential for parliamentary attention. Each policy problem seems to have a range of groups associated with it, and it is normal for those groups to be involved in some way or other, even if only as channels for communicating information to the members. More usually, the opinions of the groups are indeed taken into account.

We have reproduced as Table 6.2 a table derived from our

TABLE 6.2. *Examples of Scottish Office Consultation*

Consultation exercise	Approximate number of consultees
EC Directive on quality of water for human consumption	85
Control of Pollution Act, part 2, Pollution of Water	45
Control of pollution (anti-fouling paints)	26
Register of research on acid deposition in Scotland	35
Acid rain position paper	30
Building standards regulations	139
Access to buildings for disabled people	21
Future of building control in Scotland	228
Relaxation of building standards regulations (several cases)	42 (average figure)
Roads Bill (Scotland)	116
Misuse of drugs	12 (+58 consulted by other depts.)
Ambulance services	33
Mental health	11
Management function in NHS, Scotland	59
Speech therapy	30
EC directive on specific training in general medical practice	7
NHS management—application to units	50
Human fertilization and embryology	44

Scottish Office survey, indicating some examples of consultation exercises in 1984–6. In Appendix 6.1 we have given two typical examples of the numerous 'consultation lists' used by the Scottish Office. In total, the time and energy spent on consultation of one kind or another appears to be a significant proportion of a civil servant's working time.

Appendix 6.1

Two examples of Departmental Consultation Lists

1. *Inquiry into Human Fertilization and Embryology*

Health boards
Royal College of Physicians of Edinburgh
Royal College of Surgeons of Edinburgh
Royal College of Physicians and Surgeons of Glasgow
British Medical Association—Scottish Council
Conference of Royal Colleges and Faculties in Scotland
Scottish Joint Consultants' Committee
Scottish General Medical Services Committee
Scottish Health Service Planning Committee
Medical and Dental Defence Union for Scotland
Scottish Family Planning Medical Society
Medical Women's Federation
National Association for the Childless
Family Planning Association (Scotland)
Brook Advisory Centre (Scotland)
British Pregnancy Advisory Service (Scotland)
National Childbirth Trust (Scotland)
National Board for Nursing, Midwifery, and Health Visiting for Scotland
The Association of Scottish Local Health Councils

Reformed Presbyterian Church
United Free Church of Scotland
Congregational Union of Scotland
Episcopal Church in Scotland
Free Church of Scotland
Free Presbyterian Church of Scotland
Church of Scotland
Methodist Church in Scotland
Baptish Union of Scotland
Archdiocese of St Andrews and Edinburgh

Archdiocese of Glasgow
Jewish Faith in Scotland

The Association of Sheriffs Principal
The Sheriffs' Association
Faculties of Law of Scottish universities
Faculty of Advocates
Law Society of Scotland
Scottish Legal Action Group
Scottish Law Commission

Association of Directors of Social Work
British Association of Social Workers
British Agencies for Adoption and Fostering
Scottish Council for Single Parents

Convention of Scottish Local Authorities

Scottish Trades Union Council

2. *EC Directive on the Quality of Water for Human Consumption (80/778/EEC): Application to Private Water Supplies and to Food Business*

Aberdeen and District Milk Marketing Board
Aberdeen Fish Curers' and Merchants Association Ltd.
Association of Directors and River Inspectors in Scotland
Association of Scottish Bacon Curers
Association of Scottish Chambers of Commerce

Brewers' Association of Scotland
British Airports Authority (Scotland)
British Hotels, Restaurants, and Caterers' Association
British Oat and Barley Millers' Association
British Rail (Scottish Region)

Convention of Scottish Local Authorities

Edinburgh School of Agriculture

Federal of Bakers (Scottish Area)
Federation of British Kipperers

Glasgow Wholesale Fish Trade Association

Herring Buyers' Association
Herring Merchants' Association

Institute of Food Science and Technology (Scottish Branch)
Institute of Trading Standards Administration (Scottish Branch)
Malt Distillers' Association for Scotland

National Farmers' Union of Scotland
North of Scotland Milk Marketing Board

Queens' College, Glasgow
Queen Margaret College

Royal Environmental Health Institute of Scotland

Salmon Net Fishing Association of Scotland
Scotch Whisky Association
Scottish Association of Directors of Water and Sewage Services
Scottish Association of Master Bakers
Scottish Association of Milk Product Manufacturers
Scottish Association of Sausage and Cooked Meat Manufacturers
Scottish Association of Soft Drinks Manufacturers
Scottish Dairy Trade Federation Ltd.
Scottish Federation of Meat Traders' Associations
Scottish Fishermen's Federation
Scottish Grocers' Federation
Scottish Kippers and Herring Fishers' Association
Scottish Landowners' Federation
Scottish Licensed Trade Association
Scottish Milk Marketing Board
Scottish Milk Trade Federation
Scottish Retail Federation
Scottish River Purification Boards Association
Society of Directors of Environmental Health
Society of Scottish Directors of Consumer Protection

West of Scotland Agriculture College
Wholesale Grocers' Association of Scotland

7

'High Politics'

Introduction

Much of the analysis in this volume is concerned with what Hoffman (1966) describes as 'low politics'. He makes the distinction between those issues which have a major bearing on the viability of the nation state, which he classes as 'high politics', and those issues which are concerned with less fundamental issues, which he classes as 'low'. We would argue that the sectorization of policy-making and the development of policy communities may well work towards the disaggregation of all policy issues into 'low' and 'manageable' problems. Big, cross-sectoral issues are difficult to manage, both intellectually and politically. It is impossible, intellectually, to take account of all possible linkages between policy areas, and in political terms too many conflicting interests may be involved for a workable consensus to emerge. Thus it is no surprise that the bulk of policy-making and implementing activity is concerned with issues which might be perceived as technical and detailed.

It seems a common, even unavoidable, phenomenon that high politics are translated to implementation through specific decision processes which resemble decisions on the technicalities of low politics. Thus, for example, the Finniston Report *Engineering Our Future* (Cmnd. 7794) had at its core nothing less than 'manufacturing and national prosperity'. (It claimed, 'the paramount consideration and test of our conclusions has been: "Will this benefit manufacturing industry and future national economic needs?" ') But in practice discussion of the implementation of such dramatically 'high' objectives induced bitterly contested discussions between the Department of Industry and the chartered institutions of professional engineers, over the control of qualifications, the validation of degree courses, and the precise composition of the new Engineering Council. While everyone seems to have an opinion about 'high' politics, implementation is the province of groups deeply committed to their specialized interests and concern over detail.

It has been established that much of the concern of interest groups is with the detail of policy, as they recognize that governments are rarely willing to abandon a policy proposal completely. However, concentration on detail does not mean that groups are unable to secure major changes in proposed policies. By securing technical amendments and by affecting the *implementation* of policy, a group may well erode a policy but avoid an embarrassing 'climbdown' by government. Moreover, one man's detail is another man's point of principle, making it difficult to distinguish between 'big' issues and technical detail. For example, at one point early in 1986 Mrs Thatcher complained about the amount of time spent on the matter of a very small private company, Westland Helicopters, when an American 'take-over' was proposed. The political row, and two ministerial resignations, seemed out of proportion to the economic importance of the company.

But it is clear that there is a difference of order between consulting and negotiating with groups on, say, detailed building regulations and consulting and negotiating on the size and nature of public funding (via subsidies and tax concessions) of housing in Britain. There has been much negotiation between Mrs Thatcher's Government and the building industry on such matters as the working of the Health and Safety at Work Act, but seemingly little negotiation on the Government's dramatic cut-back of Treasury-funded public expenditure on housing. Yet another difference in policy-making procedure can be seen between that determining the level of support for house construction and the main thrust of the Government's macro-economic policy. Thus it can be argued that groups may become almost totally absorbed in the politics of minor issues whilst governments get on with taking the 'big' decisions for society. The role of the trade unions under Mrs Thatcher (to which we return later in this chapter) *may* be an example of groups being confined to relatively minor issues, where they gain significant concessions, whilst losing all the major battles.

As Stewart claimed (quoted in the last chapter), many of the big issues which divide societies have already been settled (the extension of the franchise, the establishment of parliamentary democracy, the creation of the welfare state, the shift from an agrarian to an industrial and eventually post-industrial society, the role of the Church). Thus, in general, politics in modern welfare states may be about detail rather than principle. And if political parties are, via electoral competition, drawn to the 'middle ground' and need to articulate and implement broadly similar policies when in office, then the 'stuff of politics' may be 'low' rather than high'.

However, Hoffman (1983, p. 29) does suggest that there are some issues, like macro-economic management, which are special in some sense and are perceived by governments as 'essential for the survival of the nation or for its own survival'. But, even in these areas, there seems to be a natural tendency to try to play the same kind of politics—in our terms, to operate the same policy style—in big issues, such as the management of the economy, as is played in the management of technical and detailed matters. Of particular note in the British case is the apparent tendency to try to develop tripartite structures, bringing together government, trade unions, and employers. Some of these tripartite structures can be seen as attempts to 'manage' high politics in the same way as low.

Tripartite Policy-making

In an article in 1977, Marsh and Grant analysed the degree to which 'tripartism' existed in Britain and tried to define its fundamental nature (1977, pp. 197–8). They identified four main characteristics of tripartism:

1. Obviously it would involve three parties—the Government, the CBI, and the TUC—interacting to evolve a commonly agreed industrial and economic policy within both formal and informal settings.

2. The system would be underpinned by a basic consensus: whilst there would be disagreement between the parties, such disagreement would be limited in its character and therefore capable of resolution. In particular, the parties involved would be willing to set aside any fundamental disagreements about ultimate goals in order to arrive at agreed solutions to specific problems. Without such a consensus there would seem to be little chance of arriving at policies which would be acceptable to all parties.

3. An effective tripartite system would not only involve élite accommodation. Such a system would involve the acceptance of

decisions as authoritative by both leaders and members of the groups involved. The leaderships would have to be willing and able to persuade their memberships to comply with the agreed policies. Without acceptance of the policies evolved under such a system by the membership of the groups, the chances of successfully implementing policy would be slight.

4. The three parties would each have similar degrees of influence on the evolution of policy, as otherwise the system would be tripartite in name but not in effect. If one or two parties become dominant, then not only would the term 'tripartism' be a misnomer, but also the disadvantaged party or parties would feel under no obligation to accept the agreed policies.

Having specified an 'ideal type', they suggest that the empirical evidence hardly lends support to a view that Britain has a fully fledged system of tripartism. They argue that 'a consideration of the changing nature of the relationship between the three parties since the formation of the CBI does little to indicate that any permanent basis for consensus between the three parties exists' (p. 198). An important part of their case is that it is difficult to build an effective system of tripartism on the basis of the TUC and CBI as organizations. These two 'pillars' are incapable of bearing the weight of tripartite policy-making if the system is trying to process 'high politics' decisions. For example, the TUC cannot ensure that decisions taken by the General Council are acted upon by constituent unions, let alone at the shop floor.

An example of the weakness of this particular pillar, in managing its own internal affairs, was the inability of the TUC to enforce its policy on the use of public funds for trade union ballots in 1985. The rebellion by two of the biggest unions in the TUC—the AUEW and the EETPU—in accepting public money for the organization of the election of union officers caused a bitter split within the TUC, and raised the possibility of the suspension of these unions. Attempts by the TUC to influence the electricians' union, the EETPU, were described by the general secretary of that union as 'maladroit, if not malicious, interference'. (*Financial Times*, 27 November 1985). In the event, the TUC had to recognize its inability to control powerful constituent unions. It could not enforce the decision, taken at a special conference at Wembley in 1982, that unions affiliated to the TUC should not accept government funds for internal union ballots. As a potential pillar of tripartism, the TUC is badly cracked.

Similarly, the CBI represents a very broad range of industrial and commercial interests and is itself often in difficulty in trying to maintain a united policy. As Grant and Marsh (1975, p. 93) suggested in an earlier article, 'as external demands on the organisation have increased, internal strains have worsened'. They suggested that four main lines of division have emerged, 'between different industries; between private and public sector members; between large and small firms; and most seriously, between those who favour a policy of co-operation with the government in the hope of securing policy concessions and those who would like to see the CBI taking a more aggressive stance . . .'. The question of the CBI's lobbying style was indeed the cause of a very serious split within the organization in 1981, when the CBI's director general Sir Terence Beckett argued that the CBI should engage in a 'bare knuckles' fight with the Conservative Goverment over policy differences. This speech provoked the withdrawal of the major engineering firm Babcock International from CBI membership. In autumn 1985 it was reported that British Airways was likely to withdraw from membership of the CBI when BA was privatized, thus denying the confederation some £27,000 subscription income. The considering of withdrawal was reported as being based upon the belief that the CBI was not a particularly effective voice for British industry and that BA would be a more effective lobbyist in its own right (*The Times*, 21 November 1985).

Like the TUC, the CBI lacks any really effective sanctions against its own members (let alone against government) (see Grant and Marsh 1977, p. 213.) If the CBI and TUC cannot control their own troops, then it is difficult for either organization to threaten effective sanctions against governments if open conflict between them and the government develops. Equally, governments may consider it unwise to rest policy on negotiations with organizations which may well not be able to deliver the support of their members when the policy comes to be implemented.

Despite these problems, however, there have been a few occasions when both the TUC and the CBI have been able to 'deliver' their memberships in support of an agreement negotiated with government, albeit for periods of very limited duration and with consequences for the fragile unity of both 'peak' associations.

In the case of the CBI, one of the most successful examples of it being able to 'deliver' a united membership in support of an agreement with government was the voluntary prices initiative with the Heath Government in 1971–2.

In general, as Grant and Marsh argue, the CBI has been conspicuously *unsuccessful* in the field of prices and incomes policies, 'reluctantly accepting the unpalatable economic medicine handed out by government' (Grant and Marsh 1977, p. 188). However, in early 1971 the CBI suggested that its members should limit their price increases for a twelve-month period and that as a *quid pro quo* the Government should reflate the economy (Grant and Marsh 1977, p. 192). It was hoped that this would induce wage restraint from the unions and would avoid a *statutory* prices policy, to which the CBI was opposed. Some 179 of the 200 largest private sector companies in Britain signed a document saying that they would not raise their prices for twelve months unless forced to make an unavoidable increase, in which case it would be no more than 5 per cent. Seven hundred smaller firms also supported the policy, as did many trade associations. Grant and Marsh conclude that the voluntary agreement did have a beneficial effect on the rate of inflation.

A number of strains developed, both within the CBI and between the CBI and the TUC, and between the TUC and the Government. Thus, as Grant and Marsh report, although it seemed that the TUC might be prepared to accept the limitation of stringent (price) controls to a list of key foods, another stumbling block to agreement remained. The TUC wanted concessions on such policy matters as the Housing Finance Act and, above all, the Industrial Relations Act, but *'The Government did not regard matters such as these as being negotiable within the context of tripartite talks. The government was prepared to take the effect of these policies into account, but it regarded them ultimately as matters for its own decision, subject to the approval of Parliament.'* (Grant and Marsh 1977, p. 196, our emphasis.)

In the event, the tripartite talks failed, with the result that the Heath Government introduced a statutory prices and incomes policy, against the wishes of both the CBI and the TUC. The lessons of the relative success of 1971–2 appear to be that this is rather untypical and that is general the CBI, as the 'peak' industrial association, has difficulty in 'controlling' its members. Thus Grant and Marsh's general conclusion is that the 'CBI has had relatively limited impact on the major issues which have dominated British politics since its inception' (Grant and Marsh 1977, p. 207).

In the case of the TUC, we can also see an example of a brief success in mobilizing its membership in support of a 'deal' with government, only for the experiment to collapse in some degree of acrimony and ill-feeling. Shortly after the introduction of Heath's statutory policy on wages, prices, and dividends, the TUC agreed a document with the Labour party (then in opposition) entitled *Economic Policy and The Cost of Living* (TUC 1973, pp. 312–15). This document was the basis of what was to become the 'Social Contract' between the TUC and the subsequent Labour Government elected in 1974. (For a fuller discussion of TUC/Labour party relations and of the Social Contract, see chapter 10.) By the time a Labour Government was in office, in 1974, the Social Contract loomed large as an integral part of the new Government's economic strategy. The Government, for its part, set about delivering its side of the set of bargains reached with the TUC in opposition. For example, the TUC presented the new Employment Secretary with proposals for repealing the Conservatives' two 'offensive' Acts, the Industrial Relations Act and the Counter-inflation Act. The TUC also began to pay the price of closer collaboration, becoming involved in the implementation of some form of voluntary incomes policy in return for the Government's action in repealing Conservative legislation and in introducing various subsidies on food, freezing rents, and increasing pensions and tax allowances for the lower-paid (Clark *et al.* 1980, p. 27).

The situation which the TUC had got itself into was aptly summed up by Alan Fisher, the general secretary of the National Union of Public Employees (NUPE), when he warned a special Congress held in 1976 that

If we are going to bargain continuously and effectively on all major economic issues of the day with which our members are concerned, then it is possible that we will become mesmerised by the process itself, rather than considering the results that it achieves . . . it is dangerous for the Movement to accept incorporation in the apparatus of the State, articulated through what may be loyalty to a Labour Government. (Quoted by Clark *et al.* 1980, p. 40.)

By July 1977 constituent unions were rejecting pay policies and were demanding a return to genuinely unfettered collective bargaining. Though almost in ruins, the Social Contract still had some small meaning, however. Thus, although the TUC opposed the Government's unilateral decision to impose a 10 per cent limit on wage increases, it did support a policy that no wage settlements should be made within twelve months of a previous settlement. In the following year the Government took another unilateral decision, to impose a 5 per cent limit on pay increases. This was followed by the 'winter of discontent' (1978–9), which saw a rash of politically damaging strikes (see chapter 10). Thus, as with the CBI initiative described above, the experiment in 'high politics' had some success, but was of a limited duration and carried heavy costs for participants.

The arrival of a new Conservative Government—with which the unions had poor relations—did not, however, kill the attempts to make tripartism work. Indeed, the Conservatives in opposition had seemed to be considering a more developed form of the National Economic Development Council (NEDDY), on which the Government sits along with the TUC and CBI. At that time the Conservatives seemed impressed by the reported success of German 'concerted action'.

The situation under the new Government illustrated the degree to which groups can maintain quite different sectoral relationships with the same Government at the same time. Whilst the TUC was opposed to the Government's broad economic strategy, it found issues where tripartism looked as though it might work reasonably effectively. In particular, the National Economic Development Council remained as an institution in which government and the peak economic associations could meet.

The National Economic Development Council: Tripartism and High Politics?

The NEDC (Neddy) is a rather special form of group integration into decision-making. The council meets monthly and consists of six cabinet ministers, usually led by the Chancellor (and including the Prime Minister), plus six CBI representatives, six TUC representatives, and six other members drawn from the Bank of England and other interests. When it was set up in 1962, the Conservative Chancellor, Selwyn Lloyd, expressed the view that 'experience has shown the need for a closer link between Government and industry and to make possible effective action to correct weaknesses in our economic structure' (quoted in Cassels 1985, p. 6). In other words, the NEDC was an attempt to run the economy (a matter of 'high politics') more effectively by co-ordination with industry and labour.

Middlemas (1983, p. 16) suggests that the Chancellor was not quite clear what was meant by tripartism. Indeed, he is said to have felt that 'operation of the mixed economy in the 1950s had allowed oligipoly to build up among management and labour organisations, and that a lead from government was needed to reverse the process'. Yet at the same time there was a belief that only co-operative effort through the NEDC could check Britain's industrial decline. Equally, it is not quite clear what the other parties hoped the NEDC would become. Ambivalence again seems to have been the theme.

According to Middlemas (1983, p. 18) neither unions nor employers 'expected the government to ask very much by way of obligations, and both assumed that the Council would serve them as an advantageous lobby, allowing direct and persuasive contact with the Chancellor and the Treasury'. He is probably correct in hinting that the very origins of the NEDC illustrate a fashionable assumption that institutional reform can produce results.

Thus he argues that

far from starting with a clean state . . . its very constitution incorporated the dilemma it was supposed to solve. Neither powerful nor truly independent of government, dominated by the ideologies of its long-organised partners, and pushed, largely for political reasons, into an unreasonably optimistic set of targets, NEDC began as a prime example of the belief that structures led automatically to progress. (Middlemas 1983, p. 19.)

While Mrs Thatcher's Conservative Government was widely thought—at least initially—to be hostile to the NEDC and its underlying interventionist philosophy, the CBI was by 1985 enthusiastic about its role. For example, *CBI News* (26 July) reported, 'The July (1985) meeting of the NEDC saw important success for long standing CBI campaigns.' The *CBI News* went on to talk about 'CBI's successful partnership in the NEDC'. The successful negotiation of more public infrastructure investment was ascribed to the work of specially formed tripartite groups of the CBI, TUC, and Department of Transport. Similar tripartite discussions on specific topics had been held at ministerial and departmental level on housing, hospital, and school buildings, as well as discussions in the Civil Engineering Economic Development Committee on water and sewers (see *TUC Annual Report* 1985, p. 293).

Under the NEDC are forty-five 'Little Neddys'—specific sectoral Economic Development Committees (EDCs)—covering most sectors of industry and commerce (for example heavy electrical machinery, electronic components, pharmaceuticals). Despite government participation, the EDCs can be quite critical of government policy: in 1985 the Electronic Components EDC expressed serious concern about a moratorium then in force on applications under the Government's Micro-electronics Applications Programme (NEDC 1985*a*, p. 3). The objective of the EDCs is to help improve the competitiveness of companies in each sector, and hence the performance of the sector as a whole. For example, in 1985 the Domestic Electrical Applicances EDC carried out an international comparison of reliability levels of major appliances.

About 1,200 representatives from industry are involved in the 'Little Neddy' network, including over 100 directors from *The Times*'s Top 1,000 companies. One example of a little NEDC success claimed by the NEDC's director general, John Cassels, was the Engineering Construction EDC, which 'after years of patient work' had secured the establishment of a National Joint Council for the engineering construction industry and a new comprehensive National Agreement for working practices and dispute procedures. Cassels claimed,

The NJC and the National Agreement have transformed work on large projects. Take for example, the construction of power stations for the CEGB. During the 1970s the percentage of man hours lost through disputes was 3.8% of total man hours . . . By 1983 that figure was reduced to 0.58%. The CEGB report better disciplinary procedures, an improved industrial relations climate, greater craft flexibility, rationalisation of payment and improved consultation at local levels through Project Joint Councils . . .

Cassels cites other examples of what he claims is achieved by 'patient and far sighted collaboration'. He dwells particularly on the job creation issue, where 700,000 young people were placed in the Youth Training Scheme in two years, 1983–5. He argues:

It seems to me that the tripartite character of the MSC has had a great deal to do with the speed at which it has been possible to develop the YTS. Perhaps I can illustrate this most vividly by recalling a meeting when Sir Richard O'Brien, then Chairman of the Manpower Services Commission, went to see Sir John Partridge and Sir John Methven at the CBI to say that, if the CBI would back it, he thought a Work Experience Programme should be introduced under which employers would provide six months of planned work experience for unemployed young people. Within minutes the CBI leaders committed themselves . . . That . . . made it possible to seek in turn that of the TUC which was no less readily given.

Cassels then described how the details of the scheme were worked out and claims that this and other examples show 'also the fundamental value of involvement and participation, which leads to solutions to which all those who are involved or participating contribute and, because they contribute, are committed' (Cassels 1985, p. 16).

Certainly the Cassels picture could be balanced by gloomier assessments of the record and potential of tripartism, but it is worth noting as a counter to the easy and frequent assertion that there is no British consultation in such matters. See for example Lehmbruch's view that

The declining importance or even a breakdown in a certain number of Western European countries of 'tripartite' patterns of cooperation between government and organised interests in economic policymaking . . . The rejection, by the British government, of established forms of consultation with trade unions and other groups—is only the most spectacular example of this trend. (Lehmbruch 1985, p. 2.)

The fact is that consultation still takes place with the key associations, and while the unions withdrew in 1984 over the Government's policy of banning trade unions in the GCHQ (the Government's communications interception headquarters), they 'returned to the table with a new sense of commitment and a desire to make the Council more effective' (CBI News, 26 July 1985).

The return of the TUC to Neddy took place notwithstanding the fact that the Government still refused to remove its ban on trade unions at GCHQ. The official pretext for the TUC's return to the NEDC was a joint initiative by the TUC and CBI designed to make the NEDC more effective. The TUC and CBI produced a joint paper containing some twenty points on the future working of the NEDC.

The objective was to achieve greater control over the agenda and business of the Council, to prevent it being used as a merely consultative body by the Government, to ensure that where action was agreed there was effective monitoring of the follow-up, and to allow publicity advantage to be taken of Council discussions. (TUC *Annual Report* 1985, p. 291.)

It is still open for critics to suggest that in practice it is a far less effective and harmonious body than Cassels allows, but the point is that there is something to debate about. No more can we say that there is *no* effective consultation on economic policy in Britain than we should allow uncritical accounts of Swedish or Austrian central co-ordination to go unchallenged. There is a degree of organizational integration in economic policy in Britain, though to put a measure of quantity to 'the degree' is a problem. The TUC, despite its temporary withdrawal and despite its generally bad relations with Mrs Thatcher's Government, is on record as saying that it 'took the view that the value of tripartite discussion had been to show that with the support of the CBI, not all doors were closed to TUC representatives to the Government, and the TUC had been able to alter the agenda for debate by the Council' (TUC *Annual Report* 1985, p. 293).

Cassels's invaluable piece goes on to address a matter that is at the heart of the discussion of group participation and corporatist theory (see chapter 5). He says that when the CBI and the TUC committed themselves to the idea of a Work Experience Programme,

it did not mean that every company in the land would be willing to run a WEP scheme, any more than the support of the TUC instantly converted every shop steward . . . What it did do was create an atmosphere and general disposition highly favourable . . . and to commit the CBI and the TUC to bring their powers of persuasion to bear on those of their constituents who doubted or even opposed the running of WEP schemes.

This observation, that the CBI and TUC have influence if not a guarantee of compliance over their members' actions, is predictable, but emphasizes that trying to judge whether groups 'control' their members is difficult. What is better, 'influence' that sometimes works or theoretical 'control' that can be, *de facto*, ignored? Much of the academic debate about corporatism (see chapter 5) is at too abstract a level ever to be resolved. Grant (1985, p. 20) claims that one of the 'crucial differences' between corporatism and pluralism is (and here he follows Crouch) 'the importance of groups engaged in corporatist bargaining being able to discipline and control their members to comply with agreements negotiated . . .'. He goes on, 'What corporatism offers is the possibility of arriving at *effective* bargains, in the sense that they can be secured and implemented, rather than being simply talked about . . .'.

One of the problems of such an attempted distinction is that any bargain that 'sticks' is then corporatist and any breakdown is pluralist, a distinction made after the event rather than being predictive. Moreover, there is an assumption that pluralist bargaining can take place without the prospect of 'delivery' by the participant. Delivery may be *uncertain*, but without any prospect of success negotiations will founder. And what does discipline mean? As noted above, the TUC had a clear constitutional capacity to discipline unions accepting government funds for internal union ballots, but the TUC chose not to exercise this sanction. Finally there is the aspect of ambiguity of outcomes. There can be legitimate debate about the significance of almost all Neddy activity and its shop-floor-level impact. Such ambiguity makes it difficult to measure up against the corporatist dimensions.

Caution is of course needed in assuming that where consensus does emerge, action will *necessarily* follow (Middlemas 1983, p. 19). Indeed, the NEDC has itself recognized the gap between agreement at NEDC or EDC level and action being implemented at plant level. As a result, it set up a steering group, in 1981, to help increase the impact of EDC decisions at company and plant level. A practical step was the introduction of 'ambassadors', employed by EDCs to establish contact with managers, employers, and trade union representatives. (Some thirty ambassadors now work for approximately twenty of the EDCs. See NEDC 1985a.) Here, perhaps, we see a shift in Neddy's focus from the very broad macro-economic issues which concerned it in the early years, such as formulating a national economic plan (again, 'high politics' in Hoffman's terminology), to the detail of policy—'low politics'.

The fullest study of the history of Neddy concludes that 'it has stood for steady, reasoned adjustment to national and international long-term trends, as against the oscillating, hasty patterns of reversals of government policy—or rather that party-oriented public face of policy which has often differed from what governments and departments actually did or tried to do' (Middlemas 1983, p. 186).

The differences between the processing of high and low issues is, again, important in evaluating the NEDC. There is a vast difference between the TUC arguing before the NEDC (as it did in February 1985) that 'the major course of job losses and poor economic performance has not been the pattern of wage movements, or other aspects of the labour markets. Government macro-economic policies have been responsible for a major shortfall in that demand', and, say, the Heavy Electrical Machinery EDC organizing seminars on technological change, where consensus and action might be achievable.

Neddy and New Technology: A Case study*

Some of the difficulties in making tripartism work are illustrated by a case study of attempted co-operation between the CBI and TUC on new technology. Both the TUC and the CBI have recognized that the impact of new technology will be profound. The TUC was the first to attempt to generate its own policies towards the problem. Following a resolution adopted at the 1978 Congress, the TUC set up a research group of TUC and union officials. An interim report on the possible impact of new technology on employment was published in April 1979 and was discussed by a special Conference on Employment and Technology in May of that year. The wide-ranging report, which was accepted by Congress, did not directly raise the possibility of a tripartite approach to dealing with the impact of new technology, but a hint of a tripartite approach was contained in the discussion of future work. The report stressed that, 'Much of this programme does, however, depend on a close understanding by Government and employers of the issues facing working people and the role that the trade unions can play in promoting change on the basis of consent.' The final report was considered sufficiently important by the TUC for it to be part of the TUC's submissions to the National Economic Development Council meeting held in January 1980, together with a report of a fact-finding trip by TUC delegates to the USA.

* This section is based on J. J. Richardson (1983).

This Neddy meeting proved to be a turning-point in the development of a tripartite (in the event more accurately described as bipartite) approach to the new technology. The January 1980 meeting also saw submissions from the Government, National Economic Development Office (i.e. the officials who service Neddy), and the CBI, all relating in some way to the possible impact of the microchip. The CBI had published the first in a new series of 'discussion papers' produced by CBI research staff as a basis for discussion within the CBI membership. This paper, tabled for the January Neddy meeting, was entitled *Jobs: Facing the Future*. Somewhat prophetically, as it turned out, Sir John Methven, the CBI director general, pointed out that the report did not necessarily reflect a consensus of CBI members' views. The CBI document said relatively little about new technology, but did recognize that the impact on industry would be very considerable. Though there were significant differences between the TUC and CBI approaches (in particular to new technology agreements at plant level), there was a striking similarity in approach between their two reports. The CBI argued, 'it is possible to outline a co-ordinated programme of work on employment involving government, employers and unions'. The Government's paper recognized the importance of the adoption of new technology and the NEDO paper stressed the role which the government, CBI, and TUC should play in improving the situation.

At least three things were clear, therefore, in January 1980. Firstly, the issue of the impact of new technology was firmly on the political agenda. Secondly, there was a certain amount of pressure for increased governmental intervention to encourage the adoption of new technology. Thirdly there appeared to be at least some common ground between the two key participants, management and the unions. This common ground was duly noted by government ministers. For example, Sir Keith Joseph (Secretary of State for Industry) described the TUC report as 'a first class document', and Sir Geoffrey Howe (Chancellor of the Exchequer) encouraged Len Murray of the TUC and Sir John Methven of the CBI to develop a joint approach. This was echoed by Mrs Thatcher in her summing up, when she also urged a collaborative approach. The signs were, then, that new technology as a policy area might be suitable for a further experiment in tripartism, all the more so because the TUC, possibly then the weakest element in the three pillars of tripartism, seemed particularly anxious to make progress.

This was due to the fact that more than most it recognized the uncertainty created by the new technology and because it now had the freedom of not being 'tied' to a Labour Government. When Labour was in office, the TUC saw its close ties with the Government as a way of achieving direct results (for example through the Social Contract). With the Conservatives in power it could be less inhibited in dealing with the CBI, which was itself feeling left out in the cold by the new Conservative Government. The CBI, particularly under the influence of its director general, Sir John Methven, also seemed at the time anxious to emphasize consensus in the face of a rapidly changing technological and economic environment. If tripartism is to work then it must probably be preceded by a bipartite consensus between the CBI and the TUC. On this occasion this looked a real possibility.

With the Government's encouragement, therefore, the TUC and CBI opened negotiations of 'officer level'. With hindsight, the troubles which were to cause the failure of the exercise were evident at this stage. The TUC team had what amounted to a policy statement approved by the 1979 Congress. In contrast, the CBI team had only a discussion document, not approved by the membership at large. Moreover, the CBI has a rather complex consultative process in deciding official policy, in this case involving the thirteen Regional Councils, member employer organizations, the Smaller Firms Council, the Employment Policy Committee, the President's Committee, and finally the CBI Council. CBI staff were careful to emphasize the importance of this process, and it seems likely that the point was not fully appreciated by their TUC colleagues. Equally, the TUC seems not to have appreciated the degree of opposition within the CBI membership to the principle of producing a joint statement of policy with the TUC. At least some CBI members felt that a joint statement would raise the intensity of the debate about new technology and would as a result increase the problems of managing change at plant level. Although TUC–CBI co-operation was not unknown, CBI members were also unfamiliar with the idea of national 'negotiations' between the CBI and the TUC on issues that could later directly affect their own company negotiations.

Notwithstanding these important difficulties, the CBI staff produced a draft of a possible joint statement. The normal 'sounding out' procedure was followed, namely the testing of the paper on senior members generally thought to be in touch with CBI opinion. The draft was also put to the CBI Employment Policy Committee. It was probably reasonable, therefore, for people not familiar with the complexities of internal CBI politics, to see the draft as representing CBI policy which could be taken forward for negotiation with the TUC. At the TUC, the responsibility for negotiations rested with the special Employment and Technology Group (consisting of trade union as well as TUC officials), and key decisions were referred to the TUC Economic Policy Committee. If there was a significant difference in procedure between the two organizations, it was that the TUC side was more inclined to 'clear' each stage with the 'superior' policy committee.

In fact negotiations went well and very quickly. Indeed, the speed at which events moved may have caught the CBI off-balance. It seems likely that CBI members who were directly involved in the Employment Policy Committee may not have fully realized just how flexible the TUC was proving to be, and may have felt a general scepticism for the TUC's ability to make any agreement at all. The two sides produced the first draft of an agreement by June 1980. At this point it was felt that the draft agreement should be 'cleared' again at a senior level, and a meeting was arranged between the 'Neddy sixes' (the six senior industrialists and the six senior trade unionists who sit on Neddy). This too went well, and with minor modifications the draft agreement was approved in July. Superficially such 'clearance' appeared an adequate step, and the TUC, for its part, certainly considered it so. The new 'agreement', *Technological Change*, was approved by the TUC General Council at its August meeting. It was then quickly approved by the Congress which met in September.

From the CBI's viewpoint, however, events were moving too fast and the TUC seemed to be making all the running. The TUC and CBI formal machinery had got out of phase. The TUC General Council and then the full Congress approval all happened before the CBI's complex machinery had run its full course and before the CBI Council met in October 1980. By then the TUC had published the agreement, with the subtitle *A Joint TUC–CBI Statement*. The publication (and earlier leaks) of the document itself unintentionally damaged the chances of the CBI Council agreeing to it. Some CBI members saw this as an attempt by the TUC to short-circuit the CBI consultation process by presenting the CBI membership with a *fait accompli*. Had the TUC fully appreciated the importance of CBI procedures (particularly the importance of the CBI Council), and the degree to which attitudes to the concept of tripartism varied within the CBI, then it might not have been so apparently insensitive in publishing the draft agreement. In the event the agreement was rejected by the CBI Council, thus bringing to a premature end this experiment in developing a bipartite and ultimately tripartite approach to a key area of economic and industrial policy-making.

As Marsh and Grant (1977, p. 206) suggest, for tripartism to work the participating organizational structures must have sufficient strength and internal unity to support the tripartite structures. Thus they suggested that 'both the CBI and TUC have weaknesses which make it doubtful whether they could function effectively as pillars of a tripartite system'. In this particular case there appears to have been a failure within the CBI to make the necessary clearances, and a failure to persuade sections of the membership to accept a document to which their senior representatives on Neddy had agreed.

Chance events unfortunately played a significant part in removing key actors. Sir John Methven's untimely death, together with the arrival of a new president by the time the CBI Council met in October 1980, meant that two key participants were not present to 'sell' the agreement to the membership at large. When opposition did emerge at the Council, the CBI's emphasis on internal consensus, at least by its leadership, meant that the policy was not pushed through the Council against significant opposition. Surprisingly, the TUC seems to have taken the CBI Council's rejection very mildly: the only strong reaction came in a lecture which the assistant general secretary, David Lea, gave to the Trent Business School in November. Lea argued that had the TUC failed to ratify an agreement 'which the TUC and CBI representatives had drawn up with the full support of Government and the whole of NEDC, we would have been described as Luddites'.

Despite the collapse of the potentially innovative example of collaboration between the two 'peak associations', the tripartite approach to the introduction and development of new technology is still very evident in the form of Neddy. This particular tripartite forum has managed to survive stresses and strains since its formation by a Conservative Government in 1962. Its longevity suggests that there is a fairly strong predilection for attempting to process issues of 'high politics' through consultative and negotiative mechanisms.

Conclusion

We may conclude that tripartism has a mixed record. On some issues it can be surprisingly effective, even on issues which might be regarded as high politics. Thus, for example, the workings of the Manpower Services Commission could be seen as a very effective integration of peak associations in the management of a policy area of great political salience. (See Moon and Richardson 1985, pp. 94–101.) In contrast, it has proved difficult to sustain really effective group involvement—of a bipartite or tripartite form—for such divisive issues as prices and incomes policies.

This chapter has avoided making sweeping generalizations about the effectiveness of the Neddy system, because the impact seems to vary profoundly topic by topic, and policy area by policy area. Furthermore, Neddy's component bodies must operate through influence rather than command, and such influence is difficult to quantify. Along with our determination not to over-generalize on Britain, we also noted, in chapter 5, that Marin's recent account (1985) of the Austrian 'economic and social partnership' has perhaps put some question marks against the common use of Austria as the prime case of liberal corporatism (Lehmbruch and Schmitter 1982, Schmitter 1982). For example, Marin (1985, p. 110) describes the key 'Parity Commission' in Austria as follows:

although the Parity Commission has become the kernel of the most stable and central institution of the Second Republic, not only was it established as a temporary arrangement, but it continues to be highly informal. This informality is present to an extent hardly credible to outside observers: the Parity Commission has no address or fixed meeting place, no telephone number, no independent finance, no statutes, procedural rules, membership, written agreements or even registered existence . ..

The importance of Marin's chapter on Austria is that it underlines the difficulty in operationalizing corporatist theory. We are not claiming that the 'trick' of economic and social partnership is executed as successfully in Britain as in Austria. Our point is quite to the contrary, that the vital differences between Austria and Britain are masked if political investigators hamper themselves with a definition of corporatism that suggests that they look for 'a limited number of singular, compulsory, non competitive, hierarchically ordered and functionally differentiated categories' (Schmitter 1979, p. 13).

If such an image of formal order is so irrelevant for Austria, its empirical utility is questionable in British and other cases. A common assumption is that the lack of a consensual handling of macro-economic issues in Britain has caused our economic problems. But it is at least as feasible that the economic problems have been so great that they would have eroded consensual management in any political culture.

8

Ordered and Structured Consultation

Introduction

We have elsewhere suggested that there is a natural tendency for the political system in Britain to encourage the formation of stable policy communities, one of the primary purposes of which is to achieve a negotiated and stable policy environment. The underlying value is that, wherever possible, outcomes should be negotiated between policy professionals, with each participant fully aware of the needs and desires of fellow members of the policy community. This is not to suggest that there is an absence of conflict, but that conflict is, by agreement, kept within manageable bounds, if only by concentrating on issues which are susceptible to bargaining.

There is, perhaps, a recognition that some issues just cannot be managed in this way, but one of the rules of the game for the retention of insider status is that it is 'not done' to raise issues which are bound to cause bitterness and to divide the policy community. There is a recognition—as in a family—that the occupants must live together in the years ahead, and hence there is a premium on avoiding issues which will be so conflictual as to prejudice the likelihood of that continued existence.

The experience of the NEDC, discussed in the previous chapter, suggests that policy communities work best when concentrating on smaller, more manageable issues, such as ways of bringing British manufacturers and British purchasers together in an effort to encourage import substitution. As we suggested in that chapter, it is almost certainly the case that most of the 'stuff of politics' is indeed composed of such mundane issues.

Institutionalization of Compromise

Bearing this assumption in mind, it is not surprising, therefore, that institutions and processes are devised for regulating and formalizing this bargaining relationship between groups and government. Most policy sectors exhibit what we have termed 'the institutionalization and regularisation of compromise' (Jordan and Richardson 1982, p. 92). The most simple and obvious way to effect this institutionalization is, of course, to resort to committees of one kind or another. It is almost a truism to say that government runs by committee. Thus within government, inter-departmental committees are set up in order to achieve a resolution of sectoral conflict. Outside government (or more strictly on the edge of government) we have seen a proliferation of advisory committees of various kinds. For example, an official *Report on Non-departmental Public Bodies*, published in January 1980 (Cmnd. 7797), claimed that there were over 1,500 advisory bodies in British government. The report, usually referred to as the Pliatzky Review after the name of its author, noted one possible reason for the development of the system; 'the Department's own staff cannot provide the necessary advice by themselves, or that it may be desirable to enlist the participation of outside interests in order to formulate publicly acceptable proposals' (Cmnd. 7797, p. 2).

In addition to this large number of advisory bodies, the report identified a large number of executive bodies and tribunals. Pliatzky, in his review, made the point that counting was particularly difficult and arbitrary in relation to tribunals. If anything, the figures cited understate the scale. Pliatzky discusses 67 'tribunal systems', while acknowledging that there are 2,000 National Insurance Local Tribunals *alone* each year.

If we take the report's survey of various bodies within the remit of the Department of Employment as an example, we find that it listed such executive bodies as the Advisory, Conciliation, and Arbitration Service and the Health and Safety Commission. Amongst the advisory bodies it listed the Advisory Committee on the Safety of Nuclear Installations, the Race Relations Employment Advisory Group, and the Royal Commission on the Distribution of Wealth.

A high proportion of these bodies—executive, advisory, and even tribunals—are mechanisms which allow and encourage group participation. For example, in 1983 the TUC was represented on the Advisory, Conciliation, and Arbitration Service by three members, on the Commission for Racial Equality by two members, on the Equal Opportunities Commission by three members, on the Health and Safety Commission by three members, and on the

Industrial Injuries Advisory Committee by four members. The last example is an independent statutory body for advising the Secretary of State on matters relating to the industrial injuries scheme. If we take the full membership of the last body it consists of fifteen representatives drawn from the unions, employers, and the medical profession. Normally, when the TUC is granted representation on committees and executive bodies it follows also that the CBI is included too.

Appendix 8.1 lists some of the various bodies (of differing degrees of importance in policy terms) on which the CBI is represented. This lengthy list suggests that pressure group participation via what could be termed structured and formalized consultation processes is very widespread. In addition to the Manpower Services Commission, the Advisory, Conciliation, and Arbitration Service, the Health and Safety Commission, the Commission for Racial Equality, and the Equal Opportunities Commission, the CBI is represented on 104 other bodies. Some of these other bodies (such as the Anglo-German Foundation or the Department of Education and Science Further Education Unit) may not be concerned with major political issues, but others are clearly of vital importance to the interests of the CBI (and TUC) members. For example, the Health and Safety Commission Advisory Committee on Dangerous Substances or the Review Board for Government Contracts can significantly affect the trading position of firms, the safety of workers, or indeed the safety of the public. Other bodies listed have no official government status, such as The Institute of Marketing Awards Panel, but most appear to deal with issues of concern to some group or another in society and which may well involve governmental action at some stage.

Table 8.1, which lists the distribution of non-departmental public bodies by 'parent' department, shows a concentration in the legal and economic industrial field. This fits in with Olsen's argument (1983, p. 179) for Norway that integrated participation is used primarily in economic policy-making because governmental regulation is necessary in those areas, and that such regulation is more effective when there is participation. Evidence from Moren (1974) for Norway, and from Johansen and Kristensen (1982) for Denmark is compatible in showing that the environment of integrated participation is predominantly inhabited by economic/labour interests. Again writing on Norway, Christansen and

TABLE 8.1. *Non-departmental Public Bodies*

	Executive	Advisory	Tribunal	Others	Total
Ministry of Defence	6	43	—	—	49
Department of Trade and Industry	60	25	5	—	93
Department of Environment	28	23	3	—	54
Department of Education and Science	16	13	1	—	30
DHSS	12	130	8	—	150
Department of Energy	1	4	—	—	5
Home Office/Lord Chancellor's Department	13	348	13	115	489
Department of Transport	6	5	2	—	13
FCO/ODA	13	11	2	—	26
Department of Employment	41	183	4	—	228
Central Departments[a]	3	17	3	—	23
Welsh Office	16	31	4	—	51
Scottish Office/Scottish Courts Administration	75	128	5	—	208
Northern Ireland	54	46	11	6	117
MAFF	35	52	3	—	90
Miscellaneous[b]	20	7	—	—	27
	399	1,069	64	121	1,653

[a] Includes Cabinet Office, COI, Customs and Excise, Inland Revenue, and Treasury.
[b] Includes OFTEL, Office of Arts, and Libraries.
Source: Public Bodies 1985, p. 8.

Egeberg (1979, p. 250) have claimed that the bias towards economic interests follows from the nature of subjects suitable for the committee form of participation. They claim that the operating style of committees can be characterized by 'compromise, emphasising mutual adjustment rather than confrontation . . . Certain types of problems, such as economic ones, are better suited for compromise than others. In moral–religious issues, for example, it is difficult to come to terms.' (See also Butski and Johansen (1979, p. 220) for data from Denmark confirming that functional interest groups are more active in these areas than promotional groups.)

Yet an examination of, say, the list of advisory bodies under the control of the Home Office reveals that some very important social issues are 'processed' through the advisory committee system. For example, there is an Advisory Council on the Misuse of Drugs, an

Advisory Committee on Animal Experiments, and a Race Relations Research Advisory Committee. All these provide for group representation. Through regularized participation in these structures, groups are able to shape the definition and perception of problems, influence the political agenda in those policy areas of direct concern to them, and influence the perception and emergence of 'practicable' solutions. Indeed, practicality will often be defined by policy-makers (either civil servants or ministers) as what the groups represented in the relevant advisory committee or executive body will 'stand'. The right time for a government to act on a particular problem or issue is often when the appropriate advisory committee has come to a collective agreement that there is a problem to be solved, and to a broad consensus on what should be done.

Such committees are set up because governments generally accepts that without group participation the implementation of policies is difficult. This is especially true in highly technical and complex areas, where government is itself at its weakest in terms of expertise. For example, policy development in the field of the research and development of a fifth-generation computer industry has followed a fairly conventional pattern, whereby the policy community tried to produce a climate of opinion conducive to governmental intervention. Thus in 1982 the National Economic Development Council pressed the Government to establish a more long-term policy for the information technology industry. A committee (the Alvey Committee, named after its chairman Ian Alvey) was set up with representatives from industry and academia. The committee recommended the establishment of government funding of research in industry (90 per cent subsidy was suggested by Alvey). The outcome was similar to that suggested by the committee, but with lower funding (50 per cent) (see Moon *et al.* 1986).

The implementation of the scheme is also heavily influenced by the participation of secondees from the major companies (such as GEC and Plessey) into what has become the Alvey Directorate, so much so that the programme has been criticized for favouring the large firms at the expense of smaller and possibly more innovative firms. Some important issues—such as the question of industrial property rights for those participating in the Alvey scheme—were resolved by reference to groups such as the Institution of Electrical Engineers and the Computer Services Society. Indeed, these two organizations jointly publish the directorate's official newsletter, *Alvey News* (Moon *et al.* 1986).

The pattern of group involvement in determining the shape of this important industrial policy area was continued into the next phase of the Alvey programme when, in early 1986, a new committee was set up—again drawn from the information technology industry and academia—to examine what should follow the then current Alvey programme. The committee had a wide remit, namely

the scope, balance and development of U.K. national and European collaborative research programmes in information technology, following the Alvey, Esprit 1 programmes, and the exploitation of the advanced technology stemming from programmes like Alvey and Esprit. It will pay particular attention to the needs of users of information technology and to markets that the new technology will open up. (*British Business*, 14 February 1986.)

In this case we see the main interests—the computer and IT industry—playing a central, if not dominant role in determining the shape and content of a programme of vital interest to the future of the UK.

Committees like Alvey and its successor are relatively low-profile, except for those in the industries directly concerned. Other committees—particularly Royal Commissions and the like—play a much more visible role in the policy process, though arguably they exercise less influence and have declined in usage over the last decade or so. Royal Commissions have never been that common (for example, Chapman 1973, lists only twenty-five Royal Commissions between 1945 and 1973). Royal Commissions are, however, poorly distinguished in terms of function from departmental advisory committees such as the Plowden Committee on Primary Education, which reported in 1967. Chapman (1973, p. 185) notes that 'there is a great deal of the representative element to be found in the work of commissions . . . the members are often selected on the basis of representativeness . . .'. He also emphasizes that commissions are an example of the democratic element in government. An example of this 'democratic element' was the Central Advisory Water Committee (see below), which reported in 1971. The committee consisted of members who were invited to serve in their individual capacities rather than as representatives.

Yet correspondence between the committee secretary and interested groups mentioned the need to provide 'balanced representation of many diverse interests without making the committee unwieldly' (Jordan and Richardson 1977, p. 48).

We would also emphasize that the shift during the twentieth century—and particularly since the Second World War—has been towards a much closer integration of groups in the implementation process. As Hood (1982, p. 44) suggests, much of the growth of government has not been in central government departments, but on what he calls 'indirect government'. He noted that the evidence does not really support the popular view that central bureaucracies have expanded in Britain, but suggests that there has been a growth in the number of 'fringe bodies' in recent decades. Thus he quotes Bowen's study, conducted for the Civil Service Department in 1978, and the Official Directory of Paid Public Appointments Made by Ministers (CSD 1978), which suggests that 60 per cent of the fringe bodies listed in both sources have been created in the last two decades (Hood 1982, p. 48). Deaths of such bodies appear to be infrequent, suggesting that the high percentage of new bodies is an addition to the network of bodies, rather than a process of replacement. Hood cites three policy areas (over the period 1964–5 to 1977–8). As his table demonstrates, there was a remarkable increase in the trade, industry, and employment policy area. The type of body which has been set up seems to vary from policy area to policy area. Thus in agriculture the growth has been in new research and international bodies, but in law and order the growth has been in regulatory or quasi-judicial bodies, such as the Gaming

TABLE 8.2. *Governmental Organizations Referred to in Estimates 1964–5 and 1977–8 for three Policy Areas*

Policy area	Number of organizations		Increase (%)
	1964–5	1977–8	
Agriculture, fisheries, and forestry	57	74	29.8
Law and order	21	28	33.3
Trade, industry, and employment	45	93	106.6

Source: Hood 1982, p. 49.

Board and the Commission for Racial Equality (Hood 1982, p. 49).

The arrival of a new Conservative Government in 1979 brought a new determination to reduce the number of these bodies. For example, the Pliatzty Review, cited earlier, suggests that 211 advisory bodies could be abolished. As some were due to terminate their work naturally, this figure must be regarded as much lower than Mrs Thatcher intended when initiating the review.

The Management and Personnel Office, within the Cabinet Office, produces an annual listing of non-departmental public bodies (see *Public Bodies* 1985). This shows that the 'quangocide' under the Thatcher Government has been less dramatic than is sometimes suggested (see Table 8.3).

TABLE 8.3. *Reduction in Non-departmental Public Bodies 1969–85 (Categories as used in Pliatzky Report)*

	Executive	Advisory	Tribunal	Others	Total number	Government funding (£m.)
1979	492	1,485	70	120	2,167	2,970
1982	450	1,173	364	123	1,810	3,910
1983	437	1,074	165	121	1,697	5,120
1984	402	1,087	71	121	1,681	5,160
1985	399	1,069	164	121	1,653	5,100

Source: *Public Bodies* 1985.

Some of the apparent reductions in the numbers of those non-departmental public bodies stem from redefinition of the categories. For example, the ten Regional Water Authorities were dropped from the executive category in 1984, as they were reclassified as nationalized industries.

We should not underestimate the value to groups of participating in some of these arrangements. For example, Graham Wilson (1984, p. 6) notes that employer participation in the Health and Safety Commission gives them great power over the work of the commission. He notes that

The British process for the creation of regulation had built into it by law a substantial power for employers to block new regulations: at least one-third (and in practice three out of eight) members of the HSC were to be nominated by the CBI. In practice, *employers were given a veto over new regulations, for the unions and local authority members of the HSC agreed that no regulation would be approved by a majority vote: all decisions of the HSC would be unanimous.* (Our emphasis.)

The power granted to employers, over an issue of such importance to trade unionists, is seen by Wilson (1984, p. 7) as an indication of the trust which has developed between the unions and the employers through their work on the HSC. This is a good illustration of one of the main themes of this book, that the 'relevant groups from policy communities do develop a sense of corporate identity and unity, even in the context of issues which are potentially conflictual.

Interestingly, the origin of health and safety legislation in the UK is also related to an exercise in structured and organized consultation. The Health and Safety at Work Act 1974 was in large part based upon the report of a committee on Safety and Health at Work headed by Lord Robens (Cmnd. 5034, 1972). The committee received 183 written submissions, including evidence from 23 government departments and similar bodies and from 119 'other organizations'. The 'other organizations' included the TUC, CBI, NUT, the Royal Society for the Prevention of Accidents, NALGO, the National Federation of Building Trades Employers, the Food Manufacturers' Association, and the Institute of Safety Officers. Wilson (1984, p. 10) suggests that the Robens Report 'constituted a point around which consensus built'.

The USA found much greater difficulty in achieving a workable consensus in the same policy area, in part because of the fragmentation of groups in the United States. Thus Wilson (1984, p. 17) argues that

an important consequence of the divisions and limited status of umbrella groups in the USA is that policy makers cannot entrust them with the responsibility for policy in the same way that policy makers could effectively hand safety and health policy over to the CBI and TUC. Even worse, policymakers found it impossible to find umbrella groups with sufficient authority to negotiate a settlement on behalf of employers and unions as to what safety and health policy should be.

British groups, he argues, were sufficiently cohesive, in contrast to those in the USA, for them to represent a resource rather than a problem to policy-makers.

The notion that groups can be a resource for policy-makers helps to explain the predilection for devising methods of structuring group participation. The incorporation of environmental groups in aspects of the physical planning process is a good example of the practical value of this notion. Local environmental groups have been granted an important role in the designation of conservation areas and in the construction of local physical plans, such that 'over time, as they gain political legitimacy and their arguments become more acceptable, councillors and officials may come to regard them less as *ad hoc* protest groups and more as permanent pressure groups within the planning system' (Lowe and Goyder 1983, p. 98). Typically, therefore, these groups will have achieved formalized participation in the decision-making process, as well as the opportunity to influence decisions via informal contacts. In this particular case, the groups may have been granted formal participation rights (such as Conservation Area Advisory Committees) because planners had to find ways of 'managing' the growth in environmental concern which developed in the 1970s. Yet, for whatever reason that access was granted, the groups appear to have acquired both status and influence in the specialized field.

Another, and more recent, example of structured participation is in the field of anti-unemployment policy. In that case, policy-makers have not so much been *pushed and pressured* into setting up formal structures for group participation, but have been enthusiastic to involve the groups in devising and implementing solutions to problems which national and local governments feel incapable of handling. Typical of this view is a speech delivered by Mr Michael Heseltine when he was Secretary of State for the Environment. In 1981, speaking to the Institute of Directors, he urged 'the mobilisation of all available national resources to revitalise our society, which in parts of the inner-cities is disintegrating'. He rejected the notion that government alone could provide the solutions. Thus he argued 'we [government] cannot . . . we do not have the money. We do not have the expertise. We need the private sector again to play a role which, in Britain, it played more conspicuously a century ago, than it does today.' (Quoted in Richardson 1983, p. 1.)

A number of specific institutional innovations followed from Mr Heseltine's desire to incorporate business groups formally. For example, in Merseyside a special Task Force was set up to which a team of local businessmen was seconded. At the national level, he set up, in September 1981, a team of twenty-eight managers, seconded from the clearing banks, building societies, pension funds, and insurance companies, to develop ways of securing urban regeneration. The Financial Institutions Group (FIG), as it was known, became an important element in the Government's urban policy, the whole principle of which has been to combine public and private resources in order to tackle the urban problem. Thus, though the present Government has sought to reduce the number of fringe bodies and quangos, it has not been reluctant to foster the growth of bodies which are not too dissimilar in the sense that they bring about a union of state and private interests in regularized, structural arrangements.

In practice, the same issues which gave rise to the quango phenomenon are now being handled by new instruments of public–private partnership. Concepts such as 'leverage' and 'pump-priming' appear to have become the ideologically acceptable form of public–private interdependency in meeting societal policy objectives (Richardson et al. 1986).

The most common institutional expression of this 'new' philosophy in the anti-unemployment field is seen in the flourishing local enterprise trust/agency movement fostered by such groups as the CBI Special Programmes Unit and Business in the Community (both merged in 1985). There are now well over 200 enterprise trusts or agencies in Britain, bringing together business interests, trade unionists, local authorities, and other groups to formulate and implement local plans for dealing with the unemployment crisis. Enterprise agencies might be seen as one of the new institutions of self-regulation suggested by Kemper et al. (1974) as a consensus-based structure for bringing together public and private sectors and applying their resources in the common project of managing social change and preserving stability. Whilst the Conservatives might have seen the involvement of groups in the unemployment issue as a means of 'hiving-off' the problem, it has certainly not been a means of privatizing it. In practice, the enterprise trusts are heavily dependent on access to various forms of public funding. In so far as a new partnership has developed in response to unemployment, therefore, it has brought government and groups closer together in formalized arrangements, rather than achieving a distancing of public and private.

Formalized arrangements appear in most sectors—for example, the Farm Animal Welfare Council (FAWC). When the Conservative Government constituted this body in 1979, the Council of the RSPCA refused to allow two of their executive staff members, who had been nominated by the minister, to serve. This radical policy of non-incorporation started a bitter dispute within the RSPCA. Of course a phenomenon of that field is the proliferation of groups, most of which like Animal Aid, the Hunt Saboteurs Association, and Co-ordinating Animal Welfare attempt legal direct action, while others such as the Animal Liberation Front have been involved in illegal protest. Formal participation opportunities will never incorporate all kinds and degrees of political opposition.

We would argue that there is an inherent logic to the process by which governments incorporate groups in structural arrangements for consultation, bargaining, and negotiation (Jordan and Richardson 1982, p. 81). This is because the *range* of issues in which government is more or less involved is so wide and often so detailed that relationships within groups have to be developed over time and in such a way as to withstand disagreements and changes of governments. The interpenetration of group and government is illustrated by a summary of the CBI's lobbying activity in 1984, presented in Table 8.4 (at the end of this chapter). It is worth noting that such a list excludes the daily contact between officers of the CBI and civil servants in a range of departments. Olsen (1983, p. 175) has claimed that 'peak associations', such as the CBI, find informal participation easier than formal because the latter means that the organization has to make its priorities explicit in a manner which can cause intra-organizational conflict.

Appendix 8.2 indicates that comments such as that quoted in chapter 7 about 'the rejection, by the British government, of established forms of consultation with trade unions and other groups' are not compatible with the considerable scale of TUC involvement in institutionalized relationships. The appendix lists TUC participation in over sixty public bodies. (That the figure is lower than for the CBI does not reflect insignificant difference in scale, but a more restrictive definition of 'public'.)

It is difficult to overemphasize the importance of regularized and institutionalized arrangements for the kind of relationship between group and state which Table 8.2 illustrates. Neither is the phenomenon peculiar to Britain (see below). We would not, however, wish to imply that the policy process always works so smoothly and that groups are always so effectively 'incorporated'. There are occasions when governments appear deliberately to avoid group integration in formal structures, especially when radical policy change is being envisaged. Thus formalized group participation in consultations and negotiation is extremely common, but not obligatory. Governments have a choice on whether to institutionalize and formalize group participation, just as groups have a choice in whether to seek insider status or to stay free to oppose in whatever manner they see fit.

A good example of a potentially radical reform being introduced in a manner quite deliberately designed to *exclude* groups was the Technical and Vocational Education Initiative (TVEI) introduced in 1985. The devisers of TVEI were determined to act quickly and wanted to avoid having their radical ideas smothered in a consultative morass, or at least amended out of all recognition (Moon and Richardson 1984, p. 25). For example, the Manpower Services Commission Chairman, Lord Young (who subsequently became Secretary of State for Employment) commented that 'Supposing we had decided to launch a debate about technical education, or the lack of it. We might have had a Royal Commission and it might have taken five years or even ten, to get off the ground. Now we have a pilot project due to start by September next year.' (*The Times*, 22 November 1982.) In practice little or no consultation took place (even for cosmetic reasons) prior to the decision to introduce TVEI. It was only *after* the decision that interested groups were incorporated in the policy process. It was then that a new committee was set up, the National Steering Group, which included all relevant interests.

The Finniston Report On Engineering

The TVEI case cited above illustrated that governments can get away without consultation—either formal or informal—under certain circumstances. Yet it also illustrated the need for governments—eventually—to seek to return the groups to the consultation process, in that case at the implementation stage. In the case of the attempted reform of the engineering professions in 1980, we see government running into serious difficulties in trying to formulate policy without the current and active support of the key groups involved, the professional engineering institutions. The report of the Committee of Inquiry into the Engineering Profession, chaired by Sir Monty Finniston, *Engineering Our Future*, was interesting because it proposed a radical change in the way in which the engineering profession was organized and regulated. In essence, Sir Monty wanted to achieve a big reduction in the power and influence of the institutions. The outcome was quite different to that envisaged in the report: not only did the institutions play a quite crucial role in the subsequent negotiations over what policy change should actually take place, but they also secured for themselves a continuation of their key position in determining the organization and development of the engineering professions.

The Finniston Report can be traced to a feeling that Britain's economic decline was somehow related to a failure in the manufacturing sector, coupled with a view that the 'solution' lay in improving both the quality and standing of the engineering profession through such measures as graduate entry, accrediting only acceptable degrees, or compulsory (statutory) registration of professional engineers. In particular, certain civil servants were keen to see changes in the way that the engineering profession was run, and were keen to widen the range of participation in the search for possible solutions. For example, they wanted industrialists to play a more prominent role as a balance to the influence of the professional institutions.

Notwithstanding the determination of the institutions to preserve their existing position, the Government went ahead and appointed the Finniston Committee, in December 1977. The committee was quite consciously *not* a 'representative committee'. This was a strategically important decision. On the one hand it could be argued that, as the professional institutions had failed to put their own house in order in the past it would be pointless to grant them representation on a committee that was intended to bring about reform. On the other hand, to exclude those interests risked exposing the committee's findings to the charge that they were ill-founded and that the judgements lacked experience and expertise. In the event, the latter proved to be much nearer to the reality of the post-Finniston negotiations.

Predictably, Finniston produced proposals which in essence attempted to displace the institutions from a central policy role, to leave them with only learned society functions. There followed a lengthy and extremely hard-fought campaign. A particular issue was whether any new body which might be created to oversee the profession should be a statutory body or a body based upon a Royal Charter. Finniston was heavily committed to a statutory body and the institutions were equally strongly opposed to it. The Engineering Council which subsequently emerged, in 1982, was a non-statutory body created by Royal Charter. Yet, having won their major victory, the institutions continued to fight on detailed points, securing many vital concessions in the post-Finniston negotiations. The success of the engineering institutions in arriving at an Engineering Council that they could accept can, in the main, be ascribed to the fact that the ministers were reluctant to impose sanctions against a united front. In the end, the interests of the established institutions were much easier to mobilize than those in favour of radical change.

Two contrasting views of the process which followed the publication of the Finniston Report and the setting up of the Engineering Council illustrate the dilemma of governments when facing the problem of securing significant or radical changes. The view expressed in *The Times* (31 July 1981) suggested that bargaining with pressure groups had resulted in a sell-out of the original reformist ideals. *The Times* argued that the Government's response

has confirmed precisely the complacency and institutional jockeying which the report had set out to break . . . Instead of treating the [Finniston] report on its merits the Government set out to find a consensus among the very bodies and opinions which the report sought to supersede. The result is a soggy set of compromises of the sort that always emerges from such exercises.

The best refutation to this line of argument (that virtuous reform had been betrayed) was perhaps given by Lord Caldecote, on behalf of the engineering institutions, in a subsequent letter to *The Times* (10 August 1981):

It would have been quite useless to set up a new Council . . . without the support of the majority of engineers . . . It was therefore well worth spending much time and effort to reach a workable consensus so that the new Council can be set up . . . with wide support from the engineering profession, employers and the academic world.

Lord Caldecote's view was, in essence, that it was a mistake not to set up a representative committee in the first place. To attempt change without the groups was bound to lead to further trouble and likely to result in failure. In any case, the groups had to be involved in the post-Finniston negotiations. As in the TVEI case eventually, the groups cannot be wished away.

The Finniston exercise again demonstrates that the formal integration of groups may be large-scale but that the numbers included in the several cycles of consultation (for example 764 written submissions to the Finniston Committee, 680 replies to the Department of Industry questionnaire to interested parties on the Finniston conclusions) were misleading in the sense that only a small number of the consulted had an *effective* voice. Furthermore, about a dozen drafts of the highly contentious charter for the Engineering Council were circulated. Some of these drafts were widely available, but others went out only to key groups, with the specific request that the consultation be kept private. At least twenty-seven minuted meetings between the Department of Industry and various groupings from the engineering institutions took place in the period between August 1980 and July 1981, and a much larger, but unrecorded number of informal meetings between officials took place. This episode demonstrates that influence from groups is certainly not restricted to membership of, or evidence to, formal advisory bodies, or in response to consultation invitations.

Our studies of the papers of the Finniston Committee on the reorganization of the engineering profession, and of the Central Advisory Water Committee (CAWC) on the water industry in England and Wales in 1969–70, show that outside committees are not always a means of securing outside knowledge for the department, but they are sometimes a forum in which the department's own preliminary ideas for policy change can be sounded out with the interested parties whose co-operation would be needed in the implementation of any policy change. Thus we concluded that in the CAWC exercise, the ministry was not looking for the CAWC to identify an emerging problem or to fill the exploratory role claimed in the committee's terms of reference. These tasks had already been fulfilled within the Ministry. Instead, the CAWC was a *consultative* committee conveying reactions to the ministry to its ideas for reform; the CAWC's own investigations unearthed (or at least demonstrated) more about *attitudes* to change than about the *necessity* for change itself. There was an acceptance not only that groups can legitimately complain about changes that disrupt the relationships that they have established within the existing policy framework, but that they should play a part in the decision. Certainly the department reserved the right to take the final decision, but it was to the interests on the CAWC that the department felt it had to justify itself. The intensive discussions between the department and interested groups was in great contrast to the banal scrutiny by Parliament.

A European Style?

We have argued that what J. P. Olsen (in discussing Norway) termed 'integrated participation' is a common feature of British policy-making. Yet Olsen sees Scandinavian democracies as achieving *more* integrated participation than even the UK, and much more than the USA. For example, in Norway there are approximately 400 governmental committees with group representation by 2,000 representatives (Olsen 1983, p. 166). Olsen notes that group participation prevails in crisis situations more than in others, during wars, depressions, or other national crises, as well as during crises in specific sectors of society. This is because crises emphasize the mutual interdependence of groups and government. (The increasing integration of groups in the formulation and implementation of anti-unemployment measures in the UK is a good example of this.)

Olsen (1983, p. 170) also notes that certain *types* of group dominate the structures of integrated participation. Thus he argues that large, powerful employers' associations and labour unions, together with the organizations in agriculture and the associations of the various professions, dominate these structures. This phenomenon, he believes, is common in the old Western societies. The Norwegian data are in fact rather similar to the British data on the CBI cited earlier in this chapter. In the Norwegian case, the Norwegian Confederation of Industries is represented on approximately 100 committees, compared with our own estimate of approximately 109 for the CBI. In summary, he concludes that the following factors make integrated participation more likely:

pragmatism, incrementalism, acceptance of the status quo, control by leaders, bureaucratization, professionalization of leadership, de-emphasis of activities by members, stable memberships, and of course, a lack of opposition to participation. Consequently, integrated participation appeals to organisations which are relatively centralised, with full-time, elected leaders and staffs of professionals or experts. These organisations have stable memberships of people who are not very active. Integrated participation also attracts peak organisations rather than organisations of individuals. These have significant socioeconomic leverage, affluent treasuries, and strong bureaucratic staffs. Their actual members include high proportions of their potential members.

Kvavik's (1976, p. 11) study of Norway also provides considerable detail of the incorporation of groups. He argued that few political systems are distinguished by as elaborate and active a network of interest groups, and few polities have an interest group system as pervasive and highly formalized (institutionalized). He found that groups had only limited contacts with parties and legislators, but that they were active in 'the administration's advising, managemental or policy-making commissions'.

In Sweden, Bjurulf and Swahn (1980, p. 96) have documented the significant increase in the number of bodies who are involved in their 'remiss' consultative processes, whereby the Government seeks responses from interested groups for legislative proposals. They argue that 'The sharp increase in the number of bodies to which commission reports are remitted reflects the widened spectrum of interests involved . . .' (Bjurulf and Swahn 1980, pp. 78–9). Moreover, interest groups (and the bureaucracy) have secured an increasing level of representation on the commissions themselves.

Even in France, where groups are often said to be weaker than their other Western European counterparts, there is frequently a significant degree of integrated participation. Thus Coppock (1984, p. 23), giving a US perspective on the French approach to the regulation of chemical hazards, remarks that 'what appears highly suspect in the United States because of susceptibility to undue influence is viewed in France as the unavoidable integration of relevant interests in the formulation of results'. In drawing comparisons between the United States and Western Europe, he points out that the Europeans legitimate public policy 'through a process of consultation and negotiation involving some sort of representation of the most important groups'. Pross (1986) quotes Andre Holleaux's work on French interest groups, which notes that

TABLE 8.4   *CBI–Governmental Relations in 1984*

Major Policy Statements and ministerial meetings	*Major events and submissions*
JANUARY	
Response to Draft Directive on parental leave and leave for family reasons 1984 Budget representations—Chancellor and other ministers CBI Wales meeting with Secretaries of State for Transport and Wales on Severn crossing	Response to ACARD report on advance manufacturing technology Response to White Paper *Streamlining the Cities*
FEBRUARY	
Response to Government consultative document on Draft Vredeling and Fifth Directives Secretary of State for Energy addresses CBI Council Smaller Firms Minister visits Smaller Firms Council Minister of State (DoE) at Rates Conference	Oral evidence to government inquiry on personal portable pensions Memorandum to ACARD on instrument technology Oral evidence to House of Lords Environment Subcommittee on EC air pollution policy
MARCH	
Under-Secretary of State at DoE on Rates Bill	Oral evidence to House of Commons on deficit in manufacturing with Europe Oral evidence to Treasury and Civil Service Committee of House of Commons Submission to DoE on consultative document on standardisation of local authority accounts
APRIL	
	Representations on regulations to control hazardous substances Meeting with UK Members of European Parliament's Environmental Committee Reponse to government White Paper on revised framework of insolvency law

TABLE 8.4   *CBI–Governmental Relations in 1984 continued*

Major Policy Statements and ministerial meetings	Major events and submissions
MAY	
Minister of State at Department of Employment on dock work	Representations on electricity regulations
Minister of State at Department of Environment on Rates Bill	Response to consultative document on greater security for the rights and expectations of members of occupational pension schemes
Matthews Committee recommendations to ECGD endorsed by Council	
	Response to White Paper on regional industrial development
JUNE	
President meets Secretary of State for the Environment on *Streamlining the Cities*	Response to revised EC draft directive on temporary workers
Under-Secretary of State at DoE on acid rain and the North Sea	CBI participation on DTI-led Pacific Basin Quality Mission
CBI paper on London Summit to Foreign Secretary	Oral evidence to House of Commons Environment Committee on acid rain
Minister of Trade on ECGD	
Under-Secretary of State for Industry on accuracy and use of statistics	Director-general addresses House of Lords Industrial Study Group
JULY	
Minister of State at Department of Transport on London lorry ban	Meeting with Labour Party Environment Committee
Minister of State at Treasury on VAT on imports	Response to consultative document on early leavers from pension schemes
Minister of State at Department of Environment on GLC/MCC abolition	Oral evidence to Government's special inquiry into pension provision
AUGUST	
	Evidence to House of Lords Subcommittee on draft EC directive on parental leave and leave for family reasons

Major Policy Statements and ministerial meetings	*Major events and submissions*
	Submission on DoE draft code on local authority/business rates consultation

SEPTEMBER

	Response to draft EC recommendation on positive action for women
	Paper on CBI work for multinationals approved by Council

OCTOBER

Minister for Local Government on GLC/MCC abolition	Acid rain presentation to MEPs
Minister for Industry on regional policy	Submission on modified Government proposals for changes in insolvency law

NOVEMBER

Response to Government consultative document on personal pensions	Oral evidence to House of Lords Select Committee on Overseas Trade
	Response to DTI's Metrology Review Committee
	Response to Government White Paper on the safety of goods

DECEMBER

Response to Government exercise on deregulation	Evidence to House of Commons Trade and Industry Committee on operation of ECGD
Chancellor of the Exchequer and Treasury Ministers on 1985 Budget representations	Meeting with Inland Revenue on technical budget representations
Energy Minister attends Energy Policy Committee	
Smaller Firms Minister visits Smaller Firms Council	
Lord Cockfield, Commissioner for internal market	
Minister for Industry on Regional Policy	

Source: adapted from *CBI Annual Report* 1984, pp. 6–7.

senior officials in France now see fewer and fewer individuals in the course of their working day, but rather meet delegations who are representing groups.

As we have discussed in other chapters, Heisler and Kvavik (1974, p. 57) see this regularized access as one of the central features of their 'European polity' model. They see the pattern of group access as regularized, taking a structural form, and essentially a system of co-opting. Furthermore, the act of co-opting binds the participants to the system by giving them a vested interest in the continued operation of the structure. Structured co-option becomes even more important as the numbers of participating groups expand, an expansion which has gone so far that 'most groups have already been co-opted—virtually without regard to their supportive or opposing orientations to the regime or its norms'. We would agree with Heisler and Kvavik that there is a European tradition of structured and integrated participation by groups, and that Britain is very much part of this tradition.

The dominant style of group integration is, of course, not the experience of every type of group or even of influential groups on every issue. Elsewhere (Jordan and Richardson 1982) we have identified a number of ways in which groups can participate in policy-making, *and* ways in which policies can be made independently of groups. Rhodes (1985) has argued that it is necessary to extend such a list. Ripley and Franklin (1984 edn.) also make an attempt to discuss different types of policy-making process in different issue areas. Such aspirations to more sophistication must be encouraged, but in recognizing their value we do not think that they detract from the validity of the broad pattern we offer here.

Appendix 8.1.
CBI Representation of Public Bodies 1984

1. *Major 'tripartite' bodies and functions*

National Economic Development Council The NEDC was established in 1962 to provide a tripartite forum for discussion seeking agreement on ways to improve economic performance and remove obstacles to growth.

The council is normally chaired by the Chancellor of the Exchequer and includes employer representatives chosen after consultation with the CBI, union members, and main government ministers, and several independent members.

Advisory, Conciliation and Arbitration Service The Advisory, Conciliation, and Arbitration Service (ACAS) was set up under the Employment Protection Act 1975. Its function is to promote and assist the voluntary improvement of workplace industrial relations, and to provide advice and conciliation, mediation, and arbitration services to employers, trade unions, and employees.

The service is directed by a council consisting of an independent chairman, three employed members appointed after consultation with the CBI, three trade unionists, and three independents.

Manpower Services Commission The Manpower Services Commission (MSC) was set up under the Employment and Training Act 1973 to run the public employment and training services. The commission, which is separate from government but accountable to the Secretary of State for Employment (and, in respect of its operations in Scotland and Wales, to the Secretaries of State for Scotland and Wales) has ten members who serve for a term of three years: a chairman, three members appointed after consultation with the TUC, three after consultation with the CBI, two after consultation with local authority associations, and one with professional education interests.

Health and Safety Commission The Health and Safety Commission was set up under the Health and Safety at Work Act 1974. Its function is to administer the Act in relation to the health, safety, and welfare of persons at work. It oversees the work of the Health and Safety Executive. The commission consists of a chairman and not more than nine other members, three of whom are employer members appointed after consultation with the CBI.

Commission for Racial Equality The Commission for Racial Equality was set up under the Race Relations Act 1976. Its functions are to work towards the elimination of discrimination, to promote equality of opportunity and good relations between persons of different racial groups, and to keep under review the working of the Act.

The commission has up to fifteen members, two of whom are appointed after consultation with the CBI.

Equal Opportunities Commission The Equal Opportunities Commission was set up under the Sex Discrimination Act 1975 to work towards the elimination of discrimination, to promote equality of opportunity between men and women, and to keep under review the working of the Sex Discrimination Act and the Equal Pay Act 1970. The commission has up to fifteen members, three of whom are appointed after consultation with the CBI.

2. Other Organizations

British Executive Services Overseas; British Export Trade Research Organisation; British Invisible Exports Council; British Overseas Trade Board; BOTB Area Advisory Groups (Australia and New Zealand Trade Advisory Committee; Committee for Middle East Trade; Tropical Africa Advisory Group; British and South Asian Trade Association; Hong Kong Trade Advisory Group; Korea Trade Advisory Group; Japan Trade Advisory Group; South East Asia Trade Advisory Group; British Overseas Trade Group for Israel; European Trade Committee; East European Trade Council; Sino-British Trade Council; Latin American Trade Advisory Group; North American Advisory Group; United Kingdom–South Africa Trade Association; West Indies Trade Advisory Group); British Quality Association Awards Panel; Business and Industry Advisory Committee to OECD; Business and Technical Education Council; British Standards Institution Executive Board; British Standards Institution, National Accreditation Council; British Standards Institution, Quality Assurance Council; Central Fire Liaison Panel; Central School of Art & Design; City–EEC Committee; Council of British Chambers of Commerce on Continental Europe; Council for Environmental Conservation; Council for Environmental Education; Council for the Securities Industry; DE Advisory Committee on Women's Employment; DE Disused Mineshafts Working Group; DE Joint Committee on Special Wastes; DE Race Relations Employment Advisory Group; DE Technical Advisory Committee on Dangerous Substances; DE Tripartite Steering Group on Job Satisfaction; DE Waste Management Working Group; DES Further Education Unit; DTI Industry/Education Advisory Committee; DTI Standing Advisory Committee on Patents; DTI Standing Advisory Committee on Trade Marks; EEC Advisory Committee on the European Social Fund; EEC Advisory Committee on the Free Movement of Workers; EEC Advisory Committee for Safety Hygiene & Health Protection at Work; EEC Advisory Committee on Social Security for Migrant Workers; EEC Advisory Committee on Vocational Training; EEC Group of Business Survey Experts; Export Credit Insurance (Comprehensive Guarantees Group); Export Information Steering Group; Fire Protection Association Council; Franco-British Council; Genetic Manipulation Advisory Group; Home Office Advisory Committee on Race Relations; Home Office/CBI/TUC Committee on Prison Industries; Home Office Standing Advisory Committee on Crime Prevention; HSC Advisory Committee on Dangerous Pathogens; HSC Advisory Committee on Dangerous Substances; HSC Advisory Committee on Genetic Engineering; HSC Advisory Committee on Toxic Substances; HSC Medical Advisory Committee; HSE Working Party on Dangerous Preparations; ICC Environmental Committee; Industrial Injuries Advisory Council; Institute for Marketing National Awards

Panel; Institution of Production Engineers Metrication/Standards Committee; International Chamber of Commerce United Kingdom; International Labour Organisation Governing Body; International Organisation of Employers; Joint Customs Consultative Committee; Keep Britain Tidy Group; Motability; MSC Advisory Committee on the Resettlement of Ex-regulars; MSC Advisory Group on Content and Standards of the Youth Training Scheme; MSC Special Employment Measures Advisory Committee; MSC Steering Group for the Technical Vocational Education Initiative; MSC Youth Training Board; MoD Advisory Committee on the Territorial, Auxiliary, and Voluntary Reserves; National Advisory Board for Local Government; National Advisory Council on the Employment of Disabled People; National Dock Labour Board; NEDO Advanced Manufacturing Systems Group; NEDC/NEDO Task Force on Standards and Quality; Occupational Pensions Board; Panel of Takeovers and Mergers; Post Office Users' National Council; Production Statistics Advisory Committee; Retail Prices Index Advisory Committee; Review Board for Government Contracts; Royal Society for the Prevention of Accidents; Schools Curriculum Development Committee; Social Security Advisory Committee; St John Ambulance Association Committee; SSRC Industrial Relations Research Unit Advisory Committee; Union of European Community Industry (UNICE) Council of Presidents; Watt Committee Sub-group on Acid Rain Remedial Strategies.

Source: amended from CBI *Annual Report* 1984, pp. 20–2.

Appendix 8.2.   TUC Representation on Government Committees and Outside Bodies 1986

The TUC is represented on the six major tripartite bodies listed in Appendix 8.1. The full list of outside representation, as provided by the TUC in June 1986, is reproduced below.

Advisory, Conciliation, and Arbitration Service
BBC Board of Governors
BBC Group on Industrial and Business Affairs
BBC General Advisory Council
Broadcasting Complaints Commission
British Overseas Trade Board
Production Statistics Advisory Committee
Commission for Racial Equality
Home Office Race Relations Advisory Committee
Department of Employment Race Relations Advisory Committee

Crime Prevention: Home Office Standing Committee
  Mobile Property Subcommittee
  Static Property Subcommittee
National Advisory Council on the Employment of the Disabled
Remploy Limited
Distribution Statistics Advisory Committee
Distributive Industry Training Trust
Offshore Industry Liaison Committee
Equal Opportunities Commission
Food Hygiene Advisory Council
Health Education Council
Health and Safety Commission
Health and Safety Commission: Hazard Advisory Committees
  Toxic Substances
  Dangerous Substances
  Medical
  Nuclear Installations
  Advisory Committee of Dangerous Pathogens
Advisory Committee on Genetic Manipulation
Independent Broadcasting Authority
Industrial Injuries Advisory Council
Lord Chancellor's Legal Aid Advisory Committee
Manpower Services Commission
  Youth Training Board
  Special Employment Measures Advisory Group
  Community Industry: Council of Management
  Employment Relations Limited Advisory Panel
Consumer Steering Committee
Monopolies and Mergers Commission
National Economic Development Council
National Electronics Council
National Gas Consumers' Council
Occupational Pensions Board
Patents Advisory Committee
Prison Injuries Joint Consultative Committee
Retail Prices Index Advisory Committee
National Radiological Protection Board
Social Security Advisory Committee
Territorial Army Advisory Committee
Radioactive Waste Management Advisory Committee
Sea Fish Industry Authority
Women's Employment Advisory Committee (Department of Employment)
Women's National Commission

Educational Bodies

Advisory Council to the British Library Board
British Association for Commercial and Industrial Education
BBC Further Education Advisory Council
City and Guilds of London Institute: Council
Further Education Staff College Governors
Further Education Curriculum Review and Development Unit
Local Government Training Board: Careers Services Training Committee
National Examinations Board in Supervisory Studies
Open University: Delegacy for Continuing Education
Royal College of Art: Court
Ruskin College Governors
Community Projects Foundation: Trustees
National Institute of Adult and Continuing Education
Department of Industry; Industry/Education Unit
National Advisory Body for Local Authority Higher Education: Board
Manpower Services Commission Youth Training Scheme: Contents and
    Standards Advisory Group
Schools Council Industry Project Steering Committee
Manpower Services Commission: Open Tech Programme Steering Com-
    mittee
Manpower Services Commission: Technical and Vocational Education
    Initiative Steering Group
City and Guilds of London Institute: National Advisory Committee for
    General Vocational Preparation
International Youth Year: National Co-ordinating Committee
Industry Year: 1986–Education Working Group
British Youth Council: Political Education Advisory Group
Centre for the Study of Comprehensive Schools
Standing Conference for Schools, Science, and Technology

International Bodies

Anglo-German Foundation
Great Britain–USSR Association: Council
International Automation Project: National Steering Committee
International Confederation of Free Trade Unions
    Executive Board
    Finance and General Purposes Committee
    Subcommittee
    Vice-president
    Auditor
    ICFTU Women's Committee

Economic and Social Committee
Co-ordinating Committee on South Africa
ICFTU Building Company
  Board of Directors
  General Assembly
  Auditor
European Trade Union Confederation
  Executive Committee
  Finance and General Purposes Committee
  Vice-president
  Women's Committee
Commonwealth Trade Union Council
  Steering Committee
CTUC Trust
  Trustees
  Auditor
  Trust Committee
Commonwealth Institute Board of Governors
European Community
  Economic and Social Committee
  ESC Bureau
  ESC Sections
    Agriculture
    Economic and Financial Questions
    Energy and Nuclear Questions
    External Relations
    Industry, Commerce, Crafts, and Services
    Protection of the Environment, Public Health, and Consumer Affairs
    Regional Development
    Social Questions
    Transport and Communications
  European Social Fund Committee
  Advisory Committee on Equal Opportunities for Men and Women
  Advisory Committee on Free Movement of Workers
  Advisory Committee of Safety, Hygiene, and Health Protection at
    Work
  Advisory Committee on Social Security for Migrant Workers
  Advisory Committee on Transport
  Advisory Committee on Vocational Training
  Management Board of European Centre for the Development of
    Vocational Training
  Administrative Board of the European Foundation for the Improve-
    ment of Living and Working Conditions
  Standing Committee on Employment

International Labour Organisation
  Governing Body
Royal Institute of International Affairs
Overseas Labour Consultative Committee
  OLCC Aid Subcommittee
Trade Union Advisory Committee to OECD
  Administrative Committee
United Nations Association
UK Committee for UNICEF
UNICEF Executive Committee
Council for the Overseas Development Institute.

Miscellaneous Bodies

Advisory Unit for Service by Youth
Age Concern
Aneurin Bevan Memorial Fund Trustees
Building Conservation Trust
Royal Association for Disability and Rehabilitation
British Epilepsy Association
British Red Cross Society
British Standards Institution
  Executive Board
  National Accreditation Council for Certification Bodies
  Advisory Council on Personal Safety
  Works Study Committee
  Chemical Divisional Council
  Shipbuilding Symbols Committee
  Textile Divisional Council
British Robot Association
Certification Scheme for Weldment Inspection Personnel Management
    Board
Covent Garden Market Authority
National Dock Labour Board
Hillcroft College Governing Council
Industrial Training Service
  Institute of Manpower Studies
  Vice-president
  Council
Labour Party Home Policy Subcommittee
Marine Transport Centre Advisory Board
Mary MacArthur Holiday Home Management Committee
Materials Handling Centre, National
Meat and Livestock Commission: Consumers' Committee

Post Office Users National Council
Pre-retirement Association
The Queen's Award to Industry Advisory Committee
Royal Society for Prevention of Accidents
    Committee on Industrial Safety
TUC Labour Party Liaison Committee
Working Women's Organizations: National Joint Committee
Work Measurement Standard Data Foundation
Community Projects Foundation, Trustees

9

Entry to the System: A Case Study of Women's Aid in Scotland

Gail Stedward
University of Strathclyde

Introduction

A central theme of this volume is that the British system is far more 'open'—in the sense that access to policy-making and implementing is relatively easy—than many critics allow. The emphasis on consultation and negotiation—so evident from the survey of Scottish Office procedures, for example—has produced a policy style which, if anything, is leading to overcrowding rather than to a problem of exclusion. The point we make is not new. S. E. Finer's objection to the term 'pressure group' in his book *Anonymous Empire*, first published in 1958, was based on his empirical observation that groups—if they were 'pressing'—were pressing against an open door most of the time. Yet governments are not *always* so willing to accommodate interests. For example, there is no evidence that CND has become part of any relevant 'policy community', or that any government—Conservative or Labour— has shown the slightest inclination to accommodate any of its demands. In examining the relations between Women's Aid in Scotland and government, this chapter deliberately examines a group—and a set of relations—which differ from the producer group and professionalized, consultative relations which are of major interest elsewhere in the book.

Clearly, not *all* groups gain access. Equally, not all groups wish access, if they feel so alienated from the political system or believe that the costs of participation are too high. Trade unions may feel that too close an involvement in the policy process may result in their having to enforce policies to which some of their members object, such as incomes policies.

The question of access and the acceptability of groups to

government is one of the major dimensions used to classify groups. Three approaches are particularly useful in furthering our under-standing of the dynamics of group access and of governmental attitudes to the role and importance of groups: (1) Grant's distinction (1977) between 'insider' and 'outsider' groups; (2) Olsen's analysis of group strategies in terms of the costs and benefits of formal participation in the policy process; (3) May and Nugent's suggestion (1982) that groups may adopt a variety of strategies and achieve a status in the policy process which places them on the 'threshold' of insider status.

Grant's notion of insider and outsider groups is representative of a body of literature which recognizes that some groups do have difficulty in gaining access. For example, Dearlove's study (1973, p. 166) of interest groups in Kensington suggested that the local council had adopted an attitude towards groups according to whether they were perceived as 'helpful' or 'unhelpful'. 'Helpful' groups are 'in a co-operative and favourable relationship with the council', in contrast to 'unhelpful' groups, who were 'regarded with disfavour' and had a conflictual relationship with the council.

Kogan has also suggested classifying groups according to the way they are perceived by decision-makers who can grant or withhold legitimacy. Those groups who are recognized as legitimate develop a close consultative relationship with government, whereas those who are not recognized as legitimate 'challenge accepted authority and institutions until policies are changed, (Kogan 1975, p. 75). Wyn Grant's 'insider' and 'outsider' classification reflects both the perceptions of decision-makers and the strategy adopted by the group itself as determinants of access (Grant 1977). Thus insider groups are accepted as legitimate by decision-makers and are therefore part of the regular consultative system emphasized in this volume. But the groups also deliberately pursue strategies which are more likely to gain insider status. They develop a perception of the 'rules of the game'. For example, confidentiality is an important 'rule', as is the avoidance of extreme 'non-negotiable' demands. In contrast, outsider groups are not normally consulted and take up positions radically different to those of the existing policy com-munity.

On the whole, it is reasonable to assume that most groups would prefer an 'insider' status, not only because it so obviously provides opportunities for gaining policy concessions but also because it confers status and even a sense of importance. In the context of the 'corporatist debate', it might be significant that group participation is elective and not mandatory; if the group wishes to exert influence then it really has little choice. There are very few examples of groups which deliberately decide to opt for the outsider status. While, as Grant suggests, outsider status does not *necessarily* mean a lack of influence, those groups which are clearly outsiders appear to have little influence in practice, possibly because they have not *chosen* their status as outsiders. The advantage of being on the inside track of the policy process seems overwhelming.

Yet it is possible to argue that there are circumstances when particular types of participation are *not* to the advantage of a group. The *form* of participation may be crucial to whether a group's interests are best served by enthusiastic participation or by maintaining a more distant relationship with government. Highly formalized and structured group participation may prove to be costly to a group. Thus J. P. Olsen (1983, p. 149) has suggested that formal participation (in such structures as 'the network of governmental committees, commissions, councils and boards that initiate, design and advise and decide upon, implement and administer public policies') brings with it a combination of costs and benefits. He lists eight main benefits and costs associated with formal participation as follows:

The benefits of integrated participation can include influence over policy, cartelization, efficiency, and legitimacy. Participation provides opportunities to influence governmental policies. Integration enables organizations and governmental agencies to coordinate their activities and to exchange information. Access to information may bring technical expertise that facilitates efficiency. Participation confers public recognition on an organization and gives the organization a share in policy successes.

The costs of integrated participation can include responsibilities and losses of freedom, purity, and control by members. By accepting a position in an integrated structure, an organization and its leaders become associated with the actions of this structure. The organization has to share the blame for policy failures, because it cannot credibly claim innocence. Participation sometimes compromises an organization's ideological purity. Integration reduces an organization's freedom to act, and so constrains the organization's responsiveness to its members' wishes. A participating organization usually has to give the people who represent it some rights to control the organization's actions.

These benefits and costs are neither mutually exclusive nor exhaustive, but they characterize the differences among forms of coordination. They affect an organization's spontaneity, its certainty, its willingness to compromise, its ideological identity, its social status, its acceptance of responsibility of governmental policies, its role differentiation, its responsiveness to members' wishes, and its internal conflicts of interests. These effects pose dilemmas for an organization, because benefits seem to be inextricably bound together with costs (pp. 157–8.)

In terms of the case study in this chapter, the costs of the loss of ideological identity might be seen as particularly high for some sections of the women's movement which are deeply suspicious of male-dominated society and which refuse to play politics by rules of the game which they see as devised by and for men. As Olsen suggests, reform or revolutionary organizations place a high value on purity, and this may colour their attitude towards participation. When such groups do participate, it can cause internal dissension and accusations of 'sell-outs'. This does not mean that they will not participate in the policy process at all, but that they may choose *ad hoc* informal means of trying to influence both policy and administration.

Olsen's idea that groups may eschew particularly restricting types of formal participation suggests that there may be an ambiguity in practice between insider and outsider status and that groups may adopt multiple strategies according to the particular issue or situation. As May and Nugent (1982, p. 5) suggest, 'this increasing tendency for interest groups to be drawn into the decision-making machinery has resulted in the development of a great variety of relations, ranging from the highly structured to the loose and informal, between group representatives on the one hand and politicians and officials on the other'. In discussing Grant's insider/outsider classification, they note that he may be aggregating a number of quite different elements, namely, '(i) The degree to which the *substance of demands* are moderate or radical, (ii) the *strategy* which the group adopts, especially the degree to which it seeks consultation with authorities, rather than engaging in "direct action", (iii) the extent to which a group is granted consultative *status* by authority.' They, therefore, propose that it is more useful to restrict pressure group classifications to single areas of interest, such as aims, support, strategy, status, and so on. Following this suggestion, they argue that the insider/outsider distinction should be used to describe the *strategy* adopted by a group, that the acceptable/non-acceptable distinction (as proposed by Ryan 1978) should be used to describe the *status* of a group, and the radical/ moderate distinction should be used to describe the nature of a group's demands. They, of course, recognize that even these classifications need further qualification to reflect the real world of group politics.

They propose an extension to the terminology which may be especially useful in the context of our case study of Women's Aid. The concept is of 'thresholders'. A thresholder group is a group which 'exhibits strategic ambiguity and oscillation between insider and outsider strategies' (May and Nugent 1982, p. 7). Thus some groups sometimes seek very close relations with decision-makers and at other times adopt a more hostile and distant strategy, as a means of influencing policy. May and Nugent (1982, p. 16) analyse trade unions in these terms. For example, the 1970–4 period saw unions in a much more confrontational mood with government, denoting a shift from an insider towards a more outsider strategy. However, the outsider strategy was not the only strategy used by the unions, and insider strategies continued to be used by some unions on some issues, 'thus testifying to the sense of strategic ambiguity which we have identified as characteristic of thresholder groups'. They conclude that, in the case of the trade unions, 'oscillations [in strategy], temporary or not, are becoming rather more frequent as organisational and environmental factors have changed' (p. 22).

In practice, group strategies will be determined by a number of variables relating to the environment in which a group operates, such as the structure of the decision-making, machinery of public authorities, policies pursued by decision-makers, and by variables specific to the group itself (the goals of the group, the sanctions available to the group, the nature and size of the membership, and the type of decision-making process within the group) (May and Nugent 1982, pp. 7–8).

As we turn to our case study of Women's Aid, we will see that such questions as the sanctions available to Women's Aid, the emphasis on democracy *within* the group, and especially the radical nature of some of the demands being made all contribute to the strategies adopted by Women's Aid and to its degree of influence over policy-making and policy implementation. Women's Aid illustrates the most recent 'wave' of group formation in modern post-industrial societies, when 'new' interests which challenge the existing group network are being mobilized. There are parallels between the women's movement and the environmental and black movements in that in all three cases strategies and status are ambiguous, reflecting the interactions of internal and external variables, as suggested by May and Nugent. Women's Aid is, therefore, a good example of a new group searching for a satisfactory role and of the political system itself trying to come to terms with a new interest. In essence this chapter is concerned with the *limitations* placed upon access and with the importance of the 'rules of the game' if a group is to be successful in influencing policy.

The Emergence of Battered Women as a Political Issue

In the last decade the issue of battered women has made a reappearance on the political agenda after lying dormant as a political issue for over one hundred years. Domestic violence may be regarded as a 'new' issue, but it is an old problem. The second half of the nineteenth century saw the publication of various treatises on the topic and the passing of two Matrimonial Causes Acts. The first, in 1857, made cruelty grounds for divorce (Dobash and Dobash 1981, p. 570), and the second, passed in 1878, empowered magistrates' courts to grant a separation order with maintenance to a wife whose husband had been convicted of aggravated assault upon her (Pahl 1979, p. 25). In the early 1970s there was a limited discussion of 'wife abuse' in psychiatric and sociological journals.

As has been noted by Angela Weir (1977, p. 112), 'The feature common to the agitation of the later part of the nineteenth and twentieth century is the existence of a women's movement.' Certainly, in the 1970s wider discussion of domestic violence was initiated by the Women's Liberation Movement (WLM), out of which came Women's Aid, which has since then been almost solely responsible for the mainstream airing of the topic. Before examining the activities of Women's Aid in detail, it is, however, first necessary to give a brief outline of the history of the movement.

The setting up of the first refuge for battered women in 1972, by Erin Pizzey in Chiswick, was almost accidental. What began as a general meeting-place for women also attracted women seeking refuge from violent spouses, and the centre became a refuge. This path-breaking venture was soon followed by women all over the country, and refuges were formed around Britain. Often a pattern emerged: women began meeting in the late 1960s, forming groups and discussing their lives and ideas from the developing 'second wave' of feminism. As women's groups proliferated, centres were founded for meeting and simultaneously groups began to turn away from concentrating on consciousness-raising and began to discuss putting their ideas into practice (Pahl 1978). The women's movement (WM) had taught women that 'private is political', helping a taboo subject like domestic violence to be gradually brought out into the open, as women shared their common experiences. Additionally, refuges, particularly Chiswick, received wide media publicity. Erin Pizzey 'through her husband Jack Pizzey, a producer on the BBC programme *Man Alive*, had contacts with the media' (Hanmer and Leonard 1984, p. 35).

In Scotland the impetus also came from feminists. For example, Stirling Women's Aid began as a group of university women, and the first Scottish refuge, established in Edinburgh in 1973, came out of discussions in the Edinburgh Women's Liberation Workshop. The 1974 WLM Conference, held in Edinburgh, discussed the problem of domestic violence and the provision of refuges. Following this conference, a group of feminists established Glasgow Women's Aid. The WLM Conference, held in Manchester the following year, again led to women who were concerned about wife battering being brought together and resulted in the formation of the National Women's Aid Federation (NWAF).

It was at this time that Erin Pizzey rejected the need for a national co-ordinating body, particularly a feminist one, but the thirty-five founding groups of NWAF agreed on five aims, which reveal the dual campaigning and service role Women's Aid envisaged from its beginning:

1. To provide temporary refuge on request for women and their children who have suffered mental or physical harassment.
2. To encourage the women to determine their own futures and to help them achieve them, whether this involves returning home or starting a new life elsewhere.
3. To recognise and care for the emotional and educational needs of the children involved.

4. To offer support and advice and help to any woman who asks for it, whether or not she is a resident, and also to offer support and aftercare to any women and children who have left the refuge.

5. To educate and inform the public, the media, the police, the courts, social services and other authorities with respect to the battering of women, mindful of the fact that this is a result of the general position of women in our society. (Schechter, 1982, p. 155.)

The aims of Women's Aid are neatly expressed in the title of the organization and its motto 'women helping women helping women'. The name 'Women's Aid' was carefully chosen by the founders, as Jo Sutton, first NWAF co-ordinator, has explained: 'The title "Women's Aid" makes no mention of battering or any form of violence against women. Women's Aid was aware from the outset that a woman injured by her husband was only a physical symptom of the social position of women.' (Schechter 1982, p. 156.) This explanation reflects the feminist principles which underlie the Women's Aid philosophy, which actively challenges the common assumptions about domestic violence. Some of the group's objectives are quite clearly radical, having profound implications for the likelihood of the group achieving significant policy success. In particular, it is doubtful whether the more radical demands could be processed and accommodated through the usual consultative structures.

However, as we shall see, the fact that the group's aims also incorporated a service delivery element did open up the prospect of a close relationship with government in the *implementation* of public policies. Thus Women's Aid had a set of objectives which might lead it to become a 'thresholder' group, that is, when it was emphasizing its service *delivery* functions it might be able to employ an insider strategy, but when it was challenging the fundamental nature of male-dominated society it would inevitably have to adopt an outsider strategy. The fact that it was concerned with service delivery also presented the possibility (in a political environment which was emphasizing a reduced role for the state and greater responsibilities for voluntary organizations and individuals) of governments using the group as a means of 'off-loading' (Winkler 1981) certain service functions which might otherwise have been provided by the state.

A similar 'off-loading' phenomenon is evident in the field of drug abuse, where the Conservative Government has been anxious to use various voluntary groups rather than extend NHS provision. David Ennals, Secretary of State for Health and Social Services in the last Labour Government, outlined the economic advantages of off-loading. Thus he argued that 'pound for pound, we can buy more services through the voluntary channel than through the statutory. I am ready to prove it if there are some who doubt it.' (1976, quoted in Winkler 1981, p. 125.)

The Scottish Context

Women's Aid (Women's Aid in Scotland is used here to refer to local groups, the term Scottish Women's Aid (SWA) being reserved to describe the national co-ordinating organization) began in Scotland in 1973, with the setting up of the first Scottish refuge in Edinburgh. At the outset, the aim of Women's Aid was to act as an emergency service, providing shelter for women and their children who had been subjected to domestic violence. As groups have developed, their role has widened considerably and now encompasses the advice and information to abused women who do not necessarily want refuge.

In 1975 it became apparent that a more formal organization was needed to cope with the problems that the (then ten) Women's Aid groups in Scotland had taken on. The need for an organized national office was further encouraged by the Scottish Office, who offered initial funding.

In many ways, Scottish Office support was a remarkable development, arising from the 'service delivery' objective of Women's Aid. In one sense it could be seen as the ultimate recognition that the group had quickly become an insider group; that the Government was prepared to fund certain aspects of the group's activities. As in many cases, where an umbrella organization does not exist government goes out and assists its emergence, suggesting that governments need these co-ordinating bodies with whom they can negotiate and consult. More importantly perhaps in this case, if 'off-loading' was to take place then the Scottish Office needed a viable structure to which it could devolve any service functions. (It should also be added that a 'do-nothing' strategy was not really an option for the Scottish Office, once the issue of battered women was on the political agenda. Financing Women's Aid was a means of giving some recognition to the problem without

becoming too enmeshed in the controversy—a symbolic policy
perhaps.) Thus Women's Aid found a dilemma at this fairly early
stage, whether to risk 'capture' by government through receiving
public funding. We might see a pattern here, with groups such as
environmentalists, black groups, and anti-unemployment organizations all receiving state aid of some kind and risking the
possibility of becoming dependent upon that aid, with the result
that their behaviour is modified to accept the existing rules of the
game.

Notwithstanding these risks, SWA was established (with Scottish
Office support) in 1976 as a co-ordinating body to tackle problems
which had arisen in the developing Women's Aid movement in
Scotland. SWA set out to increase contact and the exchange of
information between local groups. It also sought to deal with
administrative work, which it was felt had been neglected by local
groups striving to cope with the practicalities of providing refuge
and advice to battered women. The aims of SWA reflected the
emerging dichotomy between service provision on one hand and an
active campaigning function on the other, a conflict more fundamental than even the 'thresholder' classification might suggest:

1. To co-ordinate and assist the work done by local Women's Aid
   groups, including work with children in refuges.
2. To develop new local groups in areas without adequate
   provision.
3. To inform the public and relevant agencies nationally about the
   problem of domestic violence and the work of Women's Aid.
4. To act as a national referral and information agency for
   Women's Aid groups, women seeking help, or for relevant
   agencies.
5. To encourage research into domestic violence and means of its
   prevention.

The SWA Edinburgh office was established in 1976 with the aid
of a grant from the Social Work Services Group of the Scottish
Education Department, as was the Dundee office in 1981. Funding
for SWA was obtained in the wake of the publication of the Finer
Report on one-parent families and the Report of the Select
Committee on Violence in Marriage. As the Observations on
the Report from the Select Committee on Violence in Marriage

stated, 'The Social Work Services Group of the Scottish Education Department has this year offered a capital grant of £600 to SWA towards the furnishing of their rented premises and an annual grant of up to £6,800 towards staff and running expenses.' This figure then represented 90 per cent of the SWA budget. The staff has expanded from one national co-ordinator (appointed 1 October 1976) and a part-time secretary based in Edinburgh to seven full-time national workers, five in Edinburgh (the general and training office) and two in Dundee (the children's office), exemplifying the growth of a 'network' around a newly recognized issue. Work is divided among the general office workers, who deal with referrals, general information, publicity, education and campaigning as well as the establishment of new and support of existing local groups, and the training office workers, who provide both internal training for Women's Aid and training for relevant agencies. The children's office ensures the maintenance of a strong focus on the needs of children in refuges and promotes the interests of children who have experienced domestic violence.

Funding for the offices is only partially met by Scottish Office finance. At present the training office (two posts plus running costs) is 100 per cent funded, while the general and children's offices are 70 per cent funded. The shortfall has to be met by fund-raising. The Scottish Office Social Work Services Group (SWSG) funds SWA under the provisions laid down in Section 10(1) of the Social Work (Scotland) Act 1968, which provides financial assistance to voluntary organizations. The initial funding covers a three-year period and is reviewed annually with grant applications. The aim of initial funding is generally to aid the establishment of voluntary organizations and then gradually to decrease the financial contribution of the State, eventually leading to as great a degree of financial self-sufficiency as possible. This aim, however, cannot always be completely fulfilled, as some groups cannot achieve financial independence. Women's Aid and organizations such as Gingerbread provide what government acknowledges as valuable social services in the voluntary sector, and they continue to receive public funds.

Women's Aid aims to work collectively, and much emphasis is put on listening to what battered women themselves have to say. Women's Aid claims to shy away from the idea of service providers and clients, preferring instead the women's liberation ideal of 'women helping women'. An initial aim of Women's Aid was to have battered women running the organization, but in practice this has not materialized to the extent envisaged by the founders. There appear to be two main reasons for this. Firstly, a woman seeking help from Women's Aid may not necessarily want to become involved in the organization. The important point here is the woman's perception of the organization: she may or may not see it as either a social provision or social movement, or both (see Pahl 1979). One Women's Aid worker felt that it was perhaps naïve to expect battered women to take over the running of the organization completely. However, women who have been in refuges do play a big part in the organization. Most Women's Aid groups in Scotland employ one or two paid workers in addition to having volunteers, generally numbering between five and twenty. For example, Glasgow Women's Aid presently (1985) has ten employees, two funded by the regional council's Social Work Department plus eight funded from housing benefit revenue. (Women in refuges receive housing benefit from the district council for rent; collectively this money is used to meet running costs, overheads, wages, etc.)

Again, Women's Aid is seen to be something of an 'insider' group in that it is receiving state funding via the regional and district councils. Major decisions, especially those which might be contentious, are discussed at regular collective meetings. Groups which run refuges strongly encourage the participation of the women living there. The heavy emphasis on democracy has both advantages and disadvantages for Women's Aid's lobbying style. In some situations (such as implementation of the Housing (Homeless Persons) Act 1977), the detailed background knowledge based on experience gives Women's Aid an advantage. However, as the 'diversion' issue (examined in detail later in this chapter) has shown, in an essentially *reactive* situation the requirement of internal democracy can hamper Women's Aid from acting as swiftly as effective lobbying would require. Thus the internal characteristics of the group are an important variable, as suggested by May and Nugent, in determining the group's relationship with policy-makers and with its environment. From the policy-makers' perspective, it is much more difficult to consult, let alone negotiate with, a group whose leaders cannot act as authoritative spokespersons and who cannot make agreements stick.

In Strathclyde Region, local groups hold regional meetings every two months, where efforts can be co-ordinated to meet local circumstances and information exchanged. National policy is decided at executive meetings held every quarter at which each group (at present here are twenty-nine groups in Scotland) is eligible to attend and each has three votes. Here the work of the national staff is directed and policy is formulated. In addition SWA makes extensive use of subgroups. Subgroups were established to examine particular issues or problems in greater detail, such as pay and conditions in Women's Aid, political development, the Matrimonial Homes Act, the particular needs of Asian women, children, and training. Through the work of subgroups, which deal not only with the inception of policy but also with its implementation, local groups have possibly been able to participate more effectively in national work: for example, the finance group consists of the treasurers, representatives of two local groups, and SWA workers, meeting regularly to review SWA finances. Such combined effort has helped to keep national workers closely involved with the grass roots of the organization. Thus despite the clear dichotomy between the primary role of the local groups in service provision and the national role of co-ordination a measure of unity has been maintained, but it is important to note the danger to a reformist campaigning group in becoming bureaucratized, with its own professional social workers. The organization can easily become a supplementary professional social work service rather than a political agency. Success in some dimensions thus has costs in others.

Local groups are responsible for obtaining their own funding, and the sources from which they do secure funds vary: two groups are funded by regional councils, three by district councils, seven jointly by regional and district councils, seven by the regional council and Urban Aid, four by the district council and Urban Aid, two by the Manpower Services Commission, and four receive no funding at all from statutory bodies. Regional council funding is usually provided by the Social Work Department, and district council funding by the Housing Department. Groups also have to raise funds to supplement or in some cases wholly finance their income. The bulk (75 per cent) of SWA finance still comes from the Scottish Office Social Work Services Group, with local authority grants and donations providing a sizeable portion of SWA income. SWA also nets income from trust funds and publications, but like the local groups has to rely on fund-raising to meet the shortfall in finance. The costs to the group attached to such an arrangement are subtle but tangible. Despite the seemingly generous levels of state funding, Women's Aid finds itself in a position where it can barely keep refuges and administration running. This has meant the concomitant neglect of broader campaigning. Government funding of the 'service' function has siphoned off much of Women's Aid energy into less controversial and less confrontational pursuits. Even so, it is not unreasonable to ask whether the relatively ineffective campaigning role is due not the lack of funds but to a lack of expertise on the part of individuals not used to working through the political process. The administrative skills needed for a group orientated towards service delivery might be very different from the political entrepreneurial skills of campaigning.

At a grass-roots level, Women's Aid groups are well established. The groups, like other voluntary organizations concerned with welfare, have become part of the welfare system. For example, during 1984–5 a total of 1,088 women and 1,788 children were given refuge and an additional 4,477 women sought advice and information from Women's Aid in Scotland (figures taken from *SWA Annual Report* 1984–5). The largest source of referral to refuges (after the women themselves deciding to contact Women's Aid (30 per cent) and other Women's Aid groups (21 per cent)) has been from social work departments (18 per cent). Again we see public authorities recognizing the advantage of having groups available for 'off-loading'. One of the greatest assets of Women's Aid is the group's practical capability to react in a crisis. In providing a 24-hour service and emergency accommodation, it can actually offer better provision than the local authorities, as the state has no good equivalent of Women's Aid refuges. Some but not all local authorities have 'homeless units', which can be used in preference to 'bed and breakfast' arrangements. However, these offer a poor service in comparison with Women's Aid refuges. State provision for battered women is governed primarily by the 1977 Housing Act, and Women's Aid is involved in improving the implementation of its requirements. The work of Women's Aid—in particular the co-operation fostered between the organization and district housing departments—provides a classic example of a situation where much of the policy implementation depends upon the goodwill and co-operation of participating groups for its success (see Richardson and Jordan 1979, p. 140). The economics of co-operation are vitally important in such a scheme.

Campaigns and Issues: A Different Lobbying Style

Despite its dependency on state funding, Women's Aid has continued to lobby local and central government on issues of concern to battered women. The expansion of SWA's campaigning role is highlighted by the new aims of Women's Aid in Scotland, adopted in May 1985.

1. To encourage the provision of temporary refuge for women and their children (if any) where the women have suffered abuse (mental, physical or sexual) in their home or within a relationship with a man.
2. To offer support, advice and help to any women and their children (if any) who ask for such help whether or not they are refuge residents, and also to offer support and advice to any women and children who have left a temporary refuge.
3. To encourage women to determine their own futures.
4. To provide the opportunities for the education and emotional needs of the children to be met, particularly those resident in refuges.
5. To work to provide the opportunity for shared permanent housing for battered women and their children (if any) through Culdion Housing Association.
6. To encourage statutory authorities and other agencies to recognise their obligations, legal and otherwise towards battered women and their children (if any) and to act accordingly towards the prevention of abuse and relief of suffering.
7. Mindful of the fact that abuse—mental, physical, sexual—is the result of the position of women in society, to promote education and to inform the community and their representatives with respect to the battering of women and its prevention.
8. To encourage research into the causes, the prevention and relief of such suffering and abuse.
9. To encourage such training both for ourselves and others as will best meet the objects of SWA.

A good example of the campaigning role was the part that Women's Aid in Scotland and England played in the setting up of the Parliamentary Select Committee on Violence in Marriage in 1974, by ensuring that the issue was kept in the public eye and was forced on to the political agenda. As with state funding, the setting up of a Parliamentary Select Committee can be seen as evidence that Women's Aid (and the women's movement in general) had

achieved recognition, thus that its issues are worthy of attention. By
any yardstick of group achievements, the establishment of the select
committee must be regarded as a major 'success'. By 1976—with
the setting up of the select committee, state funding, and the report
of the Finer Committee on *One Parent Families*—the women's
movement might be said to have achieved the status of an
acceptable pressure group. (However, it is worth noting that access
to Parliament is far less restrictive than to Whitehall: for example,
the witnesses to the Social Services Select Committee on 12
February 1986 were Women in Prisons, PROP, RAP, and IN-
QUEST.)

Evidence to the select committee in 1974 was submitted by a
wide cross-section of groups, including Women's Aid, and the
findings of the committee were encouraging to Women's Aid.
Many of the recommendations have not be implemented, however,
and it is around one of the most central points made by the
committee that SWA is now actively campaigning for refuge
provision. 'The Department of the Environment must ensure that
more refuges are provided by local authorites and/or voluntary
organisations. One family place per 10,000 of the population
should be the initial target.' (*Report from Select Committee on
Violence in Marriage*, p. xxvi.) This is equivalent to 500 spaces in
Scotland, while at present there are only 179. It should be noted,
however, that such a figure may seriously underestimate demand,
as over 1,900 women had to be turned away from Women's Aid
refuges in 1984–5 due to lack of space (figures from 1984–5 *SWA
Annual Report*).

Women's Aid has been actively campaigning around the Matrimonial Homes (Family Protection) (Scotland) Act, highlighed by its
publication in 1985 of *A Guide to the Matrimonial Homes Act*.
Although the Act has improved legal protection for women, its
implementation has been problematic. On paper the Act is very
impressive: a woman suffering violence at the hands of the man
with whom she lives can apply for a court order to prohibit him
from harassing her further. The order can also prevent him entering
a stated area around the matrimonial home and in certain
circumstances can have powers of arrest attached. In practice the
Act has many loopholes and has been subject to what has been
regarded as misinterpretation by the courts. The problems surroun-
ding the Matrimonial Homes Act have not been limited to its

interpretation by the courts. Additionally, the police have often been castigated for what many see as their lax enforcement of its provisions. Donald Dewar MP (Lab.) has been among the strongest critics of the slackness inherent in the Act and in its implementation, and has been working closely with SWA to amend this situation. In the Commons Committee Stage of the Law Reform (Miscellaneous Provisions) (Scotland) Bill, three amendments to the Matrimonial Homes Act proposed by SWA and tabled by Labour MPs were accepted by the Government. Again this could be seen as evidence that Women's Aid can use existing processes to its advantage. In Scotland, Women's Aid has found the left more sympathetic to its cause, although SWA is not aligned to any political party. Both Labour and SNP party conferences have passed resolutions supporting the work of Women's Aid.

Because of the gap between legislation and implementation, Women's Aid sees a need to attempt to change practices as well as statutes. It sees police attitudes as one of the obstacles to be tackled. Again, a form of insider status has been gained, as some local Women's Aid groups have been involved in police training programmes. Sustained public pressure, an outsider strategy, has resulted in 'access'. In this way SWA had a small input into a training programme at the Scottish Police College. Women's Aid representatives were allocated one session, but found this quite inadequate to cover the multifarious aspects of domestic violence and the work of Women's Aid, and insufficient to change police attitudes. Objectively, however, access to a police training course may be perceived as a very considerable success, even if it did not produce immediate and spectacular results.

Glasgow Women's Aid has not been involved in any policy training schemes, despite the fact that Strathclyde police have established a Woman and Child Abuse squad which, amongst other issues, deals with domestic violence, specifically with the much-maligned Matrimonial Homes Act. Women's Aid was not invited to participate in the course, although Rape Crisis was. The official reason given for not asking Women's Aid for input was that it was not well organized in Glasgow (interview). In fact, Glasgow Women's Aid has three refuges and an advice centre, of which the police training hierarchy was ignorant. Thus in Glasgow Women's Aid has not been so effective in establishing itself as a recognized source of expertise.

In contrast, Edinburgh Women's Aid has contributed to several training programmes with Lothian and Borders police. Its involvement was initiated by a series of complaints it made in February 1983 about police handling of domestic violence. Around the same time a report was published which put the police in a bad light. Within six months the police contacted Edinburgh Women's Aid seeking its involvement in a refresher training course for sergeants. Again, Rape Crisis was also invited, along with other voluntary organizations. Initially Women's Aid had strong reservations about the joint nature of this venture, but found that, in practice, the violence against women message was reinforced by Rape Crisis and vice versa. Edinburgh Women's Aid has now been asked to take part in further training courses, including one with chief inspectors, and feels that the Lothian and Borders police training hierarchy now sees Women's Aid as a credible organization, but it is uncertain that actual working attitudes have altered.

This contrasts sharply with the situation in Glasgow, where the training division was quite unaware of the profile of Women's Aid in the city, although the local police on the streets were familiar with the work of Women's Aid. All local Women's Aid groups and SWA remain dissatisfied with general police procedures and attitudes and feel that they will have to do more in the way of input to training programmes in order to change attitudes to what police term 'domestic disputes'.

One of the major campaigns which Women's Aid has launched, at local and national level, has been against the inclusion in 'diversion schemes' of men accused of offences related to domestic violence. Diversion refers to 'the halting or suspending of proceedings against an accused person in favour of processing through a non-criminal disposition' (National Commission for Criminal Justice Standards and Goals, *Report of Corrections Task Force*: US Department of Justice 1973, p. 50, quoted in Scottish Office Central Research Unit Paper *Diversion from the Criminal Justice Process: Report on the Diversion Scheme at Ayr*, August 1983).

The first diversion scheme was introduced in Ayr on 1 February 1982 as a pilot scheme. As 'diversionary measures are generally confined to what is considered as less serious criminal behaviour which does not require any element of positive deterrence' (McClintock 1981, p. 191), Women's Aid was appalled at the prospect of domestic assault being included and any consequent extension of the scheme throughout Scotland. Women's Aid became involved in discussion of the scheme operating at Ayr in response to a Scottish Office report published in August 1983. Thereafter correspondence between SWA and the division organizer of the Ayr Social Work Department continued for some months. In spite of protestations from Women's Aid, domestic violence continued to be included in the scheme. Women's Aid was not consulted in the original discussion of the scheme, and the Depute Director of Strathclyde Social Work Department has said that the staff at Ayr were rather 'taken aback' by the response and indeed outrage expressed by Women's Aid.

The Divisional Organizer of the Social Work Department at Ayr echoed this surprise when he acknowledged that the department usually enjoyed 'excellent relations' with Women's Aid but that on this particular issue they had agreed to differ. Despite the correspondence between SWA and Strathclyde Social Work Department and the use of the press by SWA, at the time of writing diversion schemes have been established in eleven areas of Scotland.

A striking feature of this issue is that from the outset it would appear that Women's Aid was fighting a losing battle. The professions involved, the social workers and procurators fiscal (public prosecutors), were largely united in their aim to institute the scheme and see it extended. The lack of consultation with Women's Aid in this particular incidence appears to be symbolic of their determination not to compromise. In this particular case, Women's Aid was articulating a view not shared by other 'professionals' in the field of social welfare.

The only public debate on this issue was triggered by Women's Aid, who deliberately went to the media (resorted to an outsider strategy) in order to force more debate on the appropriateness of domestic violence for inclusion in the existing diversion scheme. Yet despite the initial impasse reached between Women's Aid and social work departments on diversion, this situation has now been overcome. Internal debate to determine its strategy on diversion meant that Women's Aid faced a classic pressure group problem, whether as an organization it should completely oppose the diversion schemes in operation or try to alter the nature of the schemes. Illustrating May and Nugent's 'thresholder' category, the group decided to change its strategy again and resolved to proffer Women's Aid training services to relevant social work departments, resulting in the production of a two or three-day training package which has been taken up by Strathclyde and Borders Regions. The training package deals with domestic violence in a broad sense, social work involvement with domestic violence, and diversion. The inclusion of Women's Aid in social work training programmes represents a notable breakthrough for the group, denoting some recognition of its specialist knowledge in the field of domestic violence. As well as the inclusion of Women's Aid training in these social work departments, meetings have also been held with the Lothian Social Work Department, and as a direct result of Women's Aid pressure the diversion scheme in Moray specifically excludes battering men. In addition, at the suggestion of the Convention of Scottish Local Authorities SWA is preparing an 'ideal model' of a diversion scheme.

Conclusion: Insider, Outsider, or Threshold?

The diversion issue provides an interesting insight into the fluidity of insider/outsider strategies. Perceived rather narrowly as a service agency on the fringes of mainstream social provision, Women's Aid was not included in any preliminary discussion of the diversion proposals and thus was at a distinct disadvantage when it sought to campaign against the scheme. Essentially, Women's Aid was not part of the exclusive policy community which made the decisions on this issue. As a pressure group, Women's Aid is faced with one overwhelming problem: to be in on the act one has to be invited, and to be invited one may have to compromise.

SWA is undoubtedly in an awkward position. On the one hand its aims are based in feminist philosophy, representing a radical challenge to the existing system. SWA seeks to change attitudes and reform parts of the system, and in this way Women's Aid remains an ideological outsider group. On the other hand, in order to influence such issues as diversion and to change police attitudes effectively, insider status is required. It would appear that Women's Aid tends to oscillate uncomfortably between these two positions, in the way that May and Nugent suggest for other groups such as the trade unions. The issue of compromise, however, remains a sensitive one and poses a more intractable problem, particularly for the women's movement, where clearly some principles are quite non-negotiable. As we noted earlier, Olsen has examined the costs and benefits of participation, both formal and informal, and why it is that some groups refuse to co-operate with government. Among his costs are loss of freedom, of control, and of pure ideological position, all of which are pertinent to Women's Aid. Benefits include legitimacy, status, and recognition as well as influence on policy, which Women's Aid has also experienced. Participation has indeed conferred legitimacy, status, and recognition, as well as increasing knowledge and experience of co-ordination with other groups.

For example, Women's Aid's retention of control of refuge provision was not at all unpalatable to the Government, as the DHSS has no wish to become more directly involved in their provision. Generally it would appear that central, regional, and local government acknowledge and 'approve' of the passive role of Women's Aid in providing refuges and advice for battered women. This is supported by the short-term grant aid allocated to Women's Aid for that purpose. Thus it is ironic that a group which is outsider in terms of its challenges to the dominant values of society serves as one of the best examples of a group performing an implementation task for government, one of the characteristics of 'insiderism'. The access and welcome enjoyed by SWA in its *service* role is eroded when it seeks a role in policy *formulation*. It is here that the contrast between Women's Aid's feminist perspective of domestic violence and the Government's interpretation of the problem can be seen most clearly.

It is quite likely that the gap between the two has actually widened in more recent years. The DHSS did sponsor research in 1977, when the Government allocated £75,000 for that purpose. At that time the department 'were more inclined to share the view of the women's movement that violence should be understood primarily in terms of sexual politics and patriarchy' (Borkowski, Murch, and Walker 1983, p. 205). However, after a DHSS conference held in 1981 and attended by representatives from Women's Aid all over Britain, as well as by professionals such as social workers, health visitors, and the DHSS Research Liaison Group, it seems that there was a distinct change of attitude. The existing policy community became more aware of, and hence wary of, the challenging and radical nature of feminist analysis and the consequent far-reaching reforms in social welfare it required.

This polarization of opinion can be seen in both theory and

practice. The state employs professional 'carers' in the field of welfare, and the line between professional and client is clearly drawn. This could not be further away from the Women's Aid philosophy, which is based on the ideal of complete participation. Belief in the authenticity of personal experience, in this case that of the battered woman, is firmly rooted in feminist theory and is put into practice by Women's Aid. Women who have experienced battering are particularly encouraged to participate actively within the organization, and women who seek help from Women's Aid are strongly encouraged to make decisions for themselves. This emphasis on self-determination is underlined by the fact that there are no wardens in Women's Aid refuges; the women themselves organize them collectively. This runs counter to professional social work practice and has aroused criticism from those who view this as anarchic and dangerous.

Future Strategies

As a campaigning pressure group it would seem that Women's Aid has a long way to go if it wishes to fundamentally alter social policy for battered women. This is primarily because it involves changing entrenched values, not only of the policy-makers but also of the general public. Women's Aid has been very successful in bringing the issue of domestic violence into the public arena of discussion, largely through its use of the media and through the use of outsider strategies. The Women's Aid movement has attained a level of credibility almost never accorded to an individual battered woman. Relations with government have not followed the same pattern. The very nature of the work of Women's Aid means that it has to liaise with many groups and agencies. Thus its recommendations on initiatives for battered women invade many policy areas. The mixed reaction to Women's Aid's contributions or attempted contributions perhaps helps to explain the status of Women's Aid as neither fully an insider nor an outsider group but as a thresholder organization, using different strategies in different situations, whether by choice or not.

Relations with local government departments (such as housing and social work) tend to be fairly open, but, as the diversion issue has illustrated, Women's Aid is not guaranteed a role in the consultation process when it adopts a policy greatly at variance with other, more established, professional groups. Similarly, Women's Aid made a large contribution to the 1975 select committee, but the close relations of the mid-1970s are no longer in evidence.

SWA's position is further complicated by the very nature of its demands, which on the surface may appear to form a single issue campaign, but in fact demand extensive feminist reforms. As noted by Dahlerup (1984, p. 38), 'feminist ideology is not always translated into proposals ready for the political agenda'. Demands from the women's movement do not come in neat manageable packages. When they arrive on the doorstep of the state the paper is torn and the contents spill out over other issues. Accommodating feminist demands more often than not requires a complete reappraisal of issues, of internal working procedures, and of policy, as well as accommodating the overspill of issues which cannot be slotted into rigid policy sectors. The experience of local authorities who have established women's committees bears witness to this.

By comparison with other feminist pressure groups, however, Women's Aid has been relatively successful. The issue of domestic violence has been placed on the political agenda in the past largely through its efforts. Wife battering has been clearly categorized as a 'woman's issue', and, given the fact that women's issues are generally considered marginal, if worthy of discussion at all, attaining any political debate on the subject has been commendable. Faced with an already overcrowded agenda and policy process, it is not surprising that government has not permanently taken on board the octopus of feminist interest groups like Women's Aid.

10

Groups and the Party System

Introduction

We have noted earlier that pressure groups in Britain tend to pursue multiple strategies of political influence. Thus most groups will recognize that close links with departments and the achievement of 'insider status' is probably the most effective strategy for influencing decisions, especially in those matters which might be termed 'low politics'. It is both banal and vital to say that groups direct their efforts to where the greatest concentration of power is to be found.

If we accept the view that to follow the group orientation is to identify the locus of power, then we might predict that the links between groups and those political institutions which are relatively weak in terms of policy-making would be of a relatively low order of priority for groups. If one takes the view that political parties, though sometimes important, are not as influential in the policy-making and implementing processes as might be imagined by the average voter, then it follows that the party system may not be one of the central areas of activity for most pressure groups. In *British Political Parties* (1955, 1967 edn., p. 649), McKenzie had described the parties as 'one of the main channels through which interest groups and both organised and unorganised bodies of opinion can bring their views to the attention of parliamentarians . . .', but, as is shown below, even by 1958 McKenzie had begun to entertain doubts about British parties performing an effective role in integrating group demands. As Moran notes (1985, pp. 117–18), British political parties are in decline as organizations. He argues that the decline 'is due to both social and political forces. Altered tastes have made party institutions less central to the leisure of the middle and working classes; disappointment with party performance in office has caused disillusionment; new styles of political participation have become popular, especially among the young.' For some party activists the party manifesto seems all-important, but, as Drucker observes (1979, p. 97), 'manifestoism is of precious little help' for Labour ministers in office. Drucker cites Headey's study (1974, p. 61) of Labour and Conservative ministers, in which he found only 6 per cent of ministers or ex-ministers who thought it was their duty to 'implement party policy or to take decisions in accordance with party policy'. As Drucker says, many issues crop up unexpectedly or are too particular for the manifesto to assist. And often, he says, the manifesto statement is impressive in an exhortatory manner but of little utility in choosing between specific courses of action. There is also the fact, as Drucker notes, that increasingly it is the case that major changes in policy, such as the decision to establish comprehensive schools, can only be made with the assent of the powerful groups affected. He argues, 'The manifesto can demand comprehensive schools but it takes the skill of the minister, not a demand or command from anyone, to carry out the policy.'

The irony, in terms of the focus of this book, is that the inexorable rise in the pressure group system has itself contributed to the decline of political parties as key organizations in the political system. Several decades ago, the late Professor Robert McKenzie, even though his main interest was political parties, suggested that pressure groups might be a *more effective channel* (our emphasis) of citizen representation than were political parties. The group system, he argued, 'provides an invaluable set of multiple channels through which the mass of citizenry can influence the decision-making process at the higher levels' (reprinted in Kimber and Richardson 1974, p. 286). For McKenzie, the central functions of political parties are to 'select, organise and sustain teams of parliamentarians, between whom the general body of citizens may choose at elections' (Kimber and Richardson 1974, p. 279). Such a view, with which we would generally concur, leaves an enormous gap in the British political system, bearing in mind what he called the rough and ready device for choosing leaders which the British electoral system represents. The gap, he argued, is filled by 'the tacit recognition of the enormous and legitimate role played by organised interests . . .' (Kimber and Richardson 1974, p. 279). Since McKenzie wrote his analysis in 1958, the number of groups has increased substantially, as has the number of citizens who join groups, whilst membership of political parties has declined. Thus, today, Lowe and Goyder suggest that pressure groups have a total membership in excess of that for the political parties (Lowe and Goyder 1983, p. 37). In 1986 CND had a membership of 90,000, and Greenpeace of over 65,000.

A further development has been the increasing volatility of voting behaviour in Britain (Franklin 1985), making the political environment that much more unpredictable for groups. Thus, in terms of group strategies, it has become more difficult to predict the outcome of elections, thereby increasing the risk factor if a group has aligned itself to one particular party in the expectation that that party will win the election. Just as membership of the EEC has added a new dimension to group activity—in the sense that policy outcomes in some cases (such as agricultural support, steel policy, car exhaust emission controls) are based upon complex and shifting coalitions at the European level—then so the increasingly volatile electorate presents groups with new problems of uncertainty.

Even when there was less uncertainty about voting behaviour, there was no certainty about the actual behaviour of political parties once they attained office. 'Accommodations to reality' by elected governments are so common as to suggest that the party as a determinant in the policy process is weak. As we outlined earlier, it can be argued that there are *twin channels of democracy*. In their review of the 'Do Parties Matter' debate, Lehner and Schubert (1984, pp. 132) argue that the decline of governmental authority is the inevitable consequence of increasing state functions and an increasing scope of politics. They present a picture of 'Government, business and organised interests operating under conditions of mutual interdependence. Consequently, they have to engage in bargaining and politico-economic accommodation.' They go on,

As a result, the constitutional structures and institutions of western democracies are paralleled by more or less formalised bargaining systems, such as tripartite consultation, various hearings and committees, joint ventures and other forms of mixed financing of private investments and activities, and contractual regulation of [the] public interest through agreements of private and public actors. Together, these and other forms of interaction . . . form a dense but segmented network which strongly influences or even determines most of government activity.

They conclude later (1984, p. 136) that

the decline in effective policy power of parties and parliaments can be explained as a consequence of the vast scope and complexity of politics and the resulting politico-economic interdependence. The provision of a large variety of public goods and services as well as the carrying out of manifold interventionist policies necessitate a high degree of bureaucratic organization of government. It also requires a high degree of professional and technocratic rationality in which bureaucracies are more skilled than parties and parliaments. Finally a high degree of politico-economic interdependence forces government to engage in bargaining with private business and organized interests, which is again much more the realm of bureaucracy than that of parties and parliament.

They indeed go on to claim that parties and parliaments often even fail to give a 'steering' sense of direction and constraint to the system. Their review reaches the conclusion that 'The severely limited role of parties and parliaments in policy-making seems to be a fact which can scarcely be disputed in empirical terms.' We broadly share their position (1984, p. 134) that even if 'parties and parliaments occasionally may play a decisive role and often may be capable of imposing restrictions on policy-making, there is no doubt that much effective policy power is concentrated in bureaucracies and organized interests'.

This parallel political system has long been recognized by groups, most of whom now eschew too close an allegiance with *one* particular party. For example, the National Farmers' Union used to have rather close links to the Conservative party (despite claiming political neutrality), but adopted a politically neutral stance after the Second World War. As Self and Storing note, the practical experience of working with a Labour Government, keen to expand food production after the war, convinced the union that it could actively work with either major political party (reprinted in Kimber and Richardson 1974, p. 59). Thus the union no longer sponsors parliamentary candidates. Friends of the Earth, a radical and campaigning group whose members might be inclined to vote Labour, make a point of adopting a non-partisan approach. Likewise, Mike Daube of ASH has claimed, that of the 100 or so Members of Parliament who participated in the Parliamentary All-Party Committee, 'I don't think any of them know which way I voted in elections' (Davies 1985, p. 120). Similarly, the National Union of Teachers has ended parliamentary sponsorship, though many other unions still sponsor Labour candidates and remain affiliated to the Labour party (see below). The essential point, underpinning the relationship between groups and the party system in Britain, is that, as Moran (1985, p. 120) puts it, 'Rich and sophisticated groups are perfectly capable, should they feel so impelled, of organising representation independently of parties. This has indeed been happening, with the result that pressure groups now seriously rival parties in the system of representation.' (And indeed Grant (1984, p. 3) shows that government would often rather deal directly with large firms than with the prism of a trade association.)

Sectional groups, in particular, have so many other means of influencing policy-making that they tend not to rely on the vagaries of party behaviour. Even promotional groups—generally considered to be the weaker type of group and least likely to attain insider status—appear to rank political parties rather low on the scale of priorities. Lowe and Goyder's survey (1983, p. 72) of national environmental groups found that only a quarter of groups

gave any ranking (and then usually a low ranking) to the role of MPs and peers as go-betweens to the political parties. This reflects the general lack of interest in party politics among environmental groups . . .

Whilst we emphasize the point that groups are an alternative and effective channel of influence for citizens, and that groups themselves emphasize different points of access, we do not wish to suggest that links with political parties *cannot* be an important aspect of group activity. Particular groups do use parties as a means of access and as a means of getting issues on to the political agenda. And in one particular case—the trade unions—party links may be said to be of central importance. It is useful to consider the general relationship between groups and parties first, and then to consider the special case of trade unions and the Labour party.

Parties as a Means of Access to Policy-Making

Anyone devising a group's strategy would find it prudent, at a minimum, at least to monitor the emergence of party policies and to see to it that the relevant party spokesmen are aware of the group's views and objectives. For example, if a party in opposition is formulating policies on nuclear energy, then it is inevitable that groups involved in the industry (and those opposed to it) will be anxious to dissuade the party from adopting 'hostile' policies which, if elected, it *might* put into practice. Alternatively, a group may be anxious to persuade an opposition party to adopt a particular policy and to pledge itself to introduce that policy if elected. For example, the road haulage industry developed very close links with the Conservative party when it was in opposition in 1945–51. The industry had a very specific objective, to persuade the Conservatives to make a public commitment to denationalize the road haulage industry (which had been nationalized by the Attlee Government) if the Conservatives were re-elected. This pledge was obtained, and indeed the Conservatives did introduce a measure of denationalization. However, this was greatly modified from their opposition pledge, when they came to face the reality of government and the views of well-organized groups opposed to the policies advocated by the Road Haulage Association.

A more modern example of such a group tactic is the activity of the anti-bloodsports lobby in persuading the Labour party to promise to take legislative action to ban hare coursing and stag hunting with dogs, if it is elected. The League Against Cruel Sports (LACS) had been anxious to avoid bloodsports becoming a party political issue, but found this unavoidable when the Conservatives refused to have a policy on bloodsports and the Labour party decided to have one (and put a commitment in the 1979 and 1983 manifestos). As the League observed, 'like it or not, animal welfare was made a party political issue'. However, other pro-animal organizations have maintained a non-partisan approach, and the General Election Co-ordinating Committee for Animal Protection, for one, has been encouraged by support from Tory MPs and those attending Conservative conferences (Thomas 1983, p. 210). (The LACS was in fact a main financial backer of the GEECAP.) The GEECAP was chaired by Lord Houghton and backed by over sixty animal welfare groups; Hollands described (1980, pp. 91–5) how it was decided 'to put animals into politics' and how the GEECAP was able to have a presence at each of the party conferences in 1978, backed up by national advertising at the same time to attract the attention of conference participants. He defended the committee's 'well-stocked bar' as the best inducement possible to gain attention at conferences.

One of the difficulties the GEECAP encountered was the problem which supporting bodies had in reconciling their membership with their charitable status, which precluded political involvement. There was also some fairly predictable inter-organizational conflict, some bodies thinking that they already effectively mounted such campaigns (Hollands 1980, p. 107).

Hollands, himself secretary to the campaign, described the difficulties of organizing such a broad-front coalition. Bodies such as JACOPIS—the Joint Committee on Pets in Society—proved impossible to mobilize, perhaps because that group incorporates the pet food manufacturing and veterinary associations as well as pet welfare bodies. The British Horse Society withdrew, because of the participation of the League Against Cruel Sports. The RSPB was one of the bodies which forced the withdrawal of the Humane Education Council, because the RSPB's own Royal charter was specifically *not* against legitimate sport.

Another example of the party approach, in early 1986, was the pressure from the Post Office Engineering Union on the Labour party, regarding the party's position in the renationalization of British Telecom. The POEU was concerned that Mr Kinnock, leader of the party, was modifying the party's renationalization policy. The POEU recognized that getting a commitment from an opposition party was no *guarantee* that the party would keep its promise if it became the Government. Once in office, the Government would have to deal with a whole range of groups and practical difficulties. Just as groups press opposition parties to make specific pledges, then the parties try to avoid being too specific, in order to maximize their room for manoeuvre if elected.

The POEU example indicates a fairly common feature of the links between groups and political parties, namely that the links are often at their closest when a particular group finds itself at odds with the Government of the day and is almost forced into the arms of the Opposition. The Opposition—in pursuit of opportunist grounds to attack the Government—is usually a ready partner. Having failed to carry its case with the Government, a group then has little alternative but to try to mobilize public opinion and/or hope that an alternative Government will emerge which is more favourably disposed towards its case. The strategy is a high-risk one—as we shall see when we discuss the special case of trade unions and the Labour Party—for if the Opposition fails to win the subsequent general election, the group can be left out in the cold for several more years and may have neglected to maintain links with the relevant government departments. Developing too close a relationship with the Opposition can reduce the chances of exercising even moderate influence over the existing Government and may be in breach of the 'rules' of insider status. The wisest strategy is, therefore, to be seen to be even-handed between parties, when circumstances allow.

Even where there are thought to be rather close links between a particular set of groups and a particular political party, the relationship may be far from trouble-free. For example, business groups have often been at odds with the Conservatives. Conservative ideology—that competition should be encouraged and that industry should not be subsidized—often runs counter to the actual desires of businessmen. Thus in the autumn of 1985 the chairman of the Association of British Chambers of Commerce, Mr James Archer, argued that the Government's assumption that industry could stand on its own two feet was no longer valid, and he called for 'an industrial strategy similar to that of other market economies' (*Financial Times*, 19 September 1985). He wanted *more* intervention on the economy—especially in the 'high tech' sector—as manufacturers no longer believed that slimming down and losing capacity was good for them. The CBI also began to move in a direction somewhat opposed to the Conservative Government in January 1986 when it emphasized that future measures to deal with unemployment and problems in the inner cities were more important than cutting taxation. In doing so it called for an extra billion pounds in public expenditure in the 1986 budget, to support cost-effective employment schemes (*CBI News*, January 1986, pp. 10–11).

The *Financial Times* had earlier reported that the Chancellor of the Exchequer, Nigel Lawson, was particularly displeased with the director general of the CBI, Sir Terence Beckett, for proposing a discussion of macro-economic policy at the National Economic Development Council (*Financial Times*, 18 November 1985). Another example of disagreement between business and the Thatcher Government was on the issue of the privatization of British Telecom. Business was in favour of privatization in *principle*, but in practice had serious doubts about the possible effects of the form of the policy on British telecommunications firms, and was active in lobbying the Government in an attempt to obtain modifications (Moon *et al.* 1986). Wyn Grant (1983, p. 173) quotes the former director general of the CBI, who had warned the incoming CBI president that 'holding office under a Tory Government would be much more testing than under Labour, much more searching, and much more vulnerable'. Grant goes on to suggest that 'When one looks at the relationship between business and the political parties, the most striking fact is the general absence of a relationship. This is particularly true of the relationship between business and the Conservative Party.'

However, it may be that Grant was looking for formal relationships, where informal relationships can be as effective. Thus there is a general mutual acceptance between élites that means that views of busiessmen can be communicated without group inter-mediation. Some ministers indeed have their private circles of businessmen who can be sounded for their reactions. There are some personal links which remain intact. Whilst there is no formal affiliation of business groups to the Conservatives, there is a degree of overlapping membership, as well as an important financial link. For example, MPs' links with business increased by 10 per cent during 1985, with the Register of Members' Interests showing some 310 registered business consultancies in that year. Most of these consultancies (though not all) were held by Conservative MPs. Typical examples were Mr Patrick Jenkin, the former Secretary of State for the Environment, who had a consultancy with Arthur Anderson & Co., management consultants; Sir William Clarke, who was an adviser to Commercial Union Assurance, Texaco, and Tate & Lyle; Robert Atkins, who was parliamentary consultant to the Japanese computer firm Wang (UK); and Robert Sheldon, who was parliamentary consultant to Panasonic (UK).

By and large, business leaders from the large firms rely on methods other than party channels for exercising political influence. With a few exceptions noted in the next chapter, Britain seems *not* to exhibit the characteristic found by J. P. Olsen in Norway, for example, where over half of the elected leaders in national economic–producer organizations had held office in a political party or represented a political party in public office (Olsen 1983, p. 203).

Though senior business leaders do not generally seek public office or play important roles within the Conservative party, the financial links between big business and the Conservatives are quite evident. Though reliable statistics are hard to come by, a significant proportion of the Conservative party funds comes from political donations by companies. However, these donations come from a minority of companies, only 27 per cent of the largest 1,250 companies in 1981 (Grant 1983, quoting a Labour party survey,

p. 177). *The Economist* (6 October 1984) claimed that in the year to the 1983 election the Conservative party (and associated bodies) received £4 million from registered companies.

It is difficult to assess the actual *policy* impact of this funding. Equally, the significance of the trade unions as a source of finance to the Labour party is no guarantee that a Labour Government will deliver. Pouring money into political parties, in the hope that it will assist a group in influencing policy, looks likely to be an irrational act, carried out for historical reasons rather than based upon an objective analysis of costs and benefits over time.

Irrespective of strategic calculations, however, there may be a 'natural' affinity between certain groups and a particular political party. McCarthy's study (1983, p. 214) of the Child Poverty Action Group suggests that there were particularly close links between CPAG and the Labour party. For example, he argued that 'The work of . . . academics in raising the issue of poverty within the Labour Party and in providing information about the problem, helped to initiate an interparty debate that persuaded Labour to incorporate an attack on poverty on its own political agenda.'

He suggests (1983, p. 222) that CPAG's 'strategy of influencing the Labour Party from within was a natural outcome of the affinity between CPAG leaders and their viewpoints and those of the party itself'. CPAG leaders were often already active in the Labour party, and had played a role in drafting the party's policy on social security—*New Frontiers of Social Security*—leading CPAG to adopt an insider strategy with the Labour party itself. The early strategy was, therefore, to influence opinion within the party, in McCarthy's terms 'to "re-educate" opinion leaders within the party about poverty, rekindle and restore the party's concern with welfare and to galvanise the party machinery for a broader assault on the problem' (McCarthy 1983, p. 223). Yet this strategy was essentially a failure because the Labour party, in CPAG's opinion, failed to 'deliver' when it gained office. Eventually, the relationship between CPAG and Labour became very strained when CPAG attacked the subsequent Labour Government, in the 1970 election, for its alleged poor record on poverty. Again in 1978 CPAG claimed that the poor had got poorer under Labour. This claim provoked a sense of bitterness amongst Labour ministers (McCarthy 1983, pp. 215–17). This case illustrates the problem of a group when it gets too close to any one particular party, which when elected finds itself faced with much broader policy and political considerations.

Marsh and Chambers' study (1983) of the abortion issue shows that groups can be avowedly non-partisan, yet in practice find their line accepted more readily in one party than another. This, they suggest, was the case with the National Abortion Campaign. They show that the NAC sought to get resolutions supporting the 1967 Act, and calling for abortion on request, introduced at union conferences and the Labour party conference. The existence of women-only structures within the Labour party—the National Joint Committee on Working Women's organizations, the National Women's Advisory Committee, the party's chief women's officer— helped 'create an atmosphere which ensured that in 1977 the Labour Party Conference overwhelmingly adopted defence of the 1967 Abortion Act as party policy'.

Marsh and Chambers describe how the Labour party women's organizations mailed MPs on the issue reminding them of party policy, how the chief women's officer of the party provided 'party supervision' of Labour MPs in the debates, and how pro-abortion members of the parliamentary Labour party used weekly PLP meetings as a channel to their colleagues. All this party contact reminded Labour members of the party's official position on the issue.

In this case the 'capture' of the Labour party—in tandem with an officially non-partisan approach—worked well. A group such as the League Against Cruel Sports had, as we suggest above, been obliged to develop a 'one-legged' stance and in 1979 to give support and money to the Labour party, but this was almost by default. Thomas (1983, p. 265) describes that, although the league wished to generate all-party support in Parliament, almost all its support came from Labour MPs.

Thomas also stresses the links between pro-hunting groups—the British Field Sports society in particular—and the Conservative party. The role of Marcus Kimball MP as chairman of the BFSS appeared critical. Thomas judges that Private Members' Bills against hunting are unlikely to prosper during periods of Conservative government, but he ascribes this as much to the personal taste of the party leadership as to the power of the pro-hunting lobby. Thomas implies that the role of Kimball and others was to remind the Conservative leadership that an anti-hunting policy, popular with the voters, would cause disruption within the party itself.

Usually the more effective 'party strategy' is to develop genuine *all-party* support for a group's aim. A typical all-party strategy is for groups to encourage the formation (and provide support for) all-party groups in the House of Commons. These groups are unofficial committees, based in the House of Commons, with the central feature of attracting all-party support. A good example of such a group is the All-Party Disablement Group, whose objective has been to press for better provision and legislative change in policy areas affecting disabled people. Such a committee can be of considerable advantage to a pressure group, as cross-bench pressure is perhaps the most effective form of *parliamentary* pressure which can be applied to a government. A government is much more likely to make concessions if it is faced with pressure from all sections of the House of Commons than if it is just faced with the expected hostile reception from the official opposition. Some all-party groups are relatively permanent, like the Disablement Group, the Civil Liberties Group, the Industrial Safety Group, the Animal Welfare Group, the Parliamentary Information Technology Committee, the Equal Opportunities Group, and the Channel Tunnel Group. Others are *ad hoc*, formed to fight on a particular issue such as opposing the third London airport. Whether or not an all-party committee exists, groups are often anxious to demonstrate all-party support. For example, in 1984 the League Against Cruel sports drafted a bill to prevent badger hunting, and made great efforts to ensure that it gained the support of MPs from all parties when it sent a delegation to see the Home Secretary. (*Cruel Sports*, no. 14, autumn 1984).

Another variant of groups developing links with parties in the parliamentary context is the link between groups and party committees in Parliament. These are especially significant on the Conservative side of the House, as the specialist party committees (such as the Conservative Trade and Industry Committee) are an important channel of back-bench influence on Conservative ministers. It is fairly common for groups to develop close links with the relevant back-bench party committee, as a means of placing added pressure on the Government, and as a means of proposing amendment to bills. Such links are rarely subject to much publicity but may be all the more effective for that. Thus a group may have very good links with the civil servants dealing with a piece of legislation, but may also maintain close links with the relevant party committee in the House of Commons. Adopting this dual strategy needs skill in order to avoid damage to the essential links with the Civil Service.

Trade Unions and the Labour Party

Martin Harrison, writing in 1974, observed that 'After more than seventy years the alliance between Labour and the Unions still rouses impassioned and contradictory assessments. On paper there would seem little room for doubt: the unions if they chose to do so could hold the Party in their grasp' (Harrison 1974, p. 69.) Yet he also continues that 'in the period since 1945 one would be hard put to produce examples of the unions dictating Labour policy on a non-industrial issue. Even on the economic and industrial questions where the unions tend to exercise their power more effectively and unsentimentally there appear to have been remarkably few major matters on which the union attitude was conclusive.'

As with the business lobby and the Conservative party, there is a financial link, so much so that it is not unfair to claim that the Labour party is as dependent upon the unions for finance as membership. The 1983 *Annual Report* of the Labour party showed 6,189,000 affiliated union members of the Labour party, with only 626,000 members being affiliated via constituency labour parties. The *Sunday Times* (13 January 1985) calculated that the unions gave the Labour party £5 million in 1983.

The unions also play a major role in the running of the party. For example, they elect twelve members to the National Executive Committee of the party (out of a total of twenty-seven elected members), and dominate in the voting for another six of the NEC places. (As individuals cannot be simultaneously on the General Council of the TUC and on the NEC, NEC representation tends to be below that of general secretary, as the TUC is seen as the more important in union circles.) They have also had, since 1983, a hand in the election of the leader of the party, having 40 per cent of the votes in the electoral college which elects the leader. The combination of membership, finance, NEC membership, and a role in the leadership election would on paper suggest enormous influence for the unions. In addition, the historical links between the unions and the party are so deep that it is quite normal for union leaders to campaign for the election of a Labour Government.

Yet the relationship is extremely complex and has been fraught with difficulties. As Harrison notes, there is little or no evidence that the trade unions can dictate to a Labour Government, and much evidence to the contrary. Labour Governments—like Conservative Governments—have to represent a much broader constituency of interests if they are to be elected and re-elected, and can only go so far in making concessions to interests with which they may have special links. At times, of course, the relationship between a Labour Government and the unions has been extremely close, such that the unions have become an integral part of the governing process. This was especially true during certain periods under the Social Contract. Ironically, it was the Conservative Government which in fact created the conditions for the development of the Social Contract during the early 1970s. It was Edward Heath's industrial relations legislation—to which the union movement was bitterly opposed—which finally led the TUC and the Labour party to take up a suggestion by Jack Jones of the TGWU and form a Liaison Committee in 1970 (Barnes and Reid 1980, p. 191).

Earlier, under a previous Labour Government, industrial relations legislation, in the form of Barbara Castle's *In Place of Strife*, had caused bitter conflict between the Government and the unions. This episode led some union leaders to the view that a much better relationship had to be reached with any future Labour Government in order to avoid a repeat of the debacle over *In Place of Strife*. The Liaison Committee has two joint secretaries, one from the TUC and one from the Labour party. The TUC has eleven representatives, the NEC eleven, and the parliamentary Labour party nine members—somewhat larger than when it was first set up—possibly making the committee unwieldy. The purpose of the Liaison Committee was to develop an alternative economic strategy to that being pursued by the Heath Government. Its early priority was to draft proposals for the repeal of the Conservatives' industrial relations policy, and it was decided that the proposals should actively be drafted in the Liaison Committee. Clark *et al.* (1980, p. 21) argue that 'This comprised a significant institutional and substantive innovation, an important departure from the traditional divisions of labour between the industrial and political wings of the labour movement.'

There is little doubt that the Liaison Committee was an

important mechanism for the unions to influence the actual content of the legislation subsequently introduced by the Labour government elected in 1974. In this case, party access proved to be a very effective channel of group influence. Statements on broader economic strategy soon emerged from the Liaison Committee, forming the basis of a 'social contract' between the unions and Labour. The policy statement *Economic Policy and the Cost of Living* was approved by the TUC and subsequently published as a pamphlet by the Labour party (see *TUC Report* 1973, p. 312). The policies advocated in this document reflect what has been described as 'unprecedented direct access to Labour Party policy-making prior to the 1974 election' by TUC leaders (Clark *et al.* 1980, p. 44).

The Labour government, in the months following the 1974 election victory, began to implement some of the key elements which had emerged from the work of the Liaison Committee, particularly in the field of industrial relations. The early years of the Social Contract must be judged a success for the TUC in that it was closely involved in government (having been forced to play an outsider role on a number of issues under the previous Conservative Government). It had secured major legislative changes—both the repeal of 'offensive' legislation and the introduction of various employment protection measures—and had secured a return to its professed objective, free collective bargaining.

However, the TUC had set itself on a path the direction of which it could not control. As the economic situation worsened, then so the pressure on the unions to deliver less welcome (to them) deals began to increase. As noted in chapter 7, the TUC found itself being drawn into an incomes policy, whether it liked it or not. As the 1975 *TUC Report* observed, the economic situation, by 1975, was critical, 'and there was a need to avert the danger of the Government being forced to take deflationary measures which would increase unemployment still further'. The shift in the relationship was made quite clear by the fact that the Labour Chancellor of the Exchequer, though hoping for voluntary agreement on a prices and wages policy, made it quite clear that he would resort to statutory means if he failed to get it (*TUC Report* 1975, p. 272). The choice, for the TUC, was not whether to support an incomes policy or not, but what role to play in its implementation (Clark *et al.* 1980, p. 34).

The involvement of the unions in the Social Contract eventually caused splits within the union movement, with considerable stress on the TUC and eventually embarrassment to the Labour Government in the winter of 1978–9 (the so-called winter of discontent), when it was clear to all that the special relationship, TUC–Labour party Liaison Committee notwithstanding, had severe limitations. The 1979 *TUC Report* (p. 285) revealed that in January the Liaison Committee had decided that 'it was important to *work towards* an early common understanding on economic, industrial and social issues . . .' (our emphasis).

The election of a Conservative government, in 1979, may have eased the task of the Liaison Committee in that a party in opposition—and also lacking the advice of the Civil Service—is more free to make policy commitments. In October 1981 the Liaison Committee agreed 'that detailed discussions with the Labour Party on the contents of the new legislation should take place in due course' (*TUC Report* 1981, p. 25). It was also agreed that the Labour Party and the TUC should again work towards a wide-ranging statement for the 1982 party conference and 1982 Congress 'similar to that which they had produced in 1973'. The TUC and Labour party are now (1986) again committed to the repeal of Conservative industrial relations legislation.

The Liaison Committee has now defined its role in the following terms: (1) to provide a forum for the TUC, NEC, and PLP to meet regularly at representative level; (2) to ensure an exchange of information and co-ordination of the policies and the campaigning work of these bodies; (3) to provide a strong critique of the central elements of the Government's thinking and policies; (4) to develop and promote jointly agreed policies (*General Council Report* 1985, p. 288). Joint policy statements have appeared, e.g. *Partners in Rebuilding Britain* in 1983 and *A New Partnership, A New Britain* in 1984.

A key issue, of course, will be the wages policy of any future Labour Government. It was reported in November 1985 that the Liaison Committee had changed the way it proceeds, 'moving away from a grand consideration of the whole economy to focussing on these two [wages and labour laws] specific-issues' (*Financial Times*, 26 November 1985). The difficulty for the Labour party is that it will need to reassure voters that its more expansionist economic strategy will not cause a rapid income inflation, and that it will not remove some of the more popular Tory trade union legislation (e.g. pre-strike ballots and ballots for trade union leaders). The problem for the TUC is that in possibly gaining concessions from the Labour party—in terms of promised legislation—it may be drawn in to helping to bring about a controversial 'voluntary' incomes policy. It is difficult to predict outcomes, especially as the TUC is itself occupied with the *internal* matters, particularly disputes between unions and the problem of some unions 'co-operating' with Conservative legislation. In early 1986 there were clear signs that the TUC might accept some of the Conservative laws as being here to stay, whatever government is in power.

In any case, as Marsh and King (1985, p. 60) suggest, there has been a general decline in the power of unions: not just because of Mrs Thatcher's Government, but because of the changing nature of world production, new international divisions of labour, and the changing composition of the workforce. In predicting a bleak future for the unions—particularly because of the arrival of new technology—they suggest that the inherent weakness of the unions 'is exacerbated by the fact that the British Trade Union movement has never attempted to develop a political strategy other than to rely on its link with the Labour Party'. Our own argument would support this view, as we believe that linking with political parties is probably one of the least effective strategies for a group to adopt in the long term. Indeed, there is evidence that the TUC itself fully recognizes this, for it continues to adopt a 'dual track' strategy of an open alliance with the Labour party and continued participation in the governmental network described in chapter 8. The Social Contract was a high point of integration in governmental decision-making, but it disintegrated with economic deterioration.

Groups and Parliament*

Professor Mackintosh (1978, p. 8) claimed in 1978 that only a limited number of pressure groups want legislative changes of a kind which MPs can influence. Wyn Grant and David Marsh (1977, p. 113) have commented, 'As the influence of Parliament has decreased, so the major interest groups in Britain have expended less effort on trying to influence its decisions.' About the CBI in particular, they wrote: 'in general Westminster is not a channel which is assiduously used by the CBI'. Grant's later work (1981, p. 31) on the growing governmental affairs function in large companies uncovered a variety of attitudes. One respondent argued that (parliamentary) contacts were of little value, as what was important was to exert influence in the executive branch before a decision was taken. Another stated that his firm largely limited its efforts to the thirty or forty MPs with a special interest in its industry.

One reason why Parliament appears to be an unpromising ground for lobbyists was put as follows by Professor Finer (1970, p. 157):

Increasingly, what the minister presents to the Commons is a package arrangement agreed between his civil servants and the representatives of the outside groups. In the House, party discipline inhibits backbenchers from challenging their government, even if it did not, the information and evidence on which the package depends are confidential and have not been disclosed; and even if they had been, the nature of the package is so well-balanced a set of compromises that if any one part were overturned in the House the entire deal would have to be renegotiated.

This kind of discussion appears at odds with the sheer volume of group activity exerted at the parliamentary level.

It is easy, however, to get out of proportion the highly visible type of group activity aimed at Parliament, the mass letter-writing

---

* This chapter is based on A. G. Jordan, 'Parliament Under Pressure', *Political Quarterly*, vol. 56, no. 2, 1985, pp. 174–82.

operations or the mass lobby. The link between 'noise' and influence is weak. Parliamentary activity is perhaps particularly important for environmental, social issue, and other cause groups without good connections to Whitehall and the Civil Service. It is because of the nature of their issues that books such as Christoph's *Capital Punishment and British Politics* or Pym's *Pressure Groups and the Permissive Society* focus so fully on Parliament. One of the advantages to the cause group in a parliamentary strategy is that the media's continuing fixation on Parliament means that parliamentary campaigns are relayed to the broad public constituency which helps further social change. The House of Lords can perform this publicity role as well as the Commons.

One aspect of using Parliament as an excuse for media attention is the mass lobby. It takes place not to win votes but to win television time. Thus in its own way the mass lobby has become ritualized and probably more therapeutic for those engaged in the lobbying than compelling to those lobbied. Rules exist to facilitate the mass lobby: so that inconvenience can be controlled. What appears to the television camera as an uncontrolled activity is probably meeting the two-page guidance 'Notes for Members of Parliament on Arrangements for Mass Lobbies', well on its way to being part of the dignified element of the constitution.

The *House Magazine* (which subtitles itself 'The Weekly Journal of the Houses of Parliament) contains the sort of 'business of the House' information that might be expected from such a title, along with articles on relevant topics such as Congress and issues such as the televising of the House. However, it is produced not by the House but by Parliamentary Communications Ltd., and appears to be financed by advertising addressed specifically at legislators. As well as corporate prestige advertising, some advertisements are in furtherance of legislation: for example, the City of Birmingham advertised in favour of its private legislation to allow a Birmingham motor road race. The magazine carries a (paid-for) Briefing and Information Directory, where causes, trade associations, and companies give contact points for members interested in their affairs. British Rail, for example, gives the name and telephone extension of its 'parliamentary affairs manager', CND offers a 'parliamentary liaison officer', British Nuclear Fuels have an 'information service for parliamentarians', and British American Tobacco lists a 'public affairs manager'.

The 'briefing on request' service is clearly one of the less active forms of pressure on the House. It can be seen as a service more than pressure, as MPs must themselves take the initiative to find out more. A similar form of self-selection of targets covers the all-party committees, of which there are currently around 100. Like the group world, the all-party world covers both cause and economic interests. Examples of the former would include the ASH (Action on Smoking and Health) Group and the Alcoholism Services and Policy Group. Examples of the latter include Cotton and Allied Textiles and the Chemical Industry Group.

The all-party groups of MPs are not usually spontaneous manifestations of parliamentary interest; they are often stimulated and indeed administered by groups. For example, the Social Science and Policy Committee stemmed from attempts by the Association of Learned Societies in the Social Sciences to improve the image of the social sciences in Parliament; the association organizes the speakers for the meetings. The creation of an all-party group on civil liberties in 1985 was linked with the National Council for Civil Liberties and was part of its campaign to broaden the political base of its cause, which had, arguably, become too identified with the left. The all-party committee was given secretarial back-up by the NCCL. Thus the common pattern is to find cause groups supporting, encouraging, interested MPs. Other examples include Age Concern and its relationship with the Pensioners Parliamentary Group (a full-time member of Age Concern is the secretary), Shelter and the Shelter Group, BLESMA and the British Limbless Ex-serviceman's Association Group . . . One of the most spectacular successes by an *ad hoc* pressure group was the Wing Airport Resistance Association's operation against the possible siting of the third London airport at Wing/Cublington in 1970. WARA managed to engineer the formation of an all-party committee with 'the express object of co-ordinating opposition to the choice of any of the proposed inland sites' (see Kimber and Richardson 1974, p. 204).

On the industrial/economic side, the Chemical Industry Group is administered through help from the Chemical Industries Association. Various other examples are administered by consultants who have relevant commercial interests: the Parliamentary Information Technology Committee, for example, is run from the office of Charles Barker Lyon, whose clients include British Telecom, Plessey, and other related companies. Charles Barker also deals with the All-Party Minerals Group, the All-Party Motor Industry Group, the All-Party Records Study Group, and the Parliamentary and Scientific Committee. CSM Parliamentary Consultants provide the secretariat for the Retail Trade Group and the All-Party Energy Committee.

The chairman of the Select Committee on Members' Interests (House of Commons 408, 1st Report, 1985, p. 10) has suggested, 'Some people think that all party groups would not exist if it were not for the fact that they are really an extension of lobbying and that they only exist because their salaried work is financed and they are only alive by the fact that visits to various countries are financed basically by external groups.'

The all-party committees are a means of group support of sympathetic members and also a means to get wider articulation of their interests. The single-party back-bench committees can also permit groups to keep members informed. One account describes the Conservative back-bench Housing and Construction Committee as operating in a similar fashion to an all-party group in that 'the members invite organisations to meetings and, in turn, receive frequent requests for consultations. In this way, the interested MPs are kept informed of developments.' (In Mackintosh 1978, p. 67.)

As an extension of access to the House though servicing all-party committees, group officials or lobbyists can be made research assistants for supportive MPs. Rolf Hermerlin, director of parliamentary affairs for MENCAP, pointed out the advantages: 'I am the honorary research assistant to one MP and therefore I can go in and out of the House freely and one meets MPs at all occasions, not just in the Chamber, not just in the committee room but in corridors, and in the cafeterias and the bars and one builds up a circle of MPs and Peers who one finds out are helpful and supportive to our causes.' (Quoted in 'In on the Act', BBC Radio 4, 17 November 1981, presented by Tony Barker.) Age Concern employs a 'parliamentary officer' who spends 75 per cent of his time in the House, technically as a secretary to Mr Andrew Bowden MP (to obtain a desk) and to Mr George Foulkes MP (to get a photopass). Apparently the RADAR (Royal Association for Disability and Rehabilitation) similarly employs a research assistant to serve the All-Party Disablement Group (see House of Commons 408, 1985, p. 53).

Another area where the groups–Members relationship is often symbiotic rather than pressuring is in the mutual interest of an Opposition and a group attempting to alter legislation. In parliamentary activity the difference in resources between the Government and the Opposition is extreme. A minister will rarely talk on the Floor of the House (in the main chamber) or in committee without his civil service advisers being present 'in the box' to his left. While the Opposition has some researchers, and can use the House of Commons library researchers, it does not have the tailor-made briefing available to the Government. This is one reason why the Opposition is often only too glad of assistance from outside groups. Case studies of non-partisan legislation also stress the role of group as support to the Members. Professor Griffith has summed up:

On important bills the affected interests outside Parliament will be anxious to help the Opposition in the hope of bringing further pressure to bear on the Government to accept amendments. And if they are powerful they will be well and expertly staffed and will have or will engage lawyers to draft amendments so that all Opposition members need to do, if they are so minded, is to sign the amendment provided and hand it in to the Public Bill Office. At times, this servicing by professionals and experts comes close in its drafting and in its briefing to the service provided for the Minister by his department. (In Walkland and Ryle 1977, p. 101.)

Marsh and Chambers' 1981 study of *Abortion Politics* (p. 115) records how the pro-abortion opponents of John Corrie's restrictive amending bill in 1979 had learned by then the lesson that 'co-ordination between the parliamentary and extra parliamentary lobby was essential'.

In the 1977–8 Session (on a new abortion bill introduced by W. Benyon MP) the pro-abortion organization had had a committee to service 'their' MPs at the Committee Stage, but this had proved inadequate, and by the time of the Corrie Bill,

a . . . group of [14] lawyers prepared a series of amendments to the Bill and new clauses . . . when the Committee Stage started in earnest there were regular Monday evening meetings between the five [pro-abortion] MPs and a group of . . . advisers including both lawyers and doctors . . . In addition members of the briefing team . . . attended each meeting of the Standing Committee in order to advise MPs when required.

Marsh and Chambers found that while the anti-abortion groups did also hold briefing meetings for MPs, these were less frequent and shorter than those held by the pro-abortion lobby. Marsh and Chambers saw the lack of a co-ordinated anti-abortion strategy as an important factor in the ultimate failure of the Corrie Bill to make abortion more restricted.

The Association of Metropolitan Authorities described its activity on the Government's rate-capping legislation (a campaign in which it used consultants for the first time) as follows:

Lobbying had started before the Bill was published and took a number of forms—with the guidance of the Association's Parliamentary consultants. Modest lunches for MPs likely to be open to persuasion, or small receptions, personal contacts, sending briefing material and alerting journalists to the issues. Unfortunately lobbying is a little like advertising— 90 per cent of it is wasted, the problem is knowing which 90 per cent.

At the same time as lobbying, thought had to be given to amendments to the Bill. Once again with the help of advisers, the Bill was examined line by line. Amendments are the *sine qua non* of the Committee stage and a large number are needed not only to wreck, improve or probe but to assist in filibustering if that happens to be the Opposition's tactic . . .

The Association supported the 'opposition' to the Bill in Committee by producing amendments and more importantly the briefs to accompany them and sustain the argument. The 'opposition' comprised the Labour side of the Committee, two Alliance MPs and Mr Anthony Beaumont-Dark, a Vice President of the Association, and one Conservative MP on the Committee representing the sizable amount of Opposition in the Conservative party . . .

Supporting the 'opposition' required attendance at the weekly meeting of the Labour side of the Committee to discuss the week's tactics and then appearing (on the public benches) at most of the Committee's sittings . . . Attendance at Committee is important, to establish links with MPs, to supplement the written briefs by oral advice, to be able to respond to Government statements etc.

. . . Some 160 amendments had been tabled, most of them coming from the Associations. The only amendments actually made to the Bill came from the Government and altered the proposals on disabled person's rating relief . . . (M. Pilgrim, *Municipal Review*, June 1984, pp. 45–6.)

Groups might organize themselves into formal or informal alliances in performing this assistance role to critics in Parliament. On the Data Protection Act (1984), the BMA, National Consumer Council, Justice, Law Society, and others worked an informal 'clearing house' system whereby they pooled all answers from ministers, proposed amendments, information, so that each could develop their case-building on the work of others. On the Insolvency Act (1985), the NCC worked closely with the CBI and the Institute of Directors, normally its opponents in the lobbying game.

The relationships between the MPs and groups interested in social or moral reforms are likely to be close. MPs successful in the ballot for a Private Member's Bill (which is the usual vehicle for such reforms) are usually given an embarrassment of choice by groups of changes to sponsor.

One reason for MPs 'leaning' on groups is that the business of drafting legislation is technical, and requires expertise. Groups themselves might well have to 'buy in' expertise at the cost of several thousand pounds for even one short bill. One lobbyist has suggested that MPs are so dependent that at a committee stage his group would make the assumption that no one (apart from the minister) had read the bill. In other words, the MPs rely upon the groups to underscore the main issues and brief them with the central arguments.

But even on general legislation, groups are active. In her description of the Committee Stage of the 1980 Housing Bill, Monica Freeman described Labour's John Tilley as having the distinction of speaking on behalf of almost every lobbying organization in the land (*New Statesman*, 21 November 1980). Graham Page (former MP) has remarked on the basis of his experience, 'When you are in Opposition you have to create your own Civil Service.' On the Town and Country Planning Bill of 1968 he organized the group interests to develop ideas against the bill. (Evidence to the Renton Committee on *The Process of Legislation*, 1975.)

Moran's study of banking (1984, p. 126) describes how 'The [Labour] Opposition in the Commons anxious to carry on the adversary battle had to rely on the banking pressure groups to brief it with informed arguments against the legislation.' As the bankers were chiefly concerned with the proposal for a Deposit Protection Fund, the debates on the DPF 'were the longest and most heated during the passage of the legislation'.

Frank Field, now an MP, but formerly director of the Child Poverty Action Group, describes with authority the ease with which even 'outsider' groups such as the CPAG can use the parliamentary links. He remarks (1982) that there was never any difficulty in getting parliamentary questions asked. This was partly because there was sympathy for the group's goals, but also because it allowed MPs an air of diligence and busyness when their sole role was to carry the questions the 100 yards from the central lobby to the Table office. Parliamentary questions allowed CPAG a spiral of advantage. The questions produced the data which let the group develop the reputation for good briefing that impressed MPs. Field also confirms the value of outside groups to the Opposition: drafting amendments and providing commentaries. He suggests that without civil service assistance the main front-bench opposition spokesmen are in a kind of information vacuum: it is in this context that it is difficult to overstate the importance of these briefs from outside bodies. 'Not only is a body like CPAG . . . quoted . . . but the most thorough use is made of their detailed briefs at the committee stage of the bills. Staff could attend the informal meetings of opposition MPs . . . and often the staff member most concerned would be present for all or part of the committee stage of the bill.' Parliamentary activity is thus often surrogate group activity.

One importance of Parliament for the lobbyist is perhaps accidental, but none the less significant. Out of office, the Opposition is often opportunistic in seeking any stick with which to attack the Government. This means its spokesmen are willing to accept the briefings and to propose the amendments of interests simply out of a wish to oppose the Government. This can give the interests useful arguments if the Opposition takes power.

Though it would be convenient to argue for omnipresent and omniactive groups, the parliamentary connections are not invariably made. And Parliament as a target for group pressure is significant only if the parliamentary process is significant. Academic opinion has tended to be dismissive of parliamentary influence in recent years. Professor Finer (1966 edn., p. 141) quoted with approval a correspondent in *The Times* who in 1963 considered that Parliament 'is already in some danger of becoming more like a pianola than a pianist, mechanically rendering tunes jointly composed by departments of state and whatever organised interests happen to be affected'.

Many of the efforts of groups in Parliament are not geared to changing legislation, and given the comparatively few cases where party rebellions force change on government, it is unrealistic for groups to expect to defeat governments. Groups, however, pay attention to Parliament—inspire questions, give evidence to Select Committees, brief MPs—because even where actual legislative change is not in sight the groups can hope to put matters on the political agenda, stimulate interest in their problems, and establish their reputation and credibility as expert sources of views in their field. Parliament can be helpful in 'climate setting', even where immediate and direct legislative benefits cannot be seen. Several quotations in Davies's book on the *Politics of Pressure: The Art of Lobbying* (1985, pp. 62–3) confirm that a picture of MPs as the victims of remorseless pressure is often materially inaccurate. The MP is only too glad to fire the group ammunition. David Myles, former Conservative MP in Banffshire, had a background in the NFU before becoming an MP. He told Davies how he maintained his NFU links and distributed parliamentary questions on behalf of the NFU:

A lot of the time, you see, Members of Parliament are so busy they really don't have time to think of the question that would be relevant . . . I would say to MPs: 'Do you want to ask a question of the Minister of Agriculture' . . . Barney Holbeche [parliamentary director of the NFU] helped me a bit. I used to tell him: 'Look send me all the questions you want asked, and I'll ensure that some of them will be asked.'

Myles also gave a good example of how he, as an MP with thirty-five whisky distilleries in his constituency, would naturally act on behalf of the industry: 'I got a note handed in from the Scottish Whisky Association [sic] . . . I went out to see them, and they said, "We've got a brief here we would desperately like to put across in the budget debate." ' Myles records how, as he queued at the Speaker's chair to ask to be called in the debate, he discovered that his fellow Conservative Maurice Macmillan was queueing behind him to ask to withdraw from the debate. Showing good thinking as well as good manners, Myles let Macmillan ahead of him in the queue, and was allocated the unexpected vacancy on the Speaker's list. Myles says, 'I was able to talk more or less on the brief I'd got from the Scottish Whisky Association.'

Commercial Lobbyists

To move on from processes which tend mainly to support the converted, there are companies and causes lobbying in an attempt to convert, and—of increasing prominence—there are specialist commercial lobbying consultants who represent a variety of interests in the way a lawyer would represent a variety of unrelated clients. That well-known Aberdeen MP James Bryce (1888, pp. 557–8), writing on lobbying in the US a hundred years ago, pointed out, 'Just as a plaintiff in a law suit may properly employ an attorney and barrister, so a promoter [of a cause] may properly employ a lobbyist.' He also noted,

the promoters and opponents of a bill will be concentrated upon the committee to which the bill has been referred: and . . . when the interests affected are large it will be worthwhile to employ every engine of influence. Such influence can be better applied by those who have a skill and tact matured by experience . . . Accordingly, a class of persons springs up whose profession is to influence committees for or against bills.

Bryce quotes the librarian of Congress who, with apparent feeling, observed,

Thus there are at Washington, pension lobbyists, tariff lobbyists, steamship subsidy lobbyists, railway lobbyists, Indian ring lobbyists, patent lobbyists, river and harbour lobbyists, mining lobbyists, bank lobbyists, mail-contract lobbyists, war damage lobbyists, back-pay and bounty lobbyists, Isthmus canal lobbyists, public building lobbyists, State claims lobbyists, cotton tax lobbyists, and French spoilations lobbyists.

He went on, 'There are even artist lobbyists, bent upon wheedling Congress into buying bad paintings and worse sculptures; and too frequently with success.' The universe of contemporary British lobbyists is more than equally large, and equally esoteric. Bryce also notes that lobbying was not entirely respectable, 'But there is plainly a risk of abuse. "In the United States", says an experienced American publicist, whose opinion I have inquired, "though lobbying is perfectly legitimate in theory, yet the secrecy . . . make[s] it rapidly degenerate into a process of intrigue . . . The most dangerous men are the ex-members, who know how things are managed." ' (p. 558).

A mark of the controversy elicited by the activities of the British commercial lobbyists was the report of the Select Committee on Members' Interests (House of Commons 408, 1985). This claimed that 'There has in recent years been a substantial increase in lobbying . . . access to the precincts of the House has become more sought after and the number of all party and registered groups has greatly increased. (p. III.) Less blandly, one journalist (David Watt, *The Times*, 27 June 1985) claimed, 'there are too many stories of undeclared interests and connections, and too much evidence that the public is turned off by the now quite frequent spectacle of MPs profiting from lobbying their fellow members and the government, even when they do declare what they are up to. It is all beginning to stink.'

Although lobbying in Parliament is now subject to more attention, in his 1966 edition of *Anonymous Empire*, Professor Finer was drawing attention to the fact that a number of PR agencies had begun to act as 'contact men' with MPs. He wrote that 'such agencies know, or claim to know, how the House of Commons "works", the organisation of its back-bench specialist committees, which members are influential within them, who is influential with what minister, which MPs are likely to be interested in particular proposals'. This would still be the sales-pitch of today's more high-profile commercial lobbyists. Part of their work is reactive, the monitoring and reporting for clients developments of relevance to them, but the more noteworthy work is where there is an attempt to alter outcomes. Where the work is more or less reporting to the client on relevant parliamentary developments, there is an overlap with parliamentary agents whose main role is to represent clients on the technicalities of private legislation (see Rydz 1979, p. 22). But such firms will also monitor Parliament, and Rydz describes how the agent might find himself advising his clients on the handling of the debate and preparing a statement for circulating to all Members.

Douglas Smith of Political Research and Communication International described his approach as follows;

First I would identify the interested MPs, those whose constituents stand to gain from what we are trying to do. Then I would convene a meeting of MPs to explain the facts of the case. Then I would get a few sympathetic MPs to go on the record. Then I would explore the issue with civil servants. Best of all, I'd get at the minister if I could . . . Recently I had to do a job on the road issue and the civil servant I wanted to talk to wouldn't meet me. So I arranged for our MP to draft something like 20 written questions, which I know he would have to do the work of answering. He soon got the message. You might call that blackmail. I call it a triumph for inspired democracy. (Quoted in *Labour Research*, July 1984, vol. 73, no. 7.)

A *CBI Supplement* (April 1984) claimed that one of the fastest-growing areas of the booming public relations industry was this parliamentary and political advice (see 'Our Man in the Lobby' by Anthony Thorncroft). Thorncroft describes how for about £2000 p.a. a company such as Charles Barker will run a basic information service which will notify clients about all parliamentary developments of relevance. More custom-made services—such as briefing MPs on amendments—presumably come more expensive, and it has been claimed that the 'going rate' for a written PQ is about £200, with oral questions costing considerably more (*Observer*, 1 July 1984). (In 1975, the House specifically excluded questions from the requirements to declare interests.) A couple of examples of commercial lobbyists having access through the research assistantship door have been the subject of media criticism. Ian Greer Associates have two assistants attached to Andrew Bowden MP and Michael Grylls MP. Ian Greer has been quoted claiming 'that having his employees as research assistants gives his company an access that they wouldn't normally have. It enabled them to get parliamentary papers with greater ease and to rub shoulders with MPs.' (*Labour Research*, vol. 73, no. 7, p. 177.) Mr Peter Luff of Good Relations Corporate Affairs frankly told the Select Committee on Members' Interests (House of Commons 408, p. 41) that his research assistantship was 'an essentially bogus relationship, one I would gladly shed if I could gain [other] access to information which my clients, I believe, have a right to have'. Douglas Smith, managing director of Political Research and Communications International, is technically a research assistant to Peter Fry MP, chairman of PRCI. *Labour Research* quoted from the *Sunday Times* as follows:

He is able to roam around the House of Commons with ease. He is also able to join the House of Commons library . . . within a few minutes people like Smith can compile records of whole groups of MPs who have quoted an interest in certain subjects . . . Smith also uses MPs to supply him with information—and he admits paying MPs for that information. 'MPs can't be expected to give us the detail of a labour of love, can they', he says. (*Sunday Times*, 13 October 1983.)

Much attention to this sort of practice has stemmed from the Bob Cryer Bill in 1982 which (unsuccessfully) sought the registration of commercial interests. Cryer quoted with relish material from

Lloyd-Hughes Associates Ltd, founded by Sir Trevor Lloyd-Hughes (Lloyd-Hughes was a journalist and later worked as press secretary to Harold Wilson and from 1969–70 was a civil servant with the post of chief information adviser):

Our success derives from confidence that we can match promises with performance. Notable specific successes have been achieved. Among them, we have saved the international motor car and motor cycle industries based in the United Kingdom millions of pounds by persuading the Government to exempt them from provisions of the Trade Descriptions Act, severely reduced demands on an American company for back-payments of British excise duties, secured British Government planning permission for an oil platform building site. (*Hansard*, 2 February 1982, cols. 127–130.)

Cryer continued with Lloyd-Hughes' claims that they had masterminded the parliamentary campaign to remove the ship repair interests from the bill to nationalize shipbuilding, and so on. The Lloyd-Hughes document claimed 'regular relationships with the British Government, Cabinet and other Ministers and their Civil Service advisers at all appropriate levels'.

Another company, Political Research and Communication International, advertise that it works for companies, state concerns, trade associations, and pressure groups. It defines its role as 'political intelligence', and advises 'This is not simply the same-day monitoring of Parliamentary papers and Committees but a knowledge of what is happening "behind the scenes"—in the political parties and Whitehall "Think Tanks". Long-term programmes, putting our client's case sensibly and consistently are our basic work. Sometimes emergency action is needed as well . . . The Parliamentary world is complex and mistakes can prove costly.'

One idea of the sort of scale of MPs' contacts with outside bodies and the climate of our political life was given by the claim made by Martin Stevens MP, when he was asked about the contradiction between his sometime role as chairman of the National Appeals Committee of the Cancer Research Campaign and his accepting the hospitality of tobacco companies at Brands Hatch and Glyndebourne. He claimed that 'each year I guess I'm the guest of 150 commercial organisations of one kind or another, as are my colleagues. I am not sure it does us any harm. I don't think Members of Parliament should be isolated in an ivory tower.' (Taylor 1984, p. 100.)

The kind of projects pursued by lobbying companies include the GLC's opposition to its own dismemberment (Roland Freeman Ltd.), AMA opposition to rate-capping (GJW), opposition to the possibility of VAT on books (Sallingbury), and The Law Society's opposition to the erosion of the solicitor's monopoly on house conveyancing (Charles Barker, Watney, and Powell). Political Research and Communications International helped Kentucky Fried Chicken get the 1982 Miscellaneous Provisions (Local Government) Bill amended to change a proposal which could have obliged 'take-away' to close by 11 o'clock. GJW Consultants also operated for Chartered Consolidated to prevent the Monopolies Commission from stopping its bid for Anderson Strathclyde. They also lobbied for a referral of the take-over bid for Sothebys to the commission in order to allow time for another bidder to emerge. Other recent cases where consultants have been active include the protection of air courier firms from being affected by the 'liberalization' of the Post Office and the removal of proposals to tax private insurance schemes from clause 30 of the 1981 Finance Bill (Greer 1985, p. 22). The latter case is an example of the limited and technical change, which, while vital to the interests concerned, is marginal and bargainable to the Government, and is negotiable. The Government itself introduced its own amendment. This was an example of government responding to pressure, without defeat in the House.

For no very clearly articulated reason, 'professional' lobbying seems to give rise to more unease than a cause or company putting forward its own case. Some idea of buying advantage seems present in discussions. Bob Cryer MP, in his 1982 speech on his bill, made clear that his proposal would not 'affect a company, co-operative, trade unionist, council tenant or ordinary individual seeking to lobby Parliament'. He continued, 'Indeed my concern is that an anti-motorway group or tenants association does not have the influence that can be sought by the big corporations which can afford to hire the services of professional lobbyists.' However, since the company or cause could itself have its own payroll lobbyists, the fact of for-hire lobbyists seems to be beside the point. (See Grant 1981 for a discussion of the growing 'governmental relations' function in industry.) It seems strange to defend lobbying only if the lobbyist promises not to be too skilled or influential.

MPs as Lobbyists

Informing Members of the background to an issue often raises controversy. For example, in May 1985, the *Sunday Times* complained that five Conservative MPs and a senior civil servant were flown first class to Brazil by British Airways as a 'freebie'. It noted that 'In the past eighteen months, parliament has seen its most intensive lobbying in recent years over aviation policy.' The *Sunday Times* also recorded other trips, claiming that other members of the Tory back-bench aviation committee had been flown to America as guests of BA. Gerald Howarth MP claimed, 'The taxpayer is not going to pay for such trips and there is no way that backbench MPs can afford to. The public is best served if the member of Parliament is better informed.'

A related lobbying controversy concerns the activities of MPs themselves in representing organizations. The activity stimulating most interest appears to be the member working for the itself controversial 'for-hire' lobbying company. The number involved here is admittedly few. The 1984 edition of the *Yearbook* of the Public Relations Consultants Association lists thirty-six organizations which offer some special capability in parliamentary relations. That number is not definitive, as some of the notable parliamentary specialists are non-PRCA members, for example GJW Consultants, founded by Andrew Gifford, Jenny Jeger, and Wilf Weeks, who had worked at various times in the offices of party leaders, David Steel, James Callaghan, and Edward Heath respectively. Nor are Lloyd-Hughes or Ian Greer and Associates in the PRCA listing. Indeed, almost any PR company could operate in Parliament on behalf of a particular client or campaign, and thus the PRCA figure of thirty-six is an underestimate.

The PRCA *Yearbook* (1984) lists seven MPs as consultants:

Tim Brinton	Communications Strategy Ltd.
Peter Fry	Baiden Barron Smith Ltd.
	Political Research and Communications International Ltd.
D. Knox	Gandalf Communication Consortium Ltd.
M. McNair-Wilson	Extel PR Ltd.
M. Morris	MPR Ltd.
Richard Ryder	Christopher Morgan Marketing and PR
Sir D. Smith	Kingsway PR Ltd.

The *Register of Members' Interests* for 1984 offers a few extra Members with general PR connections: Neville Trotter MP lists himself as consultant to Biss Lancaster; H. Dykes MP is listed as parliamentary adviser to Dewe Rogerson; M. Fox MP and K. Speed MP are directors of Westminster (Communications) Ltd., whose clients include the Motor Cycle Association; M. Forsyth MP is a director of Michael Forsyth Associates; and his colleagues William Shelton MP, Martin Stevens MP, John Gorst MP, and P. Cormack MP also head what appear to be political consultancies. Other entries are suggestive of political representation work: P. Bruinvels lists himself as a parliamentary research consultant, while Julian Critchley MP is public affairs adviser to SSCB Lintas Ltd. Tim Eggar MP was parliamentary adviser to Hill and Knowlton (UK) Ltd., P. McNair-Wilson is director of Consort PR Ltd, C. Murphy is parliamenary consultant to D'Arcy MacManus and Masius (like SSCB Lintas, an ad agency). M. Shersby MP is director-general of the British Sugar Bureau; J. Wheeler MP is director-general of British Security Industry Association: there are unusual cases of an organization leader as Member.

An article in a supplement to *CBI News* in 1983 claimed that 'Ten years ago it was considered sufficient to have an MP on the board. Today, convincing Parliament's ear demands more specialist skills.' As this comment makes plain, there is a tradition of MPs representing commercial life. This is more or less accepted, though while he was Chancellor of the Exchequer Jim Callaghan attacked critics with the comment, 'I have almost forgotten their constituents, but I shall never forget their interests.' This kind of association between MPs and economic interest is, however, so long established that it is, generally, not controversial, and indeed Members are quick to point to the advantages in being in touch with 'the real world'.

A third kind of role for Members—between representing the *ad hoc* clients of an agency and representing commercial interests as a by-product of active involvement in the firm—is where the Member is personally hired as parliamentary specialist for the concern. The annual *Register of Members' Interests* (House of Commons 249, 1984) lists the links of most MPs with outside bodies. MPs can be employed by companies or associations for reason of a relevant expertise that is unconnected with their parliamentary position: for example, Sir Humphrey Atkins is listed as consultant to Scrimgeour,

Kemp–Gee, and Co. and consultant to Street Financial Limited (Advertising and PR); Robert Adley is listed as marketing consultant to Commonwealth Holiday Inns. While such consultancies *may* utilize parliamentary knowledge, this is not totally clear from the information provided. However, some entries in the register unambiguously suggest that the MP is retained for 'Westminster' reasons; labels such as political consultant, parliamentary adviser, public affairs consultant are all reasonably clear Westminster signals. Example of the genre include James Lester MP, parliamentary consultant to the Direct Selling Association, R. McCrindle MP, parliamentary adviser to the British Insurance Brokers Association, R. Hicks MP, parliament liaison officer to British Hotels, Restaurants, and Caterers Association. Gwyneth Dunwoody's consultancy with the British Fur Trade Association only merited press attention because it is a very non-Labour cause. In certain further cases the term 'consultant' is used where we can reasonably intepret a 'political consultant role', for example, Sir Bernard Braine's position as consultant to the Police Superintendent's Association or J. Ryman's position with the National Association of Bookmakers.

Counting only self-categorized or unambiguous 'political consultancies', the *Register of Members' Interests* (1984) yielded ninety-six MPs in the political advice business. A less strict definition of 'political' consultant could easily have yielded a further twenty cases.

On the whole this is a Tory party activity. Of the ninety-six, seventy-four were Conservative. As ministers cannot hold such posts, this is a high percentage of the Tory back-benchers. If, as appears likely, there has been a growth in the role of the political/parliamentary consultant, this may stem, ironically, from the apparent tendency for full(er)-time MPs. Not having a permanent professional or business career may make MPs readier to accept such part-time duties. While some of these advisers would see their role as advising on political developments—a political intelligence role—it would appear that some are also on occasion attempting to alter developments on behalf of clients.

This is clearly a grey area. Erskine May records, *as if it is still relevant*, the resolution of 22 June 1858, 'That it is contrary to the usage and derogatory to the dignity of this House that any of its Members should bring forward, promote or advocate in this House any proceeding or measure in which he may have acted or been concerned for or in consideration of any pecuniary fee or reward (20th edn., p. 151). Erskine May also notes (p. 436) that it is now (since 1975) a rule of the House, rather than the convention that it was previously, for every Member to declare in a debate 'any relevant pecuniary interest or benefit of whatever nature'.

It must also be added that links can certainly exist between groups and companies and Members with no financial relationship. MPs will help—often being honorary officers of groups—because of a pre-existing interest in a topic or because of a constituency interest where the Member will assist the group (say the National Farmers' Union), recognizing the local importance of the issue. Members' rewards can be non-financial. It is often thought that one way to catch the Whip's eye for promotion is specialization: the group can assist the Member to become identified with 'his patch'. (One of the powers of the Whip over potential rebels in the party is a threat to try to keep them off Select Committees and out of other activities which would be important for their consultancy work.)

Another kind of relationship is of course sponsorship. The main links here are to trade unions. At the 1979 General Election almost half the 269 successful candidates were union-sponsored. This kind of link last raised serious comment in 1977 when the annual conference of the National Union of Public Employees seemed to be threatening to withdraw sponsorship from members who did not follow the union's line in opposing the Labour Government's programme of cuts. The Select Committee on Privileges decided that: 'To withdraw, or threaten to withdraw, a member's sponsorship in the circumstances set out in the conference resolution would constitute a serious contempt of the House.' (Quoted in Alderman 1984, pp. 54–5.) Alderman, in his conclusions, follows Muller (1977, p. 87), who reckoned that the Labour party Trade Union Group in Parliament had *not* been effective and that, 'As a private organisation of union-sponsored MPs, it became increasingly a social club held together by nostalgia for a shared common experience in the factory or mine.'

Returning to the issue of the power of Parliament, the kind of activities noted do not add up to a need to reconsider the decline of Parliament. Several reasons, other than the critical importance of the House, make these developments intelligible.

Firstly, on the scale of money in industrial and commercial life even the costly MP contracts (of the order of £20,000) are pretty small beer. Thus it is worth having the MP 'on board' as an insurance policy. He might not deliver much but the cost is minimal. The MP is then no more than a talisman. The MP often gives an entrance (literally or figuratively) to a political world rather more glamorous than that of commerce. Jenny Jeger of GJW Consultants has been quoted saying that 'it is extraordinary how people with the ability to make millions . . . and who can find their way around the city or ruthlessly disembowel an opponent, have bones like jelly when it comes to talking to an MP' (see Carolyn Faulder, *Good Housekeeping*, March 1984).

Secondly, while it may well be the case that some lobbying of Parliament takes place simply because the relations in the political system are misunderstood, Presthus's work in Canada found that Canadian MPs thought that the main reason lobbyists approached them was to build a bloc of opinion among party members so that party leaders could be influenced. In this light, parliamentary lobbying is seen as a two-step process, with the lobbying of Members as an indirect method of influencing the real (as opposed to formal) decision-makers. One direct benefit of parliamentary lobbying might be its Whitehall effect.

As a courtesy to a Member, a minister might well take a complaint more seriously. Alternatively, in the long term, links to back-benchers can become links to new ministers. In these senses the Parliamentary consultant is often in reality another channel to Whitehall not Westminster.

'Parliamentary lobbyists' may in fact be of prime importance as Whitehall lobbyists. To term themselves such would be even more controversial than 'parliamentary lobbyists', and thus the current label may only be the acceptable face for non-parliamentary activity. Significantly perhaps, the very first question by the Select Committee on Members' Interests (House of Commons 408, p. 1) was directed to Sir Trevor Lloyd-Hughes of Lloyd-Hughes Associates Ltd. and concerned the point made in his company's brochure that it maintained regular relationships with 'the British Government, Cabinet and other Members and their Civil Service Advisers'. The questioner, Charles Morris MP, pursued the claim as follows: 'In the country generally I think there would be anxiety about any public relations company or organisation having influence with Civil Service advisers.'

In relation to the dropping of ship repair interests from the Labour Government's proposal of nationalization of the ship-building industry, Lloyd-Hughes Associates claimed in the advertising material that they had 'masterminded the Parliamentary Campaign which rescued the UK ship repairing industry'. In fact Sir Trevor himself emphasized the *non*-parliamentary side to this famous parliamentary event:

Chris Bailey [of the Bristol Channel Ship Repair Yard] came to me and said, 'We have got a parliamentary consultant and we have got advertising people, we have no *entrée* to the Civil Service . . . They sent me a pile of papers and as usual they had been speaking to the wrong people at the wrong time . . . [I] said, 'You have it all wrong, let me do a brief to the civil servant concerned and see what he says'. This was done. I went to the civil servant—Tony Benn was the Minister at the time. The civil servant came back and said: 'You have made your case. I think in the Red Box over the weekend we will put the submission to Tony Benn and come next Monday I think you'll find Bristol Channel are taken out of the shopping list'. Lloyd-Hughes said that the press advertising campaign was done without his knowledge—'That case could have been settled without all the aggravation . . . We were the people, whatever certain Members of Parliament claim, who discovered the hybridity aspect of the thing.' [Hybridity meant that the Bill would have needed much lengthier procedures if it had included ship repair aspects]

Ian Greer (1985, p. 12) of Ian Greer Associates, one of the leading 'parliamentary lobbyists', has observed; 'by the time a Bill reaches the House of Commons it is already in the form of a draft Act . . . It has been months in preparation and most politicians and civil servants would feel that anyone with a serious interest should have known about it and made their representations . . . The time to influence legislation, therefore, is at the drafting, or better still, the pre-drafting stage.' From this perspective, use of the parliamentary channel is something of an emergency technique for rescuing causes still unwon, or solving difficulties articulated less promptly than they might have been.

A study reported in 1985 (*Financial Times*, 23 December 1985) that 41 per cent of a survey of 180 large British companies and British subsidiaries of US and Japanese companies used government affairs consultants (paying them an average of £28,200 p.a.) and 28 per cent used PR companies for work involving government (paying an average of £33,100 each). Sixty-one per cent of the sample saw a need for monitoring Parliament, and 69 per cent for monitoring Whitehall. Ninety-two per cent said they needed early warning of policies. There seemed to be more satisfaction with the links to Westminster (i.e. Parliament) than Whitehall (Government/ Civil Service). Only 8 per cent of those employing consultants saw them as useful in providing access to decision-makers in Whitehall, though 60 per cent thought them satisfactory in relation to MPs. Twenty-eight per cent of the companies replying thought that the consultants paid too much attention to Parliament, but none thought too much attention was paid to Whitehall.

Dr Geoffrey Alderman, for one, has drawn attention to some of the problems of this area. He recounts (1984, pp. 61–2) how in 1981 Sir George Young, Under-Secretary of State at the DHSS, was in favour of the statutory prohibition of tobacco advertising. Thus a Private Member's Bill introduced on the topic by Laurie Pavitt MP had a reasonable chance of the direct governmental assistance that is usually necessary for such legislation to prosper. Alderman records how no fewer than 164 amendments were put down for the bill which was being considered *prior* to the Tobacco Bill, eighty-seven of them bearing the name of Sir Anthony Kershaw, an adviser to British American Tobacco. The bill which attracted such attention concerned zoos, but the real reason for the volume of amendments was, of course, to take up so much parliamentary time that the Tobacco Bill would not be reached. Alderman quotes Sir Anthony frankly recording that 'one of my interests in that particular [zoos] Bill was to keep out the Bill banning advertising on smoking which came afterwards'. Alderman concluded (1984, p. 62) that the thirty-two MPs reputed to have financial links either directly with the tobacco industry or with advertising and PR firms which handle tobacco company accounts must 'be regarded as political arms of an industry, on whose well being their own livelihoods in part depend'. Mike Daube of Action on Alcohol Abuse has estimated that in the 1974–9 Parliament 74 MPs had direct or indirect financial links with the drinks industry, with a further number having a clear, if unpaid, constituency interest (see Davies 1985, p. 11.)

One point which can be made to balance the worry raised by Alderman is the sense of the House's own acute 'nose' in these matters. Members do discount the obvious special interest spokesman. Davies (1985, p. 60) quoted Julian Critchley's comment on the relationship between his fellow Conservative MP Eldon Griffiths and the Police Federation:

The Police Federation employs Mr Eldon Griffiths. He is known in the House as 'Constable Griffiths' who rises to his feet with great regularity whenever any matter appertaining to law and order is being related. When Mr Griffiths gets up yet again the rest of us MPs are inclined to groan slightly because we know he is doing something for which he is being paid, but having said that, he does I think, a good job for the police.

Jenny Jeger, then research officer for the Hansard Society and writing in 1978 (in Mackintosh 1978, p. 68), concluded that the bulk of established pressure groups prefer to deal with the appropriate ministry. She judged,

Approaches are made to MPs only if the pressure group has to have an item of tendentious legislation passed, if legislation is going through the House where all the group's objectives have not been fully met by prior consultation or if the group wants to get information out of the government. The groups which deal mainly with MPs are the weaker, less elaborately organised 'cause' groups and they are often inadequately equipped for the purpose.

She concluded her research report by observing that MPs have little chance of altering government policy, and thus 'contacts between MPs and pressure groups tend to be ill organised, spasmodic and not very satisfactory for any of those involved'.

We broadly agree that MPs have limited impact on mainstream policy-making, but ministers do pay attention to the House. In terms of the *actual* policy impact of Parliament, the sensitivity of civil servants and ministers is perhaps disproportionate, but a fact.

One explanation might be that ministers do usually serve a lengthy 'apprenticeship' in the Commons, and they have a direct and personal answerability in the House that means that they wish to avoid being exposed to unnecessary criticism. For that reason ministers will often not push through measures when there is clear back-bench unrest. When a Rayner scrutiny (efficiency investigation) proposed that paying state benefits by post was suggested there was considerable pressure from back-bench rural MPs because this move would threaten the viability of sub-post-offices. The DHSS dropped the proposal. There was no immediate threat of parliamentary defeat, but ministers did not want the hostility.

In 1986 the Government dropped the proposal to sell off British

Leyland after pressure from Conservative Midlands MPs who saw this as a threat to their re-election. Later, in April 1986, the Government was actually defeated on the Shops Bill, which proposed to allow wider Sunday trading. Sixty-eight Tory MPs voted against the Second Reading and others abstained on a 'three-line whip'. One reason for the defeat is that policies which are not central to the Government's programme can now (after several precedents) be safely defeated without threatening the Government's tenure. It may also have something to do with the accumulation in the House after eight years of Conservative government of back-benchers with no prospect of promotion. A party that becomes factionalized cannot count on loyalty at the margins of its programme.

Part Three
CONCLUSION

Groups and Governance: Governing with Groups or Governing by Groups?

The central theme of this book has been that, broadly speaking, pressure group activity—of different styles—is normal, commonplace, unavoidable, and normally desirable. The incorporation of some types of groups into the process by which policies are formulated and implemented has become routinized in a complex web of informal and formal arrangements. In chapter 1 we emphasized that our central concern was not only with formal membership-based groups but with *pressure between bodies* as a *process* of governing. Here we attempt a preliminary assessment of that process in terms of democratic practice. Hayward (1966, p. 1) has noted that for those with a constitutional, institutional approach to the study of politics the sort of informal, behavioural approach in use here in recording interest group activity presents a challenge, and that for 'institutionalists' a consultative body 'is regarded as of minor interest because it does not—and they hasten to add should not—dispose of formal decision making power'. We are quite happy to follow Hayward's belief that importance need not equate with formality.

Hayward (1966, pp. 1-2) points out that the relations between interest groups and traditional political institutions can follow any of three broad patterns:

First there are attempts to persuade, manipulate, cajole or coerce interest groups into conformity with official policy, presented as the dictate of the general, national or public interest. Secondly, there are attempts by the interest groups to persuade, manipulate, cajole or coerce the official decision-makers into action or inaction which may be presented as in conformity with the public interest 'as a whole'. Finally, there are attempts to promote cooperation between the interest group spokesmen and the official policy makers by coordinating or 'concerting' their activities within a formal or informal consultative system so as to achieve a consensus which can be presented as in the public interest.

As Hayward points out, the public interest means different things for groups in different contexts—particularly the first and second. The first 'public interest' is established by official policy-makers independently of 'sinister' interest group pressure. In the second sense the 'public interest' is a label for the balance of interests at any one time. Hayward (1966, p. 5) argues that an antithesis between consultation and legislation has been one of the casualties of the increasing interdependence between government and interest groups. He argues that the nominal power of the formal decision is less relevant than the real source of the actual decision. In chapter 1 we discussed the twin channels of democracy and a possible decline in the importance of the concept of numerical (electoral) democracy. This contrast was perhaps first made by Hayward in his observation that 'it is on the badly lit backstage of consultative "closed politics" rather than under the stage lighting of the public performance of conventional "open politics" that the answers to . . . vital questions generally lie' (p. 6).

Not all commentators take such a benign view of group activity as we (broadly) hold. The theme of the role which groups can play in resisting desirable policy change has been taken up by Mancur Olson (1982) in the context of an analysis of the reasons for the rise and decline of nations. His thesis is based upon the theoretical foundations of his earlier work, *The Logic of Collective Action*, combined with 'micro-economic' theories about the behaviour of individual firms, consumers, and industries. He believes that it is impossible for societies to achieve 'optimal' outcomes (or indeed 'equity') through a process of bargaining. Thus he claims that some groups such as consumers, taxpayers, the unemployed, and the poor do not have either the selective incentives or the small numbers needed to organize (Olson 1982, p. 37). The best-organized groups will press for policies which maximize their benefits, even if the policies are inefficient for society as a whole. They can do this because the costs will fall disproportionately on society as a whole and not on themselves.

If we take Olson's view that organizations are maintained by a system of selective incentives within the organization, then this (he argues) has implications for the longevity of groups. He suggests that 'Selective incentives make indefinite survival feasible. Thus once established such groups usually survive until there is a social upheaval or some other form of violence or instability' (Olson 1982, p. 40.) The more stable a society, the longer that established organizations will survive.

Olson goes on to consider the possible implications of his theories about group formation and group behaviour for the prosperity of the nations in which the groups reside. Clearly, it can be assumed that virtually all groups in society want to be in an efficient and increasingly wealthy society, whatever the particular concerns of the group. But according to Olson (1982, p. 42), organizations have two main ways of serving the interests of their members. They can attempt to increase the total wealth in the society—or they can attempt to maximize the share of the wealth enjoyed by their members. Olson is convinced that the first method will rarely be chosen. Groups will normally try to increase their share of the existing pie, rather than devote their efforts to increasing the size of the national pie. This is so, he argues, because increasing the pie is rather like trying to increase the supply of a *collective* good. He uses the example of an organization which wants to eliminate the losses in economic efficiency that arise because of differential tax rates. For the campaign to be effective, the organization would incur significant costs to itself. But if the campaign is successful it will receive but a tiny proportion of the benefits, as everyone would share in those, as a result of a more efficient society.

In Olson's view,

The organisation that acts to provide some benefit for the society as a whole is, in effect, providing a public good for the whole of society, and it is accordingly in the same position as an individual who contributes to the provision of a collective good for a group of which he or she is a part. *In each case the actor gets only a part (and often a tiny part), of the benefits of its action, yet bears the whole cost of that action.* (Olson 1982, p. 43, our emphasis.)

Assuming that an organization represents only a relatively narrow section of society, it will have few incentives to act in the interests of society as a whole. Even when the broader social costs to society as a whole are great, and exceed the benefits to the group by a large margin, the group will still press for those benefits which are peculiar to itself. There are, as a result, rather few organizations which exist to increase national wealth or output, and many organizations which exist to influence the distribution of existing wealth: they are 'distributional coalitions (Olson 1982, p. 44). Because of these groups, distributional issues tend to dominate political life.

The distinction between large, encompassing organizations and narrow, specialized organizations is important for the implications of Olson's theories concerning the prosperity of societies. For example, enterprise-wide or industry-wide unions are most likely to agree to more efficient working practices than are narrow craft unions, according to Olson's theoretical prediction. In societal terms, however, society will only benefit from more broadly based organizations if these organizations encompass many different industries. Thus peak associations (such as the CBI and TUC) require to take a less parochial view of issues than do individual member bodies. However, as we noted in chapter 7, these peak associations can be quite weak *because* they are so broadly based and as a result lack coherence. The CBI is particularly prone to criticisms that it has tried to become an all-encompassing organization. Most firms look to their more narrowly focused trade associations as the most effective means of influencing public policy. As Olson (1982, p. 59) also notes, 'peak associations, frequently lack the unity needed to have any great influence on public policy, or even coherent and specific policies'.

The central difficulty for societies, from this perspective, is that the narrower, more self-interested groups are generally more successful than the more broadly based encompassing groups. Special interest groups, Olson argues, slow the rate of growth of economies which might result from, for example, the introduction of new technologies and other changes such as the reallocation of resources from one activity or industry to another, as the groups defend their narrow interests against the interests of society as a whole.

The sum total impact of the activity of distributional coalitions in society has profound implications for the nature of government and society. In a key passage, Olson (1982, p. 73) argues that 'The accumulation of distributional coalitions increases the complexity of regulation, the role of government, and the complexity of understandings, and changes the direction of social evolution'. Thus the complexity of regulation is increased by lobbying because groups demand and secure special provisions and exceptions for themselves. Once regulations are established, certain groups will defend the continuation of the regulations (such as specialized accountants, lawyers, and consultants, who are hired to deal with the regulations and will profit from their continuation). What Olson (1982, p. 71) calls 'cartelistic organisations' end up bargaining with each other. The result is that, 'Given the slow decision-making, crowded agendas, and cluttered bargaining tables, it takes some time before negotiators agree on anything. But once agreements are reached, the same considerations suggest that they should not be changed without compelling reason.'

Olson goes on to assess the *practical* consequences which he believes follow from his theoretical analysis. In summary, he sees the main outcome of highly developed and stable interest group systems (such as we have described for Britain) as economic decline. Countries that have had democratic freedom of organization, uninterrupted by upheaval (by a revolution, say, or war, or invasion), will have developed interest group networks which defend sectional ends and impose societal costs. In a telling passage on Britain, he argues that this helps to explain why we have had such a poor growth rate. We have had the longest immunity from dictatorship, invasion, and revolution. In short,

Britain has precisely the powerful network of specialised interest organizations that . . . would lead us to expect in a country with its record of security and military stability . . . In short, with age British society has acquired so many strong organisations and collusions that *it suffers from an institutional sclerosis that slows its adaption to changing circumstances and changing technologies.* (Olson 1982, p. 78, our emphasis.)

Olson's belief that the blame for economic and other forms of inertia can be laid at the door of interest groups is echoed by other commentators. Samuel Beer concluded (1982, pp. 24–5) that 'pluralistic stagnation' resulted from the cumulative effect of the defence of 'a quiescent *status quo*'. Party government, according to Beer, is undermined by the continued proliferation, and increased power, of groups. Parties may end up simply competing for group support with no other objective than winning elections: 'The upshot is that immobilism and incoherence in public choice against which part government was supposed to be the safeguard.'

At a general level is Hardin's argument of 'The Tragedy of the Commons', which suggests that if every interest seeks to maximize its advantage the overall result means that they share a diminishing resource (Hardin 1968). (The analogy in the title of course suggests that if those with grazing rights to common ground are allowed to maximize their grazing each year, the 'common'—the common ground—will deteriorate.)

In his book *The Role and Limits of Government*, Samuel Brittan (1983, p. 7) has also drawn attention to the impact of particularistic demands by interest groups. He argues that

Much of what purports to be criticism of the conduct of the public services is really a cry by particular interest groups for more distribution towards themselves, enhanced and rationalised by an excessive expectation of what governments can do to boost their nation's economy so that other identifiable groups do not have to be asked too obviously to pay the cost.

Referring to Hayek's work, Brittan (1983, p. 24) notes that the main theme of that work is that 'democracy has degenerated into an unprincipled auction to satisfy rival organised groups who can never in the long run be appeased because their demands are mutually incompatible'.

Brittan (1983, p. 79) argues, in a similar view to that of Olson, that the sum total of the restrictive practices and special deals which interest groups negotiate is harmful to the interests of society. Thus one group might gain a special tariff on foreign imports, another gains protection from the threat of new domestic entrants, a third gains a delay in the introduction of new methods in order to maintain employment—and so on. Each 'bargain' is only mildly damaging to the rest of the community, and 'The defects of politics viewed as an accommodation of interest-groups are thus not probed until it is too late.'

However, Brittan (p. 212) does—more explicitly than Olson—admit the benefits of a group democracy. He acknowledges (p. 212) that associational life may strengthen the cohesion of society by creating a network intermediate between the citizen and the state, but he concludes that the economic costs are high. He qualifies (p. 238) the pessimism of the overarching argument in two important ways. By relating the British disease to a particular stage in economic and political development, he shows that it is likely that other advanced democratic economies will meet similar problems, which at least will ease Britain's relative problem. Secondly, he considers that as the output costs of inertia grow, then so does the obvious incentive to break down restrictive practices. There is some evidence for his first qualification. As we suggest in chapter 8, there is a widely held view that a high degree of interest group integration is a Western European—not just a British—policy style. On the second qualification, we can only speculate that here too there may be some UK evidence (and evidence in other Western democracies) that we are entering a phase in which existing distributional coalitions (in Olson's terms) are being dismantled. For example, this is true to varying degrees in telecommunications, transport, the stock exchange, labour relations, and even in some of the established professions, such as conveyancing and opticians.

Other objections to the Olson type of analysis include the fact that there are countries with stability and strong interest group systems that have also had economic success, Sweden being the most notable example. Olson's answer is to suggest that the nature of groups in Sweden (and Norway) is rather different to that in Britain. In Sweden, groups are, he argues, 'highly encompassing'— 'more so than in any other developed democracies' (Olson 1982, p. 90). This means that (in his view) the interest organizations in Sweden have been less damaging to society's interests because, as his theory predicts, encompassing organizations are less parochial. In his more technical terms, encompassing organizations are more likely to internalize the costs of inefficient policies and are more likely to give some weight to economic growth and the needs of society as a whole. (This argument is not too dissimilar to Truman's concept of moderation through overlapping membership, discussed in chapter 2.) There is certainly some point to Olson's analysis, but it is not thoroughly convincing. For example, although British 'peak associations' may not be as 'all-encompassing' as in Sweden, in international terms they are well developed. An article in *Scandinavian Political Studies* in 1986 by Rasch and Sorensen argued that Norwegian data suggested that small specialist groups are quite likely to indulge in productive strategies. They suggest that while Olson's theory was parsimonious and precise, 'When it comes to realism and accuracy of implications, the score seems lower.' They draw attention to the apparent paradox that while 'Norway's growth rate during the seventies was quite respectable', union membership had grown dramatically in the twentieth century (1986, pp. 54–6). In the same issue of *Scandinavian Political Studies* (pp. 35–5), Agne Gustafsson underlined that Sweden had for many years had strong interest groups—and in GNP was one of the wealthiest countries in the world. He says, 'predicting from the new Olson theory, Sweden should long ago have suffered from national decline'. As Gustafsson notes, Olson can only salvage his theory by a special theory for the deviant Swedish case. The general

Olson argument thus not infrequently looks controversial when the details of the parts are examined.

The Olson theory is simply too broad-brush to explain important aspects such as the substantial *variability* over time in productivity rates in the British economy. Olson (1983, p. 116) writes that Britain does relatively badly in the older industries and heavy industries that are especially susceptible to oligopolistic collusion and unionization. It may be that it does badly not because of the unionization, but the age. Heavy, old-style industry on the Ruhr has done as badly as in Britain. Shipbuilding in Britain might have been hampered by union demarcations, but other factors such as the decline in markets, growth of competition, high (oil-boosted) exchange rates, are all relevant.

Although Olson presents intimidating statistical support, there is at the core a simple world-view that people defend their own interests. For example (1982, p. 117), he speculates that troubled industries have had excessive numbers of vice-presidents and other corporate bureaucrats with handsome prerequisites.

Olson over-generalizes on the nature of groups. Different types of group will have different impacts, and indeed at different times or on different subject-matters groups will be pushing for change. Olson does not equate change with improvement. However, there are many instances whereby 'obstruction' by groups is, with hindsight, the preferable position.

And what is the alternative to group inefficiency? Electoral inefficiency? It is not simply that government backs off from reform in face of group recalcitrance, but government is as reluctant to offend electoral interests as any other. Thus it is easy to think of decisions made by government for reasons of electoral popularity rather than economic rationality: examples are the location of Invergordon aluminium smelter or of enterprise zones.

The United Kingdom is often cited as an extreme example of the power of groups in preventing necessary change in society. We would agree that there are economic costs of a system which, *de facto*, permits veto groups, but most of us would view the erosion and suppression of *our* influence in matters which affect us as political costs.

There may be a very generalized trade-off between democratic costs and economic costs. As Damgaard (1984, p. 97) has argued, any democracy has to reconcile the interests of its constituent groups with the interests of society as a whole. Thus he points out that

terms like participation, representation, and interest articulation point to the need for open input channels. On the other, decision-making, governance, leadership, and steering refer to the instruments of political control. Without widespread participation there can be no democracy. Without some kind of governance, there can be no democratic role.

Danish data suggest that the development of interest groups and modern bureaucracies poses particular challenges to political parties, traditionally regarded as central to our notions of democratic government. For example, data on membership of interest groups and political parties show that the former are much more important than the latter (Johanson 1980, quoted by Damgaard 1984).

Although Danish MPs generally expressed favourable attitudes regarding contacts wth interest organizations (in Damgaard's survey 93 per cent of MPs felt that in a democratic society it was necessary to listen to affected interests), they also expressed concern about the close connections which develop between interest groups and the bureaucracy (Damgaard 1984, p. 103). Similarly, in our chapter on groups and parties we suggested that parties were generally not a primary channel of influence for groups, as the groups had more effective means of influencing policy in their own right. One of our central themes is that the continual development of the group system has itself been a central factor in the declining influence of traditional institutions such as parties, elections, and Parliament.

It must be acknowledged that there are limits to interest group involvement in some areas of policy-making. Damgaard (1984, p. 107) notes that interest groups are rarely participants in the policy process which leads to increased taxation: 'parties remain responsible for at least the unpopular parts of economic policies. The need for governance thus sets limits for representation of interests, the alternative being chaos or anarchy.' The main thrust of Damgaard's analysis is that in Denmark there is more interest representation and less governance than there used to be.

In the British case, Mrs Thatcher's two Governments since 1979 have reminded us that the 'mix' between governance and interest representation can vary, depending on circumstances and political will. Thus we have seen rather more examples of what we have elsewhere termed 'non-negotiable' policies, in which negotiation as a process is somewhat peripheral to the main action. (We would, however, still argue that the Thatcher Governments have, for the main part, not been as radical a departure from the traditional policy style as their self-cultivated image and their critics would claim.) Equally, one cannot totally ignore the influence of Parliament, which, even with Mrs Thatcher's huge majority (or perhaps because of it), has managed a few successful raiding-parties on the power normally shared between government and interest groups. Thus, just as the degree of governance may vary, then so might the degree of parliamentary influence. Certainly, in the Canadian case there seems evidence that the decline of the legislature—largely due to the close liaison between groups and and government—has not continued. Thus Pross (1985, p. 238) suggests that Canadian pressure groups now pay far more attention to Parliament than they did in the past. Canada, like all Western democracies, has seen a proliferation of groups and their achievement of a very prominent role in the policy process. But Pross (1985, p. 245) argues that the current phase of Canadian politics is a diffusion of power.

This diffusion process has changed the nature of bureaucratic politics such that interest groups are more inclined to seek public support and to seek legitimation via Parliament. Pross (1985, p. 256) argues that 'A system of pressure politics in which access sprang from the ability to provide specialised information has been changed into one in which legitimation is equally important.' The greater emphasis on legitimation in the system has the effect of enhancing the role of Parliament. This slight shift back towards Parliament is, it should be noted, 'a modest amelioration of a situation that has been described as "Intolerable". In a sense, parliament's lot has improved because that of other more powerful policy actors has deteriorated considerably.' (Pross 1985, p. 264.) It is not too difficult to imagine that the British House of Commons might achieve at least this shift, should an election result in a 'hung' parliament. Similarly, some issues are not resolved in the bureaucratic–interest group arena, but are resolved in more public forums (the Westland aircraft issue and the student grants issue being two examples in 1985).

To point out that variations in the distribution of power in society can and do occur between groups (as it does between institutions) is one thing. To suggest that these shifts represent fundamental changes in the nature of the policy process is quite another. These shifts do not change the fundamental nature of the system from that which we have described in this volume. John P. Olsen's title of his book on political institutions in a welfare state (Norway) neatly captures our own view of British democracy (*Organized Democracy*, 1983). Thus we would argue that modern British society is characterized by organizational participation in policy-making and that this participation is deeply entrenched. As we suggested in our introductory chapter, we accept Truman's argument of the prevalence of groups, and believe that the agenda of group/government world is not that of Parliament and the media. What we describe here is not a new phenomenon. As early writers have argued, Britain has long had a highly developed interest group system.

Consultation is not a threat to democratic institutions, it is an alternative form of democracy. Recently, Goodin (1987) has suggested that in Britain 'consultation and cooperation are decisively preferred over compulsion; advice and accommodation are decisively preferred over adversarial relations'. He observes that there are practical reasons why such consultation takes place. He begins by quoting Derek Walker-Smith in a debate in Parliament in 1947: 'In this democratic community of ours, an ounce of cooperation is worth a pound of regulation and a whole ton of compulsory sanctions.' Like us, Goodin notes that while consultation is endemic it takes place with a potential of asymmetrical power: Government *could* proceed without consent. He notes,

A centrally important feature of these negotiations is that they are characteristically conducted under the threat of unilateral action on the part of the government, should these negotiations break down . . . Push come to shove, the government can make policy on its own, and the implications of that point are seldom lost on either party to the negotiations.

However, the puzzle is why governments are so reluctant to push, far less shove . . . the answer appears to be self-restraint based on a belief that consultation has a higher legitimacy than imposition.

What we now lack is a means of reconciling the empirical world of government–group relations with traditional notions of democracy, accountability, and parliamentary sovereignty. The decline of numerical democracy leaves everyone slightly uneasy. We accept, however, the argument that group involvement in policy-making *strengthens* democracy. Groups are also a political resource for governments *in* the governing process as well as a political problem for government by their articulating of demands. Governing with (and through) groups is not the same as a government immobilized by fear of group sanctions. Although 'leverage', 'manipulation', 'bargain' are not terms required in a description of formal government, they are the vocabulary of effective governance.

One important idea introduced by Hayward (1966) is found where he quotes J. K. Galbraith's 1952 work on *American Capitalism*. Galbraith argued that 'the provision of state assistance to the development of countervailing power has become a major function of government—perhaps *the* major domestic function . . .'. That is to say that government can respond to numerical pressure to restrict the privileges of the better-orphanized groups (like manufacturers) over the disorganized (but electorally numerous) consumers.

Mechanisms do have to be found to maintain the benefits of this group system, whilst ensuring that it does not do the damage which Mancur Olson believes that it does. In considering possible restraints on the power and influence of groups, it is of course important to remember that the rapid extension of the group system, which seems to have occurred in all Western democracies in the last two decades or so, is in part due to the perceived failure of those 'democratic' proceses and institutions which some observers see as threatened by excessive interest group influence today. As J. P. Olsen (1983, p. 13) suggests, one way in which the alleged crisis in representational democracy reveals itself 'is through the mushrooming of collective political behaviour outside the established institutions of government and representation'. In particular, the phenomenon of 'citizens' initiatives' seen in many Western European democracies may be seen as a threat to the older political systems.

In Britain, we have not really witnessed either the phenomenon itself, or the debate, as increased citizen involvement has tended to be via fairly conventional pressure group formation and incorporation in the decision-making process. For example, the thrust of the analysis of environmental groups by Lowe and Goyder (quoted earlier) was that group formation at the local level had been extensive, as had the accommodation of those new groups by existing decision-making processes. This suggests that the absorption capacity of the British system is rather high. If Mancur Olson's view that Britain has the oldest and most stable group system is correct, then it is equally correct that, by and large, this sytem has proved capable of absorbing new issues and new groups. For example, rather challenging groups like Women's Aid managed to secure significant governmental funding at an early stage in their history, as Gail Stedward's chapter indicates. Perhaps the most surprising aspect of the group process in the UK is the continued suspicion of it, even though it is clear that citizens see resort to the group process as a more effective means of participation than electoral or party politics. As Alderman (1984, p. 123) notes, there is probably no facet of British politics that has generated more suspicion, mistrust, and even fear than the activity of groups.

Perhaps the best that can be hoped for is that the more the system is revealed, the more citizens will come to accept that government bargaining with groups is a perfectly natural phenomenon. Indeed, our argument (following Bentley and Truman) is that this *is* the governmental process. We may have reached a somewhat contra-dictory position within the political culture in which citizens cling to traditional notions of parliamentary and electoral democracy, yet recognize the reality of political power by joining (and forming) more and more groups. We are still moving towards a situation where virtually all interests are organized, albeit in the context of an uneven distribution of power. We face new political problems of managing the consequent complexity.

This is not a situation of stalemate in which policy change is impossible. It is interest groups who have effectively produced some of the changes in society that are generally well regarded. Reforms such as the abolition of slavery, the reduction of lead in petrol, more effective controls on the introduction of new drugs, improved consumer protection, all owe some debt to the activities of interest groups. The problems which governments address on an already crowded political agenda are often identified by groups (e.g. acid rain, nuclear radiation from power stations) and would be ignored by governments but for group activity. Even very powerful economic interests which have a times been thought to exercise a veto over governments and electorates are in fact subject to policy

changes which they oppose. For example, there was much talk of
the 'excessive' power of the trade unions in the 1960s and 1970s,
yet this all seemed very dated by 1986, with Britain's unions subject
to a new range of laws and restrictions thought impossible fifteen
years earlier. Similarly, business interests have had to accept much
tougher pollution control laws, health and safety laws (notwithstanding their still powerful position in the implementation of these
laws), and employment protection laws. Both unions and firms
now employ more lawyers and spend more time trying to cope with
an increased regulatory 'burden'. This 'burden' has not been
accepted with enthusiasm but has been imposed on them by society,
via elected governments and often in response to the demands of
other groups, such as environmentalists and conservationists.

Mature political societies are characterized by a diffusion of
political power. Olson, Beer, and others can legitimately draw the
inference that groups will use this fragmentation of political power
in defending their own ends, but do we still have confidence that
policies evolved without group participation will meet the circumstances in which they need to be put into practice? Government's
can use the process of group integration to educate and even seduce
group leaders into assisting in the management of society.

Our conclusion about the merits of groups in the political system
is to accept that group influence is both inevitable and generally
positive. There may well be problems in this group democracy. Is
the group contest biased? Do single-issue groups erode the belief in
compromise needed in a multi-group society? Can the system cope
with the increase in the number of mobilized interests?

Our main conclusion about the political science aspect of this
book is that no coherent category of 'pressure group' is identifiable.
And wherever the appropriate boundaries are drawn they are not
likely to follow superficial characteristics, such as being membership-
based or not. Generally, one does not join something like
Greenpeace to make group policy, but in order to support clear
aims which have already been articulated. Most groups tend to
resemble 'cadre'-based parties (which are leadership-dominated)
more than 'mass parties', where there is an assumption that
members make policy.

We write no blank cheques in support of the group system.
Instead our message is that the system can work—can be worked—
better or worse. Some pressures will be undesirable—but that

judgement will depend on political goals sought. Sometimes groups will frustrate government, but at other times they will stimulate or carry out governmental policy. Whether governments utilize the capacities of groups skilfully or turn the opportunities into opposition is the test of successful governance.

References

Adler, M. and Asquith, S. (eds.) (1981), *Discretion and Welfare* (London: Heinemann).

Alderman, G. (1984), *Pressure Groups and Government in Britain* (London: Longman).

Almond, G. (1983), 'Corporatism, Pluralism and Professional Memory', *World Politics*, 25, 2, 245–60.

Ashford, D. E. (1981), *Policy and Politics in Britain: The Limits of Consensus* (Philadelphia: Temple University Press).

Barbrook, A. (1979), *Protest and Pressure: The Public Interest and Pressure Groups in the USA*, Hull Papers in Politics, no. 11.

Barker, A. (ed.) (1982), *Quangos in Britain* (Basingstoke: Macmillan).

Barnes, D. and Reid, E. (1980), *Governments and Trade Unions* (London: Heinemann).

Bechhofer, F. and Elliot, B. (1981), 'Pathways of Protest', paper presented to conference on 'Capital, Ideology, and Politics', Sheffield, 13 Jan. 1981.

Beer, S. H. (1955), 'The Future of British Politics', *Political Quarterly*, 26, 33–42.

——, (1965, 1969 edn.), *Modern British Politics* (London: Faber & Faber).

——, (1982), *Britain Against Itself* (London: Faber & Faber).

Benewick, R. (1973), 'Politics without Ideology: The Perimeters of Pluralism' in Benewick, R., *Knowledge and Belief in Politics: The Problem of Ideology* (London: Allen & Unwin).

Bentley, A. F. (1908, 1967 edn.), *The Process of Government*, ed. P. Odegard (Cambridge, Mass.: Belknap Press).

Berger, S. (ed.) (1981), *Organizing Interests in Western Europe* (Cambridge: Cambridge University Press).

Berry, J. M. (1977), *Lobbying for the People* (Princeton, NJ: Princeton University Press).

——, (1984), *The Interest Group Society* (Boston: Little, Brown, & Co).

Birch, A. H. (1984), 'Overload, Ungovernability and Delegitimation: The Theories in the British Case', *British Journal of Political Science*, 14, 2, pp. 135–60.

Bjurulf, B. and Swahn, U. (1980) in Heidenheimer, A. and Elvander, N. (eds.), *Health Policy Proposals and What Happened to Them* (New York: St Martin's Press).

Blank, S. (1973), *Government and Industry in Britain* (Farnborough: Saxon House).

Borkowski, M., Murch, M., and Walker, V. (1983), *Marital Violence: The Community Response* (London: Tavistock).

Borthwick, R. and Spence, J. (eds.) (1984), *British Politics in Perspective* (Leicester: Leicester University Press).

Brittan, S. (1983), *The Role and Limits of Government* (London: Temple Smith).

Bryce, J. (1888), *The American Commonwealth*, vol. I (London: Macmillan).

Butski, J. and Johansen, L. (1979), 'Variations in organisational participation in Government', *Scandinavian Political Studies*, 2, 3, 197–220.

Cassels, J. S. (1985), 'Can Tripartism Compete?', *The Three Banks Review*, no. 146.

Cater, D. (1964), *Power in Washington* (New York: Vintage).

Cawson, A. (1982), *Corporatism and Welfare* (London: Heinemann).

——, (ed.) (1985), *Organised Interests and the State* (London: Sage).

——, (1985a), 'Corporatism and Local Politics' in Grant, *The Political Economy of Corporatism* (London: Macmillan).

CBI (1983), *Working with Politicians*.

—— (1984), *Annual Report*.

Chandler, G. (1984), 'The Political Process and the Decline of Industry', *The Three Banks Review*, no. 141, 3–18.

Chapman, R. (ed.) (1973), *The Role of Commissions in Policy Making* (London: Unwin University Books).

Christensen, R. and Ronning, R. (1977), '*Organisational Participation in Governmental Politics*', paper prepared for the workshop in 'Interest Group Strategy' (Berlin).

Christensen, T. and Egeberg, M. (1979) 'Organised group–government relations in Norway', *Scandinavian Political Studies*, 2, 3, 239–60.

Christoph, J. B. (1962), *Capital Punishment and British Politics* (London: Allen & Unwin).

Chubb, J. E. (1983), *Interest Groups and the Bureaucracy* (Stanford: Stanford University Press).

Clark, J., Hartmann, H., Lau, C., and Winchester, D. (1980), *Trade Unions, National Politics and Economic Management* (London: Anglo-German Foundation).

Clark, P. B. and Wilson, J. Q. (1961), 'Incentive Systems: A Theory of Organisations', *Administrative Science Quarterly*, 6, 129–66.

Coates, D. (1984), 'Food Law' in Lewis, D., and Wallace, H. (eds.), *Policies into Practice* (London, Exeter: Heinemann Educational Books), pp. 144–60.

Colby, P. W. (1983), 'The Organisation of Public Interest Groups', *Public Studies Journal*, 11, 4, 709–11.

Cole, G. D. H. (1931), 'The Method of Social Legislation', *Public Administration*, 9, 4–14.

Collins, W. P. (1980), 'Public Participation in Bureaucratic Decision-Making: A Reappraisal', *Public Administration*, 58, 465–77.

Connolly, W. E. (ed.) (1969), *The Bias of Pluralism* (New York: Atherton Press).

Cooke, S. (1930s edn.) *This Motoring* (AA Publications).

Coppock, R. (1984), 'Control of Chemical Risk and Hazards: Risk Analysis, Conceptual Outlooks and Political Traditions in Selected Countries', *Journal of Public and International Affairs*, fall/winter.

Crenson, M. (1971), *Unpolitics of Air Pollution* (Baltimore: Johns Hopkins University Press).

Crick, B. (1959), *The American Science of Politics* (London: Routledge & Kegan Paul).

Crossman, R. (c.1938), *How Britain Is Governed* (Labour Book Service).

——, (1977), *The Diaries of a Cabinet Minister*, vol. iii (London: Hamish Hamilton & Jonathan Cape).

Crouch, C. (1983), 'Pluralism and the New Corporatism: A Rejoinder', *Political Studies*, 31, 3, 452–61.

——, (1984), 'Corporatism', *Political Studies*, 32, 1, 113–17.

Chubb, J. E. (1983), *Interest Groups and Bureaucracy* (Stanford: Stanford University Press).

Dahl, R. (1956), *A Preface to Democratic Theory* (Chicago: University of Chicago Press).

——, (1967), *Pluralist Democracy in the United States* (Chicago: Rand McNally & Co.).

——, (1982), *Dilemmas of Pluralist Democracy* (London: Yale University Press).

——, (1983), 'Comment on Manley', *American Political Science Review*, 77, 386–7.

——, (1984), 'Polyarchy, Pluralism, and Scale', *Scandinavian Political Studies*, 7, 4, 225–40.

——, (1985), *A Preface to Economic Democracy*, (Cambridge, Mass.: Polity).

——, and Lindblom, C. (1953, 1976 edn.), *Politics, Economics and Welfare*, (New York: Harper & Row).

Dahlerup, D. (1984), 'Overcoming the Barriers: An Approach to how Women's Issues are Kept off the Political Agenda' in Stiehm, J. (ed.), *Women's Views of the Political World of Men* (New York: Transnational Publications).

Daintith, T. (1985), 'The Executive Power Today: Bargaining and Economic Control' in Jowell, J. and Oliver, D. (eds.), *The Changing Constitution* (Oxford: Clarendon Press).

Damgaard, Eric (1984), 'The Importance and Limits of Party Government:

Problems of Government in Denmark', *Scandinavian Political Studies*, 7, 2, 97–110.

Davies, M. (1985), *Politics of Pressure* (London: BBC).

Dearlove, J. (1973), *The Politics of Policy in Local Government*, (London: Cambridge University Press).

Dobash, R. Emerson, and Dobash, Russell P. (1980), *Violence against Wives: A Case against the Patriarchy* (London: Open Books).

——, (1981) 'Community Response to Violence against Wives: Charivari, Abstract Justice, and Patriarchy', *Social Problems*, 28, 5, 563–81.

Dogan, M. (ed.) (1975), *The Mandarins of Western Europe* (New York: Wiley).

Dowding, K. M., and Kimber, R. (1984), 'The By-product Theory of Groups', *Keele Research Paper*, no. 18.

Drucker, H. (1979), *Doctrine and Ethos in the Labour Party* (London: Allen & Unwin).

——, Dunleavy, P., Gamble, A., Peele, G. (1983), *Developments in British Politics* (London: Macmillan).

Dudley, G. (1984), 'Implementation Dynamics and Discontinuities within the "Imperfect" Policy Process', *Strathclyde Papers on Government and Politics*, no. 11 (Glasgow).

Dunleavy, P. (1983), 'Analysing British Politics' in Drucker *et al.*, *Developments in British Politics* (London: Macmillan).

Eckstein, H. (1960), *Pressure Group Politics: The Case of the BMA* (Stanford: Stanford University Press).

Ehrman, H. W. (1967), *Interest Groups on Four Continents* (Pittsburgh: University of Pittsburgh Press).

Field, F. (1982), *Poverty and Politics* (London: Heinemann).

Finer. H. (1931), 'Officials and the Public', *Public Administration*, 9, 23–5.

Finer, S. (1958, 1966 edn.), *Anonymous Empire* (London: Pall Mall).

——, (1970), *Comparative Government* (London: Allen Lane).

Finniston, Sir Monty (1980), *Engineering our Future*, Cmnd. 7794.

Foley, E. J. (1931), 'Officials and the Public', *Public Administration*, 9, 15–21.

Franklin, M. (1985), *The Decline of Class Voting* (Oxford: Oxford University Press).

Freeman, J. Leiper (1965), *The Political Process* (New York: Random House).

Fritschler, A. L. (1975), *Smoking and Politics* (New York: Appleton–Century–Crofts).

Frohlich, M., Oppenheimer, J., and Young, O. (1971), *Political Leadership and Collective Goods* (Princeton: Princeton University Press).

Gais, T. L., Peterson, M., and Walker, J. (1984), 'Interest Groups, Iron Triangles, and Representative Institutions in American National Government', *British Journal of Political Science*, 14, pt. 2, 161–86.

Galbraith, J. K. (1952), *American Capitalism* (London: Hamilton).

Gamble, A., and Walkland, S. A. (1984), *The British Party System and Economic Policy 1945–1983* (Oxford: Clarendon Press).

Garson, G. D. (1978), *Group Theories of Politics* (Beverly Hills: Sage Publications).

Goldthorpe, J. H. (ed.) (1984), *Order and Conflict in Contemporary Capitalism* (Oxford: Oxford University Press).

Goodin, R. E. (1982), 'Banana Time in British Politics', *Political Studies*, 30, 1, 42–59.

——, (1987), 'The Principle of Voluntary Agreement', *Public Administration*, 65, 1, spring.

Grant, W. (1977), 'Insider Group, Outsider Group and Interest Group Strategies in Britain' (unpublished paper).

——, (1981), 'The Development of the Government Relations Function in UK Firms', discussion paper for IIM/Labour Market Policy (Berlin).

——, (1983), 'The Business Lobby: Political Attitudes and Strategies', *Western European Politics*, 6, 4, 163–82.

——, (1984), 'The Role and Power of Pressure Groups' in Borthwick and Spence (eds.), *British Politics in Perspective* (Leicester: Leicester University Press).

——, (1985), *The Political Economy of Corporatism* (London: Macmillan).

——, and Coleman, W. (1984), 'Business Associations and Public Policy: A Comparison of Organisational Development in Britain and Canada', *Journal of Public Policy*, 4, pt. 3, 209–37.

——, and Marsh, D. (1974), 'The Politics of the CBI: 1976 and after', *Government and Opposition*, winter.

——, ——, (1975), 'The Politics of the CBI: 1974 and After', *Government and Opposition*, 10.

——, ——, (1977), *The CBI* (London: Hodder & Stoughton).

Greenwald, C. S. (1977), *Group Power* (New York: Praeger).

Greer, I. (1985), *Right to be Heard* (London: Ian Greer Associates).

Griffith, J. A. G. (1949), 'Delegated Legislation: Some Recent Developments', *Modern Law Review*.

Guither, H. D. (1980), *The Food Lobbyists* (Lexington: Lexington Books).

Gustafsson, A. (1986), 'Rise and Decline of Nations: Sweden', *Scandinavian Political Studies*, 9, 1, 35–50.

Ham, C. and Hill, M. (1984), *The Policy Process in the Modern Capitalist State* (Brighton: Wheatsheaf Books).

Hansen, J. M. (1985), 'The Political Economy of Group Membership', *American Political Science Review*, 79, 1, 79–96.

Hardin, G. (1968), 'The Tragedy of the Commons', *Science*, 162, 1243–8.

——, Hardin, R. (1982), *Collective Action* (Baltimore: John Hopkins University Press).

Harrison, M. (1974), 'Trade Unions and the Labour Party' in Kimber,

R. & Richardson, J. J. (1974), *Pressure Groups in Britain* (London: Dent).

Harrison, M. L. (ed.) (1984), *Corporatism and the Welfare State* (Aldershot: Gower).

Hayward, J. E. S. (1966), *Private Interests and Public Policy* (London: Longmans).

Headey, B. (1974), *British Cabinet Ministers* (London: Allen & Unwin).

Heclo, H. (1978), 'Issue Networks and the Executive Establishment' in King, A. (ed.), *The New American Political System* (Washington, DC: American Enterprise Institute).

Heisler, M. (1979), 'Corporate Pluralism Revisited: Where is the Theory? *Scandinavian Political Studies*, 2, 3.

——, (1980), 'Towards A Theory of Mixed Polity: Corporate Pluralism In Contemporary Democracy', paper prepared for ECPR workshop of 'Interest Groups and Governments' (Florence).

——, and Kvavik R. B. (1974), 'Patterns of European Politics: The European Polity Model' in Heisler, M., *Politics in Europe* (New York: David MacKay).

Herring, E. P. (1929), *Group Representation Before Congress* (Baltimore: Johns Hopkins University Press).

——, (1930), 'Great Britain has Lobbies too', *Virginia Quarterly Review*, 6, 3.

——, (1936), *Public Administration and the Public Interest* (New York and London: McGraw–Hill).

Hoffman, S. (1966), 'Obstinate or Obsolete: The Fate of the Nation State and the Case of Western Europe', *Daedalus*, 95, 3, 862–915.

——, (1983), 'Reflections on the Nation State in Western Europe Today', *Journal of Common Market Studies*, 21, 1–2, 21–37.

Hollands, C. (1980), *Compassion is the Bugler: The Struggle for Animal Rights* (Edinburgh: Macdonald).

Hood, C. (1982), 'Government Bodies and Government Growth' in Barker, A. (ed.) *Quangos in Britain* (Basingstoke: Macmillan).

Howell, D. (1985), 'Information Technology and Relations between Government and the Public: Some Hopeful Reflections', *Catalyst*, 1, 4, 75–87.

Jennings, I. (1939), *Parliament* (Cambridge: Cambridge University Press).

Jergesen, A. D. (1978), 'The Legal Requirements of Consultation', *Public Law*, pp. 290–315.

Johansen, L. and Kristensen, O. (1982), 'Corporatist Traits in Denmark 1946–76' in Lehmbruch, G., and Schmitter, P. C. (eds.) *Patterns of Corporatist Policy-Making* (London: Sage Publications).

Johnstone, D. (1975), *A Tax Shall Be Charged* (London: Civil Service Studies, HMSO).

Jordan, A. G. (1981), 'Iron Triangles, Woolly Corporatism and Elastic

Nets: Images of the Policy Process', *Journal of Public Policy*, 1, pt. 1, 95–123.

——, (1984), 'Pluralistic Corporatisms and Corporate Pluralism', *Scandinavian Political Studies*, 7, 3, 137–52.

——, (1985), 'Corporate Pluralism and Corporatist Concertation', *Scandinavian Political Studies*, 8, 4.

——, (1987), *The Engineer in the Economy* (forthcoming).

——, and Richardson, J. J. (1977), 'Outside Committees and Policy-making', *Public Administration Bulletin*, 23, 41–58.

——, ——, (1982) in Richardson, J. J. (ed.), *Policy Styles in Western Europe* (London: Allen & Unwin).

——, ——, (1984), 'Engineering a Consensus', *Public Administration*, 62, 383–400.

——, ——, (1987), *British Politics and the Policy Process* (London: Allen & Unwin).

Kelso, W. A. (1978), *American Democratic Theory* (Westport, Conn. and London: Greenwood Press).

Kemper, T., Macmillan, K., and Hawkins, K. (1974), *Business and Society: Transition to Change* (London: Allen Lane).

Kimber, R. (1981), 'Collective Action and the Fallacy of the Liberal Fallacy', *World Politics*, 33, 178–96.

——, and Richardson, J. J. (eds.) (1974), *Pressure Groups in Britain: A Reader* (London: Dent).

King, A. (ed.) (1976), *Why is Britain Becoming Harder to Govern* (London: BBC).

——, (1985), 'Governmental Responses to Budget Scarcity', *Policy Studies Journal*, 113, 3, 476–93.

King, R. (1983), 'Corporatism, Capital and Local Politics', paper presented to the annual conference of Political Studies Association, Newcastle, April.

——, (1985), 'The Organisation, Structure and Political Function of Selected Chambers of Commerce', end of grant report H 430/1 ESRC.

Kogan, M. (1975), *Educational Policy-making* (London: Allen & Unwin).

Kvavik, R. B. (1976), *Interest Groups in Norwegian Politics* (Oslo: Universitetforlaget).

La Palombara, J. (1964), *Interest Groups in Italian Politics* (Princeton: Princeton University Press).

Latham, E. (1952), *The Group Basis of Politics* (New York: Cornell University Press).

——, (1952a), 'The Group Basis of Politics', *American Political Science Review*, 46, 376–97.

Lehmbruch, G. (1984), 'Concertation and the Structure of Corporatist Networks' in Golthorpe, J. H. (ed.) *Order and Conflict in Contemporary Capitalism*, Oxford: Oxford University Press).

——, (1985), 'Neocorporatism in Western Europe', paper presented to IPSA 13th World Congress, Paris.

——, and Schmitter, P. C. (eds.) (1982), *Patterns of Corporatist Policy-making* (London: Sage Publications).

Lehner, F., and Schubert, K. (1984), 'Party Government and the Political Control of Public Policy', *European Journal of Political Research*, July, 131–47.

Lindblom, C. (1959), 'The Science of Muddling Through', *Public Administration Review*, 19, 79–88.

——, (1977), *Politics and Markets* (New York: Basic Books).

——, (1980 edn.) *The Policy-making Process* (Englewood Cliffs: Prentice Hall).

——, (1982), 'Another State of Mind', *American Political Service Review*, 76, 1, 9–21.

——, (1983), 'Comment on Manley' *American Political Science Review*, 77, 2, 384–86.

Lowe, P., and Goyder, T. (1983), *Environmental Groups in Politics* (London: Allen & Unwin).

Lowi, T. (1964), 'American Business, Public Policy, Case Studies, and Political Theory', *World Politics*, 16, 677–715.

——, (1969), *The End of Liberalism* (New York: W. W. Morton).

McBride, S. (1985), 'Corporatism, Public Policy and the Labour Movement: A Comparative Study', *Political Studies* 33, 3, 439–57.

McCarthy, M. (1983), 'Child Poverty Action Group: Poor and Powerless?' in Marsh, D. (ed.), *Pressure Politics* (London: Junction Books).

McClintock, F. H. (1981), 'Some Aspects of Discretion in Criminal Justice' in Adler, M., and Asquith S. (eds.), *Discretion and Welfare* (London: Heinemann).

McConnell, G. (1966, 1970 edn.), *Private Power and American Democracy* (New York: Vintage Books).

McFarland, A. (1976), *Public Interest Lobbies* (Washington: AEI).

McKenzie, R. T. (1955, 1967 edn.), *British Political Parties* (London: Heinemann).

——, (1958), 'Parties, Pressure Groups and the British Political Process', *Political Quarterly*, 29, 1, reprinted in Kimber, R. and Richardson, J. J. (1974), *Pressure Groups in Britain*, (London: Dent), 276–88.

Mackintosh, J. P. (ed.) (1978), *People and Parliament* (Farnborough: Saxon House).

Manley, J. F. (1983), 'Neo Pluralism: A Class Analaysis of Pluralism I and Pluralism II', *American Political Science Review*, 77, 368–83.

Mann, T. E. and Ornstein, N. (eds.) (1981), *The New Congress* (Washington and London: AEI).

Marcuse, H. (1965), 'A Critique of Pure Tolerance' in Woolf, R., *et al.*, (eds.), *A Critique of Pure Tolerance* (London: Cape), 1969.

Marin, B. (1985), 'Austria: The Paradigm Case of Liberal Corporatism' in Grant, W., *The Political Economy of Corporatism* (London: Macmillan).

Marsh, D. (1976), 'On Joining Interest Groups', *British Journal of Political Science*, 6, 257–71.

——, (1978), 'More on Joining Interest Groups', *British Journal of Political Science*, 8, 280–4.

——, and Grant, W. (1977), 'Tripartism: Reality or Myth?', *Government and Opposition,* 12, 2, 194–211.

——, (ed.) (1983), *Pressure Politics* (London: Junction Books).

——, and Chambers, J. (1981), *Abortion Politics* (London: Junction Books).

——, ——, (1983), 'The Abortion Lobby: Pluralism at Work?' in Marsh, D. (ed.), *Pressure Politics* (London: Junction Books).

——, and King, J. (1985), 'Trade Unions Under Thatcher', *Essex Papers in Politics and Government*, no. 27 (Colchester).

Martin, R. (1983), 'Pluralism and the New Corporatism', *Political Studies*, 31, 1, 86–103.

May, T. and Nugent, N. (1982), 'Insiders, Outsiders and Thresholders', paper presented to Political Studies Association annual conference, University of Kent.

Middlemas, R. K. (1979), *Politics in Industrial Society: The Experience of British Society since 1911* (London: Deutsch).

——, (1983), *Industry, Unions and Government* (London: Macmillan).

Miers, D. R. and Page, A. C. (1982), *Legislation* (London: Sweet & Maxwell).

Miliband, R. (1969), *The State in Capitalist Society* (London: Weidenfeld & Nicolson).

Mills, C. W. (1959 edn.), *The Power Elite* (Oxford: Oxford University Press).

Mitchell, E. J. (1974), 'Research on Energy Policy-making' in Hans H. Landsberg *et al. Energy and the Social Sciences: An Examination of Research Needs* (Washington DC: Resources for the Future).

Moe, T. (1980), *The Organization of Interests* (Chicago: University of Chicago Press).

——, (1981), 'Towards a Broader View of Interest Groups', *Journal of Politics*, 43, no. 2, 231–43.

Moon, J. (1986), 'Neo-corporatist Decision-making Structures and Radical Government: Reflections on the Thatcher Government's Unemployment and New Technology Policies' (mimeo).

——, and Richardson, J. J. (1984), 'The Unemployment Industry', *Policy and Politics*, 12, 4, 391–411.

——, ——, (1985), *Unemployment in the UK*, (London: Gower).

——, ——, and Smart, P. (1986), 'The Privatisation of British Telecom: A

Case Study of the Extended Process of Legislation', *European Journal of Political Research* 14, 339–55.

Moran, M. (1984), *The Politics of Banking* (London: Macmillan).

——, (1985), *Politics and Society in Britain* (London: Macmillan).

Moren, J. (ed.) (1974), *Den Kollegiale Forvaltning* (Oslo: Universitetsforlaget).

Morriss, P. (1984), review of Dahl (1982), *Political Studies*, 33, 164.

Muir, R. (1930), *How Britain is Governed* (London: Constable & Co.).

Muller, W. D. (1977), *The 'Kept Men'* (Brighton: Harvester Press).

NEDC (1985), *Annual Report 1985*.

Newman, O. (1981), *The Challenge of Corporatism* (London: Macmillan).

Odegard, P. (1928, 1966 edn.) *Pressure Politics* (New York: Octagon).

Olsen, J. P. (1981), 'Integrated Organisational Participation in Government' in Nystrom, P. C. and Starbuck, W. D. (eds.), *Handbook of Organisational Design*, II. (Oxford: Oxford University Press).

——, (1983), *Organized Democracy: Political Institutions In a Welfare State* (Oslo: Universitetsforlaget).

Olson, M. (1965), *The Logic of Collective Action* (Cambridge, Mass.: Harvard University Press).

——, (1982), *The Rise and Decline of Nations* (New Haven: Yale University Press).

Pahl, J. (1978), *A Refuge for Battered Women: A Study of the Role of a Women's Centre* (London: HMSO).

——, (1979), 'Refuges for Battered Women: Social Provision or Social Movement?', *Journal of Voluntary Action Research*, 8, 1–2, 23–35.

Paloheimo, H. (1984), *Politics In The Era of Corporatism and Planning* (Finnish Political Science Association).

Pennock, J. R. and Chapman, J. W. (eds.) (1975), *Participation in Politics* (New York: Lieber–Atherton).

Peters, B. G. 'Insiders and outsiders: the politics of pressure groups influence on bureaucracy', *Administration and Society*, vol. 9, no. 2 (August 1977), pp. 191–218.

Pliatzky, L. (1980), *Report on Non-departmental Public Bodies*, Cmnd. 7797.

Polsby, N. W. (1963), *Community Power and Political Theory* (New Haven: Yale University Press).

——, (1979), 'Empirical Investigations of Mobilization of Bias in Community Power Research', *Political Studies*, 27, 4, 527–42.

——, (1981), 'The Washington Community, 1960–1980' in Mann. T. E. and Ornstein N. J. (eds.) *The New Congress* (Washington and London: AEI).

Potter, A. (1961), *Organised Groups in British National Politics* (London: Faber).

Poulantzas, N. (1973), *Political Power and Social Classes* (London: NLB).

Presthus, R. B. (1974), *Elites In The Policy Process* (London: Cambridge University Press).

Pross, P. (1981), 'Pressure Groups: Talking Chameleons' in Whittington, M. and Williams, G., *Canada in the 1980s* (Toronto: Methven).

——, (1985), 'Parliamentary Influence and the Diffusion of Power', *Canadian Journal of Political Science*, 18, June, 236–66.

——, (1986), *Group Politics and Public Policy* (Oxford: Oxford University Press).

Pym, B. (1974), *Pressure Groups and the Permissive Society* (Newton Abbot: David and Charles).

Rasch, B. E. and Sorensen, R. J. (1986) 'Organisational Behavior and Economic Growth: A Norwegian Perspective', *Scandinavian Political Studies*, 9, 1, 51–63.

Rhodes, R. (1985), 'Power Dependence, Policy Communities and Inter-governmental Networks', *Public Administration Bulletin*, no. 49, 4–29.

Richardson, J. J. (1982), 'Tripartism and the New Technology', *Policy and Politics*, 10, 3, 54–61.

——, (1983), 'The Development of Corporate Responsibility in the UK', *Strathclyde Papers on Government and Politics*, no. 1 (Glasgow).

——, and Jordan, A. G. (1979), *Governing Under Pressure* (Oxford: Martin Robertson).

——, Moore, C., and Moon, J. *Business and Society in Britain: The Politics and Practice of Corporate Responsibility*, forthcoming.

Ripley, R. and Franklin, G. (1976, 1980, 1984 edn.), *Congress, the Bureaucracy and Public Policy*, (Homewood, Ill.: Dorsey).

Rokkan, S. (1966) in Dahl, R. (ed.), *Political Opposition in Western Democracies* (New Haven and London: Yale University Press).

Rose, R. (1984 edn.), *Do Parties Make a Difference?* (London: Macmillan).

Rosie, G. (1978), *The Ludwig Initiative* (Edinburgh: Mainstream).

Rumbelow, R. M. (1983), 'Partnership in Practice', *Management in Government*, 38, 1, 28–31.

Ryan, M. (1978), *The Acceptable Pressure Group* (Farnborough: Saxon House).

Rydz, D. L. (1979), *The Parliamentary Agents* (London: Royal Historical Society).

Salisbury, R. (1969), 'An Exchange Theory of Interest Groups', *Mid West Journal of Political Science*, 13, 1, 1–32.

——, (1984), 'Interest Representation: The Dominance of Institutions', *American Political Science Review*, 78, 1, 64–78.

Saunders, P. (1982), 'Review of Simmie', *Local Government Studies*, July/August, 16–69.

Schattschneider, E. E. (1935), *Politics, Pressure and the Tariff* (New York: Prentice Hall).

——, (1942), *Party Government* (New York: Farrar & Rinehart).

——, (1960), *The Semi Sovereign People: A Realist's View of Democracy in America* (New York: Holt, Reinhart & Winston).

Schechter, S. (1982), *Women and Male Violence* (London: Pluto Press).

Schmitter, P. (1979), 'Still the Century of Corporatism' in Schmitter and Lehmbruch, *Trends Towards Corporatist Intermediation* (Beverly Hills: Sage).

——, (1982) 'Reflections on where the theory of Neo Corporatism has gone . . .' In Lehmbruch and Schmitter, P. (eds.) *Patterns of Corporatist Policy Making* (London: Sage Publications).

——, (1984), 'Neo Corporatism and the State', *EUI Working Paper*, no. 106.

——, (1985), 'Neo Corporatism and the State' in Grant, W. *The Political Economy of Corporatism* (London: Macmillan).

——, and Lehmbruch, G. (eds.) (1979), *Trends Towards Corporatist Intermediation* (Beverly Hills: Sage).

Schubert, G. A. (1957), 'The Public Interest in Administrative Decision-making', *American Political Science Review*, 51, 346–68.

Schwartz, B., and Wade, H. N. R. (1972), *Legal Control of Government* (Oxford: Clarendon Press).

Self, P., and Storing, H. (1962, 1971 edn.), *The State and the Farmer* (London: Allen & Unwin).

Simmie, J. (1981), *Power, Property and Corporatism* (London: Macmillan).

Smith, M. (1986), 'The Lobbyist's Business', *Government and Industry*, no. 1, section 3.1.

Spencer, R. (1928), 'Significance of a Functual Approach in the Introductory Course in Political Science', *American Political Science Review*, 28, 4, 954–66.

Stewart, J. D. (1958), *British Pressure Groups* (Oxford: Clarendon Press).

Stewart, R. B. (1975), 'The Reformation of American Administrative Law', *Harvard Law Review*, 88, 8, 1669–813.

Streeck, W. (1982), 'Organisational Consequences of Neo-corporatist Co-operation in West German Labour Unions' in Lehmbruch, G., and Schmitter, P. *Patterns of Corporatist Policy Making* (London: Sage Publications).

Suleiman, E. (1974), *Politics, Power and Bureaucracy in France* (Princeton: Princeton University Press).

Taylor, P. (1984), *Smoke Ring: Politics of Tobacco* (London: The Bodley Head).

Thomas, R. (1978), *The British Philosophy of Administration* (London: Longman).

Thomas, R. H. (1983), *The Politics of Hunting* (Aldershot: Gower).

Truman, D. B. (1951), *The Governmental Process* (New York: Knopf).

——, (1960), 'On the Invention of "Systems",' *American Political Science Review*, 54, 494–5.

TUC (1973), *General Council's Report*.

TUC (1985), *General Council's Report*.

Vogel, D. (1983), 'Cooperative Regulation: Environmental Protections in Great Britain', *Public Interest*, no. 72, 88–106.

Walker, J. (1983), 'The Origins and Maintenance of Interest Groups in America', *American Political Science Review*, 77, 390–406.

Walkland, S. (1968), *The Legislative Process in Great Britain* (London: Allen & Unwin).

——, and Ryle, M. (eds.) (1977), *The Commons in the Seventies* (London: Fontana).

Wapshott, N. and Brock, G. (1983), *Thatcher* (London: Macdonald & Co.).

Wardroper, J. (1981), *Juggernaut* (London: Temple Smith).

Wass, D. (1984) *Government and the Governed* (London: Routledge & Kegan Paul).

Weir, A. (1977), 'Battered Women: Some Perspectives and Problems' in Mayo, M., *Women in the Community* (London: Routledge & Kegan Paul).

Whiteley, P. and Winyard, S. (1983), 'Influencing Social Policy: The Effectiveness of the Poverty Lobby in Britain', *Journal of Social Policy*, 12, 1, 1–26.

——, ——, (1984), 'The Origins of the "New Poverty Lobby" ', *Political Studies*, 32, 1, 32–54.

Wildavsky, A. (1964), *The Politics of the Budgetary Process* (Boston: Little Brown).

——, (1978), 'Changing Forward versus Changing Back', *The Yale Law Journal*, 88, 217–34.

Williamson, P. J. (1985), *Varieties of Corporatism: Theory and Practice* (Cambridge: Cambridge University Press).

Wilson, D. (1983), *The Lead Scandal* (London: Heinemann Educational Books).

Wilson, G. K. (1977), *Special Interests and Policy-making* (London: Wiley).

——, (1981), *Interest Groups in the USA* (Oxford: Clarendon Press).

——, (1984), 'Legislating on Occupational Safety and Health: A Comparison of the British and American Experience', paper presented to ECPR Workshop, Salzburg, April.

——, (1985), *Business of Politics* (London: Macmillan).

Winkler, J. T. (1981), 'The Political Economy of Administrative Discretion' in Adler, M., and Asquith, S. *Discretion and Welfare* (London: Heinemann).

Wolfe, A. (1977), *The Limits of Legitimacy* (New York: Free Press).

Woolf, R. (1965) in Woolf, R., Moore, B., jun., and Marcuse, H., *A Critique of Pure Tolerance* (London: Cape), 1969.

Yates, D. (1982), *Bureaucratic Democracy* (Harvard: Harvard University Press).

Young, H. and Sloman, A. (1984), *But, Chancellor* (London: BBC Publications).

Young, S. (1974), *Intervention In The Mixed Economy* (London: Croom Helm).

Zeigler, H. (1964), *Interest Groups in American Society* (Englewood Cliffs: Prentice Hall).

INDEX